Place Names: T.....
Origins and Their
Meanings

© 2020 Mark Adams

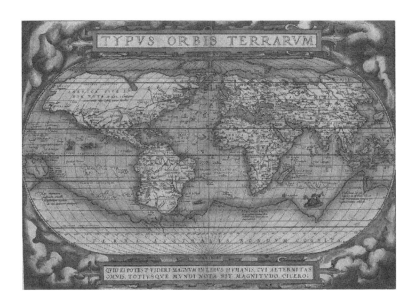

This easy-to-read non-fiction will appeal to anyone interested in history, geography, or language. It is unique in that it gives you, not only the origin of the place-name, but additional information that would be of interest to travelers. There are 1100 entries, many of which have more than one possibility for the meaning of the name.

Many have wondered how nations, states, cities and physical features on the map have gotten their names. This book has the answers.

Contents

Acknowledgement...ii

Introduction..iii

Chapter 1. Place Names Within New York City: The Five
Boroughs..1

Chapter 2. Geographical Names Within the United
States...56

Chapter 3. European Place
Names...114

Chapter 4. Place-Names of the
World...182

Bibliography..236

Travel Guide
Bibliography..244

Acknowledgement

I would like to thank the New York Public Library, the Brooklyn Public Library (Main and Park Slope branches), and the Brooklyn Historical Society for the use o their materials, without which the completion of this book would not have been possible. Thanks are due to Fred Heller, Erna Heller, and Peter Adams for their helpful suggestions. My appreciation also goes out to Joseph Wolf, who put my manuscript into print.

Introduction

My purpose is not the publication of an encyclopedic volume on geographical nomenclature, but simply a book for the reader of light non-fiction. Anyone who has an interest in far places, near places, or language should find this work both interesting and informative.

Those who travel frequently may want to carry a copy along, so as to get just a little more understanding of the city, state, or country that they are visiting.

The entries that I have selected are well-known and may be located on any standard map. I have avoided names that are so obscure that they will mean nothing to most readers as well as names that are so obvious that no explanation would be required. The names of continents, countries, states, major cities, large bodies of water, and great mountain ranges have been included.

Chapter 1 deals with the city of New York, the five boroughs. I decided to devote one of the four chapters to New York for two reasons. First, it is a feature that makes this book different from others of its kind. Works on American or foreign geographical names do not include the streets and neighborhoods of any particular city, and materials on New York do not divert their focus beyond the city limits. Second, I have chosen New York because it is a major American metropolis of many diverse neighborhoods each with its own unique history and culture. The many millions of people who live in the New York Metropolitan area and the many more who have lived or will live in it should find this chapter an added attraction.

My concentration on the United States and Europe in the second and third chapters, respectively, may appear out of balance considering the fact that only one chapter (Chapter 4) covers the remainder of the globe. The American reader has, no doubt, a greater familiarity with the United States and Europe than with other parts of the world, and American tourists are more likely to travel within the United States or Europe than to the other continents. As a way of introducing geographical names, I shall say a few words on some of the criteria that lie behind them and what they can tell us about the history of any particular locality.

Names on the map may be described as linguistic fossils, since so often they were left by the earliest inhabitants of a region. Native American names abound on the landscape of the United States as names of states, rivers, lakes, and mountains. The same phenomenon may be found in Europe, where the names of topographical features are those given by the pre-Indo- European speakers thousands of years ago. New settlers may have modified the name and adapted it to their own language, but without having altered its basic structure.

The name of a political division, such as a nation, a state, or a city often tells us something about its past. Peoples, tribes, individuals, ways of life, and even mythology have been immortalized on the map. Bodies of water, mountains, deserts, and other natural landmarks bear names that describe a notable characteristic such as "slow," "muddy," "flat," "blue," "swampy," etc. The presence of certain kinds of plants or animals can also be a determining factor in the choice of a name. The political, economic, cultural, or natural history of a locality is recorded in its name.

The entries that I have chosen are illustrative of the ways in which geographical nomenclature gives us clues about the past, and they will provide us with a glimpse of languages that have been out of use for many centuries. Hopefully, this book will further our knowledge and understanding with respect to our cultural heritage.

Chapter 1. Place Names Within New York City: The Five Boroughs

The Bronx

The Bronx The Bronx is the only one of the five boroughs that is part of the North American mainland. The borough takes its name from Jonas Bronck, the Dutch settler who owned much of the land back in the seventeenth century. When his family had the land settlers who were living in the area would refer to it as the Bronck's. Even after the Bronck family had gone, the name was still used. The designation "the Broncks," retaining the article ("the"), remained through habit or custom, but the spelling changed to "Bronx" probably in order to simplify it.

Arthur Avenue This street in west-central Bronx, in the vicinity of Fordham University, was named for President Chester A. Arthur. Most of it was originally known as Broad Street, while a smaller section of it was called Central Avenue. In the late nineteenth century a woman by the name of Catherine Lorillard Wolfe owned some land adjacent to Broad Street. When her land was divided into lots she requested that Broad Street be named after President Arthur. Arthur Avenue, today, may be described as the "Little Italy" of the Bronx with its many Italian stores and restaurants.

Big Tom Island Located in Eastchester Bay, off the coast of the eastern Bronx, this rock was named possibly for Thomas Pell. He was the first Lord of Pelham Manor in the 1650's.

Bruckner Boulevard This street in the south Bronx, formerly called Eastern Boulevard, was renamed in July, 1942 in honor of Henry Bruckner, a Bronx Borough President, Congressman, and State Senator.

Castle Hill During the eighteenth century this section of the south Bronx was an important fort and settlement of the Siwanoy Indians. It was located on a hill overlooking Westchester Creek. Surrounded by a strong stockade with palisades, it was called "Castle Hill" by the European settlers.

Clason's Point This section of the eastern Bronx was partially owned by Isaac Clason at the end of the eighteenth century. Clason was one of the early settlers of the Bronx. Part of Clason's mansion later became a part of the Clason Point Inn.

Crotona Park Originally Crotona Park was going to be named Bathgate Park after the Bathgate family, the former owner of the land. There was a disagreement, however, between the Bathgate family and the engineer of the Parks Commission which resulted in a change to "Crotona" after Croton. Crotona Park, in the southwestern Bronx, was named in 1883.

Cuban Ledge This sandy island with rocks at one end is located in Eastchester Bay. It is visible at low tide, but at high tide it is submerged. There are four possible explanations for its name. One possibility is that it was named for a ship called the *Cuban Lady* which carried lumber. On one trip, however, the ship was carrying rum. The crew drank some of the rum, became intoxicated, and ran the ship onto this island. According to another theory, the island was named in 1898 when the Hutchinson River in the Bronx was being widened. A barge carrying a cargo of rocks was floating under Pelham Bridge when a man standing on the bridge announced that the *Maine* had been blown up in Havana, Cuba. The men on the barge tossed the rocks into the water and went to join the navy. The rocks formed part of what would be called "Cuban Ledge." The third possible explanation also relates to the Spanish-American War. One possibility is that it was named for a ship called the *Cuban Lady* which carried lumber. On one trip, however, the ship was carrying rum. The crew drank some of the rum, became intoxicated, and ran the ship onto this island. According to another theory, the island was named in 1898 when the Hutchinson River in the Bronx was being widened. A barge carrying a cargo of rocks was floating under Pelham Bridge when a man standing on the bridge announced that the *Maine* had been blown up in Havana, Cuba. The men on the barge tossed the rocks into the water and went to join the navy. The rocks formed part of what would be called "Cuban Ledge." Throgs Neck, a part of the southeastern Bronx near Eastchester Bay, was being divided into streets at the time of the war (1898). The island was named to commemorate some of the fighting that was taking place in Cuba. One other explanation for the name. One possibility is that it was named for a ship called the *Cuban Lady* which carried lumber. On one trip, however, the ship was carrying rum. The crew drank some of the rum, became intoxicated, and ran the ship onto this island. According to another theory, the island was named in 1898 when the Hutchinson River in the Bronx was being widened. A barge carrying a cargo of rocks was floating under Pelham Bridge when a man standing on the bridge announced that the *Maine* had been blown up in Havana, Cuba. The men on the barge tossed the rocks into the water and went to join the navy. The rocks formed part of what would be called "Cuban Ledge." The third possible explanation also relates to the Spanish-American War. Throgs Neck, a part of the southeastern Bronx near Eastchester Bay, was being divided into streets at the time of the war (1898). The island was named to commemorate some of the fighting that was taking place in Cuba. One other explanation for the name is the fact that the island has the shape of Cuba when depicted on a map.

Fordham Road Fordham Road in the western Bronx was named after Fordham Manor, one of the original manors of Westchester County. The manor which was granted by the English king in 1671 included part of what is presently the Bronx. Fordham Road is in a very busy commercial area with many shops and small restaurants.

Hunt's Point This neck of land extends into the East River from the south Bronx. Edward Jessup, one of the proprietors of West Farms, had a daughter, Elizabeth, who married Thomas Hunt. Eventually Hunt became owner of the neck of land which was later to bear his name. (see West Farms) Hunt's Point is presently an economically depressed industrial neighborhood within some residential sections. It is the site of the *New York City Terminal Market*, the main market for wholesale fruits and vegetables.

Hutchinson River The Hutchinson River was named for Anne Hutchinson who came from England and settled in Boston in 1634. She had to leave Boston because of her religious views. In 1643 she arrived in the Dutch New Netherlands and settled at Pelham Neck in what is now the Bronx. The Hutchinson River flowed very close to her house. She and her settlement perished in an Indian conflict. The Hutchinson River flowed very close to her house.

Jerome Avenue This street is located in the Jerome Park area of the western Bronx, and the Jerome Park Reservoir is in the immediate vicinity. The name commemorates Leonard W. Jerome, one of the founders of the Jerome Park race track. The race track was opened in 1876, but was terminated in 1890. The Jerome Park Reservoir is where the track used to be.

Katonah the name of the Katonah section of the northern Bronx may have been derived from the Native American name *Ketatonah* which means "great mountain." It had a variety of forms such as *Catonan*, *Catoonah*, *Katoonah*, and *Kotonah* during the latter part of the seventeenth century. There was also a chief of the Delaware Indians by the name of Katonah who sold much of his land in Westchester and Connecticut to the English at the end of the seventeenth century. There is also a town of Katonah in Westchester County where this chief was buried.

Kingsbridge This part of the western Bronx was named after a bridge known as King's Bride which was built in the vicinity in 1693, and named in honor of English royalty.

Major Deegan Expressway Running along the Harlem River in the western Bronx, this important road was named for Major William F. Deegan, a Tenement House Commissioner. In April 1937 the road received the name Major William F. Deegan Boulevard and in 1956 the name was shortened to Major Deegan Expressway.

Melrose In the late 1850's this part of the Bronx was surveyed by Andrew Findlay who was of Scottish descent. He called the area Melrose after Melrose Abbey, a work by Sir Walter Scott. Also, the name was popular at this time. Alexander's Department Store had its start in Melrose where it opened for the first time at 2952 Third Avenue.

Morrisania The name of this community in the southwestern Bronx commemorates the Morris family, a prominent family in colonial New York. The estate of Gouverneur Morris was located there.

Mosholu Parkway *Mosholu*, a Native American word signifying "smooth stones" or possibly "clear water," was originally the name of Tibbett's Brook which flowed through southwestern Westchester County down into the western Bronx. Mosholu Parkway is not far from the New York Botanical Garden, one of the nation's earliest and largest Botanical Gardens with its two hundred and fifty acres of unspoiled terrain.

Mott Haven This neighborhood extends from East 137th Street to East 141st Street along Alexander Avenue in the southwestern Bronx. It was named for Jordan Mott, the inventor of the coal-burning stove and the owner of the Mott Iron Works which was located at 134th Street. Mott also owned some property in this area during the 1820's and 1830's. Mott Haven has always been industrial, but in recent years it has suffered economically. The neighborhood, however, has begun to improve since 1990.

Pelham Pelham is a section of the northeastern Bronx to the north of the Long Island Sound The land, originally part of Pelham Manor, was purchased by Thomas Pell from the Indians in the 1650's. (see Big Tom Island) Pelham is known for Pelham Bay Park, with its facilities for golf and horseback-riding. Orchard Beach is a part of this park.

Pugsley's Creek Pugsley's Creek is situated in the eastern part of the Bronx not far from Westchester Avenue. Known also as Wilkin's Creek, it was named Pugsley's after a local farmer. Westchester Avenue formed a causeway which spanned some wet meadows over Barrett's Creek. Barrett's Creek as well was known as "Pugsley's."

Roberto Clemente State Park This park in the south Bronx was originally called Harlem River State Park. In 1974 it was renamed to honor a baseball player for the Pittsburgh Pirates. Roberto Clemente died while flying to Nicaragua to help the victims of an earthquake. His plane crashed into the sea.

Schuylerville Settled in the 1840's, this part of the southwestern Bronx was home to Irish stone masons who worked on the local estates. Some worked at Fort Schuyler. The neighborhood most likely took its name from the fort.

Throggs Neck Throggs Neck is a peninsula leading from the southeastern corner of the Bronx into the Long Island Sound. In 1642 John Throckmorton (or Throgmorton) along with thirty-five English families petitioned the Dutch authorities of New Netherlands to allow them to settle in what is now the southeastern tip of the Bronx. The Dutch called this locality *Vriedlandt* ("land of peace"). The Dutch granted the English permission to settle on the neck of land to the south of Eastchester Bay. The English called it Throckmorton's Neck or Throgmorton's Neck after their leader. Eventually it was shortened to Throggs Neck. Sometimes the name was mistaken for "Frog's Neck." Throggs Neck, today, is a community of about thirty thousand people and has the atmosphere of a small fishing village with its small bungalow-like homes. Fort Schuyler, Maritime College of the State University of New York, is at Throggs Neck.

Tremont Avenue This Bronx street is divided into East and West Tremont Avenues. East Tremont in Morrisania was planned in the 1850's. Postmaster Hiram Tarbox named the street Tremont because of the three hills in the vicinity. West Tremont Avenue traverses the lower end of Archer Manor, the lands of the earliest proprietors of Fordham.

Van Cortlandt Park Located in the northwestern Bronx, the park was named for a prominent Dutch family. The family arrived in New Netherlands in 1638 and acquired large tracts of land. Some family members became traders and shipbuilders.

Van Nest Pieter Pietersen van Neste came from Holland and settled in the Bronx in 1647. One of his descendants, Reynier van Nest, owned a saddlery shop during the early nineteenth century. Reynier's son, Abraham, served as director of the suburban line of the New York, New Haven and Hartford Railroad. There is a Van Nest Memorial Park which was dedicated in honor of the family members who had died in World War I. The park is located on the road which connects Bronxdale with the Westchester Turnpike.

Webster Avenue During the 1860's this Bronx street was surveyed between East 162nd Street and East 165th Street. In 1879 it was opened up as far as East 184th Street, and it extended to Fordham Road by 1882. The street may have been named for Albert L. Webster, an engineer in the Department of Public Works at the time that the street was lengthened. The only other possibility is that the street was named for Joseph Webster who was a surveyor. Most likely, both of these individuals were considered when the street was named.

Weir Creek This stream flowed from the Long Island Sound, north of Throggs Neck, to Middletown Road (northern branch of the stream) and to Lawton Avenue (southern branch). The English settlers called it Weir Creek because of the weirs of plaited reds from which they were able to weave fish traps. The traps were placed across the mouth of the creek in order to catch the fish. This method of fishing was introduced to the Europeans by local Native Americans.

West Farms Originally the patent of West Farms was the territory to the west of the Bronx River and north of the Long Island Sound. In 1663 Edward Jessup and John Richardson of Westchester bought the land from the Indians. Jessup and Richardson divided their land into twelve parcels and called it "Twelve Farms." Because they were located to the west of Westchester, the name "West Farms" eventually caught on. The patent was confirmed by Governor Nicholls in 1666.

Williamsbridge This Bronx neighborhood was at one time the village of Williamsbridge in the northwestern part of Fordham Manor, not far from the Bronx River. There was a bridge at that spot spanning the Bronx River as early as 1670. During the eighteenth century there was a farm near this bridge which was owned by John Williams. The bridge was known locally as "William's Bridge."

Brooklyn

Brooklyn The name was originally *Breuckelen*, named by Dutch settlers after a town in the province of Utrecht, not far from Amsterdam in the Netherlands. *Breuckelen* means "broken land," that is, land cleared for farming. With approximately 2,231,000 people, Brooklyn is the most populous of the five boroughs. Among some of the famous people who have lived there are Mickey Rooney, Mae West, Jackie Gleason, Woody Allen, Barbra Streisand, Floyd Patterson, and Isaac B. Singer.

Albermarle Road At the turn of the century parts of the country were experiencing an interest in England and in English tradition. Developers caught on and began giving streets British sounding names. Originally Avenue A, the name was changed to Aussable Avenue, and then shortly afterwards to Albemarle Road (December 1897). Albemarle Road is a residential street in the Flatbush section of Brooklyn.

Bay Ridge Bay Ridge is a section in southwestern Brooklyn. In 1853 James Weir proposed the name because of certain geographical features that characterized this neighborhood. It borders on Gravesend Bay and a ridge of land exists between Colonial Road and Ridge Boulevard.Originally the area was known as Yellow Hook because of the color of the soil. The Ovingtons, a local family, formed the Ovington Village Association and the Ovington Syndicated company for the purpose of developing the neighborhood. They agreed with Weir on the name "Bay Ridge" because they believed that it would attract new residents. Bay Ridge is basically a residential neighborhood with many small businesses along both 86th Street and 5th Avenue. This ethnically diverse area has people of Italian, Norwegian, Greek, Irish, and Asian descent.

Bedford-Stuyvesant Bedford was a small Dutch community in the seventeenth century and was known as Bedford Corners. It was within the Dutch town of *Breuckelen*. Later on a network of roads that crossed Brooklyn, Queens and the rest of Long Island reached Bedford Corners. The name Stuyvesant comes from Peter Stuyvesant, one of the Dutch director-generals or governors of New Netherlands. Stuyvesant was governor from 1646 until 1664, when he had to surrender the Dutch colony to the British. Bedford Avenue and Stuyvesant Avenue are the two major streets in this part of Brooklyn.

Bensonhurst This Brooklyn neighborhood was named for Egbert Benson who owned a large tract of land there in the nineteenth century. For many years Bensonhurst has been a residential Italian neighborhood with numerous restaurants and bakeries. The comedians, Dom De Luise and Phil Silvers, are both natives of Bensonhurst.

Bergen Beach Bergen Beach, located on Jamaica Bay, is named for one of the first Dutch families of Brooklyn.

Boerum Place This street in downtown Brooklyn was named for a Dutch family that settled in the area during the seventeenth century and had acquired a large amount of land. Boerum runs perpendicular to the Fulton Street Mall, the main commercial area of downtown Brooklyn. It separates the mall from Borough Hall and Brooklyn Heights.

Borough Park The name of this section in southwestern Brooklyn is derived from a land development of the same name. In the 1880's the Litchfield family, owner of a large piece of land, began to develop the area called Blythebourne which was close to the Borough Park development. When Eastern European Jews started to reside in Borough Park the land values rose and the neighborhood began to expand. Presently only the Borough Park Post Office is still called Blythebourne. Borough Park is currently an Hasidic Jewish community and is basically residential in character. There are, however, plenty of shopping areas where all kinds of stores can be found.

Brighton Beach It was named after the well-known English seaside resort of the same name. In 1868 William A. Engeman, who was spending some of his time at the beach in Gravesend, decided to buy several hundred acres of land. He spent twenty thousand dollars for the land which he turned into a resort. He called this new seaside community Brighton Beach. This area has for many years been an Eastern European Jewish neighborhood. The most recent group of Russian immigrants (mostly Jewish) have been settling in Brighton Beach since the 1970's. The main commercial street has many Russian restaurants as well as stores of all kinds.

Brownsville The Brownsville section of Brooklyn was at one time the village of Brownsville, named for Charles S. Brown who bought the original land title in the 1860's. Brown divided the land into lots and sold them. Brownsville has always been ethnically diverse, but the largest group in this neighborhood during the first half of the twentieth century has been the Eastern European Jews. Presently, this basically residential area is African-American and Hispanic.

Bushwick Sandwiched between Brownsville and Greenpoint, this Brooklyn neighborhood was one of the original Dutch towns. The Dutch name was *Boswyck* which means a "town" or "village in a bushy place" or "grove." *Bos* is grove or thicket and *wic*, *wich*, or *wyk* in Germanic languages such asDutch suggests a village, town, or hamlet. Several breweries were established here by German immigrants during the nineteenth century. Most of them have been demolished, but some of the mansions of the brewers and manufacturers are still standing.

Buttermilk Channel This small channel of water separates Governor's Island from Brooklyn. The unusual name comes from its use by women from Brooklyn to bring buttermilk to the market. On its Brooklyn shore, shipbuilding yards, wharves, and other industrial facilities have been established.

Cadman Plaza located in downtown Brooklyn, it was named for Samuel Parkes Cadman (1864- 1936). Cadman was an English-born clergyman who became pastor at the Central Congregational Church in Brooklyn (1900-1936). He was one of the first clergymen to be heard on radio.

Canarsie Among the suggested meanings of this Native American name are "the fenced-in place" and "long, small grasses." The Canarsee Indians were living in southeastern Brooklyn during the seventeenth century. When the Europeans arrived some of the Indians living in what is today called Canarsie began to move farther east on Long Island, while others remained in Canarsie through the eighteenth century. The last reported Canarsee Indian residing in Brooklyn was a man by the name of Jim de Wilt (Dutch for "Jim, the Wild Man") who died in 1830. *Wilt* (pl. *Wilden*) was the Dutch word for the Indians of New Netherlands. Canarsie remained a rural area through some of the present century until it became suburban with the coming of the automobile which made it possible for more people to live there. Two-family row houses became very popular as the neighborhood attracted new residents.

Caton Avenue This Flatbush street was called Johnson Street until 1916 when it received its present name. It was probably named for the Caton or Catin family. There was a Mrs. Caton who lived (c. 1840) at what is presently the corner of Flatbush and Caton Avenues.

Chauncey Street The street was named to commemorate Isaac Chauncey (1772-1840) who served as a naval officer during the War of 1812. Chauncey was in command of the American Navy on Lakes Ontario and Erie.

Clarendon Road The choice of this British name for a street in Flatbush exemplifies the interest in England expressed by many Americans at the turn of the century. (See Albemarle, above) Originally Avenue C, it was renamed Clarendon Road at this time.

Clark Street Clark Street in Brooklyn Heights was planned in 1806, and named for a Captain Clark whose son married into a local family. Captain Clark also lived in the neighborhood just south of the street that bears his name. Previous to 1806 Clark Street existed as a small lane which dated back to at least 1766, if not earlier. Clark Street is the main subway stop on the I.R.T. in Brooklyn Heights, and it is the site of what was at one time the St. George Hotel which was known for its swimming facilities.

Clarkson Avenue This Flatbush street was named for the Clarkson family, an old Brooklyn family that participated in the American Revolution. The sources mention David Clarkson, David Clarkson, Jr. and Matthew Clarkson (1758-1825) who was a soldier during the Revolutionary War and later supported civic improvements in New York City.

Classon Avenue Classon Avenue runs from east to west in the western part of Brooklyn. The name is derived from Claasen (also spelled Claesen and Klaesen), an early Dutch family. There were many members of this family living in Kings County during the seventeenth century. Some of them were in Flatbush while others were in the town of Brooklyn. In 1657 Hendrick Claasen settled in Brooklyn not far from the present-day Navy Yard. He owned land in the vicinity of what is now Bedford Avenue, fairly close to Classon Avenue.

Coney Island This is the English form of the Dutch name *Conyen Eylandt* ("rabbit island"). Coney Island was originally within the town of Gravesend. The Dutch settler Gysbert Op Dyck had a patent for it in 1642. The amusement park and the beach with its boardwalk have made Coney Island known throughout the country.

Cropsey Avenue Cropsey Avenue runs through Borough Park and commemorates a family that settled there in the seventeenth century. At that time, it was part of the Dutch town of New Utrecht which included present-day Bay Ridge, Bensonhurst and part of Borough Park. The name of the family was originally Casperse and they arrived in Brooklyn from the Netherlands in 1652. Jasper Casperse built his house at what is now 69th Street in Bay Ridge. Through mispronunciation, the name Casperse eventually became Cropsey or Cropsy. There was a Jacobus Cropsey and a Hendrick Cropsey in the Revolutionary War. The Cropsey family was engaged in farming and fishing.

Crown Heights During the seventeenth century, Crown Heights was part of the Dutch town of Brooklyn. The earlier name of this area was Crow Hill. The designations "hill" and later "heights" are descriptive of the neighborhood's physical character, a succession of hills. In the early twentieth century, "Crow" became "Crown," but there is no known explanation why or how the final *n* was added. Despite the conflict that took place in the summer of 1991, Hasidic Jews and African-Americans have been living there peacefully for the past thirty-five years.

DeKalb Avenue This street in downtown Brooklyn was first noted on a map in 1835. The name was chosen to honor General De Kalb who participated in the American Revolution.

Dean Street Traversing the Prospect Heights section of Brooklyn, Dean Street first appears on an 1835 map. The name comes from Silas Deane, another soldier of the Revolution.
DeWitt Avenue This Brooklyn street was opened in 1929 and named for George DeWitt of the Topographical Bureau.

Ditmas Avenue The name of this Flatbush street comes from Henry S. Ditmas, a local farmer during the middle of the nineteenth century.

Dreier-Offerman Park Situated in Bensonhurst, the land was ceded by New York City from the German Home for Recreation of Women and Children on December 18, 1933. Katherine S. Dreier was the corresponding secretary for the German Home in 1925, and Grace Offerman was the district nurse for the Brooklyn Bureau of Charities in 1918.

Dyker Beach Park This park adjoins the Brooklyn neighborhoods of Bay Ridge and Bensonhurst. It was named for the family of John Tomasse van Dyke, local Dutch settler who arrived there in 1654. Johan Tomasse became a magistrate of the town of New Utrecht in 1661.

East New York In 1835 a Connecticut merchant, John R. Pitkin, passed through this part of Kings County noticing how close Brooklyn was to New York City. He was impressed by the local landscape and thought of founding a new city to be a commercial rival of New York. Having purchased some farms, he divided the land into streets and lots. He called the new community East New York because it was to the east of New York City. Pitkin sold many of his lots but the economic panic of 1837 put an end to his plans, forcing him to sell back all of his property to its former owners. He held on to the section between Wyckoff and Alabama Avenues, an area that retained the name of East New York. In 1853 Horace Miller and James Butler bought fifty acres to the east of Wyckoff Avenue and erected homes which sold for moderate prices. The new homes attracted people to the village of East New York which had approximately eight thousand residents by 1880. East New York has been an ethnically diverse neighborhood since the middle of the nineteenth century. It is, today, primarily African-American and Hispanic.

Eastern Parkway It was known at first simply as Parkway and extended from Prospect Park Plaza to a point between Ralph and Howard Avenues. Later on it was lengthened from the point between Ralph and Howard to Highland Boulevard, and the older portion began to be called Eastern Parkway. After a while the entire street was being called by the new name. The construction of Eastern Parkway from the plaza to Ralph Avenue was completed in 1874, and the extension was added in 1906. Eastern Parkway is a wide and busy street with apartment buildings on both sides. The Brooklyn Museum, the Brooklyn Botanical Gardens, and the Brooklyn Public Library are all on this street.

Emmons Avenue This street in Sheepshead Bay takes its name from a family by the name of Emmans (also spelled Emans and Imans). Andries Emmans, the first member of this family to come to Kings County, arrived from Holland and settled in Gravesend in 1661. Present-day Emmons Avenue is very close to where Andries Emmans had lived. It is the main street running along the bay with its many restaurants. The original Lundy's Restaurant had closed, but a new Lundy's has opened at the same spot very recently.

Farragut Road During the nineteenth century this street in Flatbush was Avenue F, but in 1901 the name was changed in honor of Admiral David Farragut.

Flatbush The English form "flat" is derived from the Dutch *vlachte* which means a plain. The Dutch *bos*, meaning bush, was easily Anglicized. *Vlachte bos*, or "plain in the woods," shortly became Flatbush. Modern Flatbush is a large, ethnically diverse, residential section with many busy commercial streets. Jamaicans, Haitians, Hasidic Jews of Eastern European origin, Syrian Jews, and Asians are among the many groups that live there.

Floyd Bennett Field This small airstrip in the vicinity of Jamaica Bay was named for a navy pilot and friend of Admiral R. E. Byrd. Bennett accompanied Byrd on his polar explorations in the 1920's. Floyd Bennett Field is now a part of the Gateway National Recreation Area.

Fort Greene Fort Putnam was originally the name of the bastion which protected the Americans against the British during the Revolution. It was situated at what is today Fort Greene Park in downtown Brooklyn. British troops wanted to capture it in August 1776, at the time of the Battle of Brooklyn. Many years later, during the War of 1812, Fort Putnam was renamed Fort Greene to honor General Nathanael Greene (1742-1786), a Revolutionary War leader. Fort Greene is near the Manhattan Bridge and downtown Brooklyn's Fulton Street Mall. It is also the home of the Brooklyn Academy of Music.

Fort Hamilton Fort Hamilton is in southern Brooklyn close to the Verrazano Bridge. On the day that the Declaration of Independence was signed in Philadelphia, a small American battery at the spot that would later be Fort Hamilton was attacked by the British warship, **Asia**. On August 22, 1776 the British army landed at that same place. During the War of 1812 the new battery built there was fortified with thirty guns and named Fort Lewis. In 1819 the Army decided to plan the construction of a fort which actually began on June 11, 1825. The defense work was named in honor of Alexander Hamilton. The Fort Hamilton Veteran's Hospital and the Harbor Defense Museum, New York City's only military museum, are presently both there.

Foster Avenue This street in Flatbush, Brooklyn, was named for a family living in Jamaica, Queens, during the colonial period. There is no apparent reason for a street to be named for a family living so far away. One possibility is that they owned land in this part of Flatbush during the colonial period or at a later date.

Avenue E east of Flatbush Avenue became Foster Avenue in 1902. Foster Avenue runs through an ethnically diverse, residential Flatbush neighborhood.

Gates Avenue The name first appears on an 1835 map and most likely refers to the General Horatio Gates who took part in the Revolutionary War. Part of Gates Avenue was called Magnolia Street during the nineteenth century. Gates Avenue is in the Bedford-Stuyvesant section of Brooklyn and is primarily residential.

Gerritsen Avenue Between Sheepshead Bay and Flatlands, Gerritsen Avenue is named for the family of Wolphert Gerritsen van Cowenhoven. Wolphert came from Amersfoort in the Dutch province of Utrecht and settled in New Amersfoort, the present Flatlands section of Brooklyn.

Gowanus Gowanus is a form of the local Delaware Indian word *yauwin* which means to sleep or sleeper. It shows up as *Cujanes* on a 1646 document and as *Cowanoes* on a 1666 map. The form *Gouwanes* appears frequently in seventeenth-century sources. Gouwanes or Gowanus would refer at different times to a bay, a creek, a neighborhood, and a road in downtown Brooklyn, not far from Red Hook. The creek eventually became the Gowanus Canal. The first European settlers bought the land from the Indians in the 1630's, but the Indians continued to fish at Gowanus Creek into the eighteenth century. Wharves and gas tanks were built along the canal in modern times. There was also a paint factory near the canal, and when the vats were cleaned, the water turned from dark green to red and gold.

Gravesend Gravesend was settled by the English under the leadership of Lady Deborah Moody in 1643. The Dutch gave them the religious toleration that they were denied in New England. There are two

Hoyt Street The Hoyt family, for which this downtown Brooklyn street is named, came to Brooklyn from the Netherlands in the seventeenth century. They still owned land in Brooklyn during the early part of the nineteenth century. There was a hill in downtown Brooklyn to the west of Red Hook Lane which was known as Prospect Hill or Hoyt's Hill. It was named for Charles Hoyt who owned the land at that time. Hoyt started to build streets in the area during the 1820's. Hoyt Street, today, is in the heart of downtown Brooklyn's busy Fulton Street Mall, with its many discount stores, "fast-food"restaurants, and street merchants.

Humboldt Street Originally it was Wyckoff Avenue, but later on it was changed to Smith Street or Smith Avenue. It was opened in 1851 and extended from Flushing Avenue to Greenpoint. The name was changed to Humboldt Street sometime between 1868 and 1880 in honor of Alexander Humboldt.

Joralemon Street Joralemon Street in Brooklyn Heights was named for Tunis Joralemon who came from New Jersey, lived for a while in Flatbush, and settled in downtown Brooklyn in the early nineteenth century. Joralemon owned land in the village of Brooklyn and served on the village board a number of times. Joralemon Street is characterized by its beautiful Greek Revival row houses.

Keap Street Keap Street was named for Thomas McKean, a signer of the Declaration of Independence. The name was mistaken for "Thomas M. Keap" and was never corrected. Keap Street was opened in WIlliamsburg from Lee Avenue to Division Avenue in 1858.

King's Highway Brooklyn at one time had many trails connecting the Native American villages. There was a large path leading from the village of *Keshaech-queren* in present-day Flatlands to the village of *Techkonis* in what is now part of Bensonhurst or

Borough Park. The Native American name for this road was *Mechawanienk* which means "an ancient pathway." The trail was first recorded in a deed of land conveyance in 1652. In 1682 the road was widened for wagon traffic The English began to call it "the King's Highway" in 1704 in honor of British royalty. King's Highway is a busy commercial street at the end closest to Coney Island Avenue, but it becomes much more residential in the direction of Flatbush Avenue.

Leif Ericson Drive It was named for the Scandinavian sailor, Leif Ericson. The Board of Aldermen met in April 1925 to establish a park in Bay Ridge which they named Leif Ericson Park. The name of the drive was derived from that of the new park. The Board of Aldermen chose the name of Leif Ericson due to the large number of Scandinavians residing in Bay Ridge.

Liberty Avenue During the nineteenth century this road in East New York was free for the use of farmers. There were no tolls, hence "Liberty."

Lorimer Street Lorimer Street in Williamsburg was named for the local developers, John and James Lorimer Graham.

Marcy Avenue This street in WIlliamsburg was opened in 1856 and named for William Learned Marcy, a captain in the War of 1812, Secretary of War (1845-49), Secretary of State (1853-57), and Governor of New York (1833-39).

McCarren Park Located in Greenpoint, it was originally Greenpoint Park. The Board of Alderman renamed it in 1909 probably to honor Patrick Henry McCarren (1847-1909), a New York State legislator. McCarren was a Brooklyn democratic boss during the first decade of the twentieth century, and he prevented Tammany Hall from getting control of the borough.

McDonald Avenue McDonald runs near Greenwood Cemetary in the direction of Flatbush. At first, it was called Gravesend Avenue, but was renamed by the Board of Aldermen in 1933 for John R. McDonald, a chief clerk at the Surrogate Court and father of District Attorney Miles F. McDonald. It is presently a residential street with small private houses.

Meserole Street Meserole Street was opened in 1848 from Union Avenue to Bushwick Avenue. There was a Meserole family in early Williamsburg, owners of land in the area.

Midwood All of Flatbush was called *Midwout*, *Midwoud*, or *Medwoud* by the Dutch when they first arrived in the area. The name means "middle woods" and describes the forested character of Flatbush in the seventeenth century. This section of Brooklyn has both an Eastern European and a Middle Eastern Jewish community with a large number of religious schools. The Syrian Jews are settled primarily in the vicinity of Ocean Parkway.

Mill Basin Mill Basin is in the neighborhood of Jamaica Bay. The name comes from the tide mills that were erected there, mills run by tidal currents for the purpose of clearing lands of tidal water. Mill Basin is a relatively newly developed residential area with small houses and suburban-looking street

Montague Street This street in Brooklyn Heights was at one time known as Constable Street. Henry Evelyn Pierrepont, a prominent resident of Brooklyn, had the name of the street changed to Montague in honor of Mary Wortley Montague, an authoress. The change was made around 1850. Montague Street is the main commercial street of Brooklyn Heights, with a variety of stores and restaurants which blend in well with the neighborhood and do not detract from its appearance.

Nevins Street Nevins was the name of a prominent family in nineteenth-century Brooklyn. Patrick Henry Nevins was in charge of repairs at the Brooklyn Fire Department and his son, Dr. Thomas Francis Nevins, was a physician. Part of this street traverses the busy Fulton Street Mall area.

New Lots Avenue Part of the Dutch town of Flatbush was called *Oost-wout* or "East Woods." As the population of Flatbush grew, *Oost-wout* was cleared of its forest and was designated "the New Lots," hence New Lots Avenue.

New Utrecht Avenue New Utrecht was one of the original towns of Brooklyn established by the Dutch in the seventeenth-century. It was named after Utrecht, a town in the Netherlands. New Utrecht included what are today Bay Ridge, part of Bensonhurst, and part of Borough Park. New Utrecht Avenue traverses Bensonhurst.

Nostrand Avenue Nostrand Avenue in Brooklyn runs from Bedford-Stuyvesant to Sheepshead Bay. It was named for the van Nostrand (originally van Noordstrandt) family from Nordstraat or Nordstrandt in Holstein. Eventually van Noordstrandt was Anglicized to Nostrand. This street has some busy commercial sections with shops and small restaurants of all kinds.

Osborne Street This Brownsville street was at one time called Ocean Avenue. It was renamed in 1887, at a time in which many street names were being changed by the Common Council of the City of Brooklyn. The name probably comes from either Dr. Samuel Osborne or Dr. Samuel Johnson Osborne a son of Dr. John Osborne of Middletown, Connecticut, but there is a possibility that it was named for both of them. Samuel became a physician and settled in Brooklyn, where he became prominent. He was in Brooklyn during the Yellow Fever epidemic of 1809. Later on, he moved to New York City. Dr. Samuel Johnson Osborne came from

Pennsylvania and studied medicine in New York City during the 1840's. He started his practice in Brooklyn in 1844, and in 1851 he became president of the Medical Society of King's County. Four years later he moved to Wisconsin. Some of his family may have remained in Brooklyn, for there was a Harriet Osborne listed in a directory for the years 1865-66.

Pitkin Avenue The street commemorates John R. Pitkin, a Connecticut merchant who visited this part of Kings County in 1835. It was here that he wanted to establish a new city that would rival New York. (see East New York) In the past, Pitkin Avenue was a busy commercial street with a variety of stores, but in recent years the area has become depressed economically.

Prospect Place At one time a part of Warren Street, the Brooklyn Board of Aldermen renamed the largest portion of it in March 1872. The Board selected the new name because the street was near Prospect Park. Prospect Place is a residential street running through the Prospect Heights and Crown Heights sections of Brooklyn.

Ralph Avenue An 1835 map shows Ralph Avenue running from Division Avenue to the Brooklyn-Flatbush border. Today the street traverses Bedford-Stuyvesant and continues on through Flatbush. It was probably named after Ralph Lane who owned property in the area during the nineteenth century.

Redhook Wouter van Twiller succeeded Peter Minuit as Governor of New Netherlands. He took title to the promontory on Long Island (Brooklyn) called *Roode-Hoek* or "Red Hook." The name was descriptive of the soil's color. Redhook has always been a rather poor and isolated neighborhood. The Port Authority Shipping Terminal and the Erie Basin Terminal should bring some economic improvement. Redhook is known as having been one of the places in which Al Capone and his family resided.

Remsen Street and Avenue The former is in Brooklyn Heights and the latter in East New York. The Remsen family was one of the first to arrive in Brooklyn from the Netherlands. Originally settling near the present Navy Yard, Remsen and his descendants became the largest landowners in colonial Brooklyn.

Rutledge Street Rutledge Street in Williamsburg was named for Edward Rutledge, a signer of the Declaration of Independence. Rutledge (1749-1800) was also a member of the First and Second Continental Congresses as well as Governor of South Carolina.

Schermerhorn Street This street in downtown Brooklyn was named for one of the first Dutch families in the borough. Schermerhorn runs parallel to the Fulton Street Mall between Fort Greene and Brooklyn Heights. It is a large commercial street, but it is never very crowded.

Sheepshead Bay The name does not come from the shape of the bay, but rather from the name of a fish that used to be caught there in abundance. Earlier in the century this fish, known as the "sheepshead," was a popular local food. For a long time, Sheepshead Bay has been both a residential and recreational area. There are fishing boats which go out every day and bring in flounder and bass. Sheepshead Bay has many Italian and seafood restaurants for visitors and residents.

Snyder Avenue Snyder Avenue in Flatbush used to be Grant Street, named most likely for President Grant. It became Snyder Avenue in 1903 in commemoration of a Dutch family that owned land there for a long period of time.

Sterling Place Sterling Place was named in honor of William Alexander, known as Lord Stirling (1726-83). Lord Stirling served as a brigadier-general during the American Revolution, during which he was in command of New York City and played a leading role in the Battle of Long Island (August 27, 1776). The military activity on Long Island entailed much fighting and marching throughout Kings County. Sterling Place runs through the Prospect Heights and Crown Heights sections and it has always been a completely residential street.

Stillwell Avenue Stillwell is in Bensonhurst, not far from Coney Island. The street was named after a family that owned property in the vicinity since the late seventeenth century. Richard and Nicholas Stillwell were among the earliest settlers.

Sumner Avenue Sumner Avenue is located in the Bedford-Stuyvesant section of Brooklyn. It received its present name in 1887. One possibility is that it was named in deference to Jethro Sumner, a Revolutionary War soldier who served George Washington at Brandywine Creek, Germantown, and Valley Forge. The other candidate is Charles Sumner, a United States Senator and abolitionist. The likelihood is in favor of Charles Sumner because in 1887 his name would be more timely, since he was prominent during the Civil War period and more familiar to people at this time than was Jethro. Before the street was renamed, it was known as Yates Avenue.

Sunset Park Sunset Park is in southwestern Brooklyn, flanking New York Bay and Greenwood Cemetery. Irish immigrants came in the 1840's, followed by Poles and Scandinavians after 1880. The name Sunset park came into use in the 1960's. There is a local park by this name which rests high on a hill overlooking the streets and New York Bay. The name probably refers to the good view from the park which faces west, in the direction of the sunset. Before the present name came into fashion, the part of the neighborhood closest to the shore was called "South Brooklyn"

and the southern part of the area was considered an extension of
Bay Ridge. Sunset Park today is still ethnically mixed with
Hispanics, Arabs, and Asians in addition to the older European
groups. There are many row-houses which date back to the
nineteenth century. Greenwood Cemetery, in which Mae West,
Boss Tweed, and Henry Ward Beecher are buried, is situated in
this neighborhood.

Sutter Avenue At one time Union Avenue, it was renamed for
Peter D. Sutter, a leader in the democratic party.

Thatford Street G.S. Thatford, an important resident of East New
York during the nineteenth century, donated land for a church. The
street was probably named after this individual. Thatford Street is
presently within a rather economically poor area.

Throop Avenue This street was named for Enos T. Throop
(1784-1874) who served as New York State governor in the early
nineteenth century.

Tillary Street Tillary Street in downtown Brooklyn was named
for a Dr. Tillary who owned a large amount of land in Brooklyn. It
is not far from the bridges which span the East River, and it is
close to the Cadman Plaza and Borough Hall area.

Van Siclen Avenue The name does honor to the van Sigelen or van
Siclen family, early Dutch settlers in Brooklyn.

Van Sinderen Avenue Dominic Ulpianus van Sinderen, a
member of an old Dutch family, served as a minister of the Dutch
Reformed Church in Flatlands. During the Revolutionary War the
British soldiers would listen to his sermons, for there was no

English church in the area. The sermons were in Dutch and the British soldiers did not realize that he was praying for the American forces to win.

Voorheis Avenue Voorheis was the name of a prolific family in colonial Kings County. Alternative spellings of the family name were Voorhees, Voris and van Voorhies. The Sheepshead Bay racetrack used to be near Voorheis Avenue and Villepigue's Inn, a famous seafood restaurant, opened there in 1886 and stayed in business until after World War II.

Wallabout Channel Wallabout Channel forms part of the East River near the Navy Yard. Most of the early settlers of Brooklyn were Dutch, but there was also a small group of people called Walloons. They were from what is today the French-speaking section of Belgium. Some of them had fled to Holland for religious freedom, but due to the crowded conditions of the Netherlands, they came to America along with the Dutch. The Walloons settled near the present Navy Yard and the area became known as *Wallabout*, while the channel was called "*Wallabout* Creek." The name means "Bay of the Walloons," or "Waals" as they were called in Dutch.

Williamsburg This section of Brooklyn was named to honor King WIlliam III of England (reigned 1689-1702). William belonged to the Dutch dynasty of Orange-Nassau. It was a common practice in early New York to give names commemorating this royal family. Williamsburg has been both an Hasidic Jewish and Hispanic neighborhood for many years. It is an old residential area with shopping sections for the people who live there. The neighborhood is rather isolated from the rest of Brooklyn, but the Williamsburg Bridge connects it to Manhattan and the rest of the city.

Willoughby Avenue Most likely, Willoughby Avenue was named for a prominent local family. There is the possibility, however, that it was named specifically for Mrs. Willoughby, daughter of John Duffield. Duffield was the name of another important local family. Willoughby Avenue is in an old residential section of Brooklyn.

Windsor Terrace This neighborhood is to the immediate south of Prospect Park. It was named "Windsor" after Windsor in England and "Terrace" because of the extensive terrace work that had to be done in order for the area to be developed. Windsor Terrace is a quiet residential area with private houses and some small apartment buildings. Close to its western end is Prospect Park West and near its eastern end is Ocean Parkway. Prospect Park Lake is also in the immediate vicinity.

Manhattan

Manhattan The island of Manhattan took the name of the local Indian tribe. It is also possible that it means "island mountain" in the Algonquian language. Manhattan is 12.5 miles in length and 2.5 miles wide, the smallest of the five boroughs in area. It is the third largest in population with close to 1.5 million people.

Allen Street In lower Manhattan, Allen Street is named for Captain William Henry Allen, who served in the Navy during the War of 1812. Allen was instrumental in capturing a number of British ships and he died in action. Allen Street, today attracts visitors because of its many antique stores.

Astor Place John Jacob Astor was the wealthiest man in the United States when he died in 1848. The family residence was on this street'

Avenue of the Americas Formerly Sixth Avenue, this street was renamed after the Organization of American States, in honor of the other nations of the Western Hemisphere.

Battery Park At the end of lower Manhattan, the name is derived from a battery of artillery erected on a platform at this spot in 1693 by the English to stave off a possible French attack. It was a military post later on, during the War of 1812. The battery was at Battery Place which is next to the park. At the time of the Civil War the park was a prison camp for captured Confederate soldiers.

Bayard Street Bayard Street in lower Manhattan was named for one of two likely candidates, Nicholas Bayard (1644-1707) and William Bayard (1761-1826). Nicholas, the more likely choice, was a nephew of Peter Stuyvesant and served in the Dutch colonial government as a secretary of the province. He was also a customs surveyor as well as a mayor of New York City during the 1680's, after the English had taken over. The other possibility, William Bayard, was a New York merchant and partner in a major shipping company.

Bedloe's Island Governor Lovelace, a British governor of colonial New York, appointed a man by the name of Bedlow as commissioner for the purpose of hearing the complaints of colonists who were protesting some of the policies of the Duke of York. The island was named for this British official.

Beekman Street This Manhattan street was named in remembrance of Willem Beeckman who came to New Netherlands in the middle of the seventeenth century. Beeckman owned a large amount of property in Manhattan, held the position of clerk in the Dutch West India Company, and served as mayor for nine terms.

Bleecker Street Named for a nineteenth-century writer by the name of Anthony Bleecker, the street traversed the Bleecker family property. Bleecker wrote for periodicals during the early part of the nineteenth century, and he knew both Washington Irving and William Cullen Bryant.Bleecker is the main street of Greenwich Village, with its night clubs, theaters, and cafes.

Bowery The Bowery (*bouwerij* in Dutch) was named for Peter Stuyvesant's farm. There was a road that joined his property to the main part of New Amsterdam. It was an aristocratic neighborhood during the eighteenth century, but by the middle of the following century the area had become squalid. For decades it has been associated with hobos and cheap hotels.

Bowling Green In the early eighteenth century three men rented this piece of land from the colonial government to use for bowling. They would rent the property for ten years at the price of one peppercorn a year. Bowling Green is close to Battery Park and the Wall Street area, and is usually very crowded during the day.

Broadway Broadway used to be much wider in lower Manhattan than it is now, hence its name. Known as Heere Street in Dutch times, it was possibly used by the Indians before the Europeans had arrived. Broadway is one of Manhattan's main attractions because of its theaters and restaurants, but the section of it that runs through the vicinity of Times Square had deteriorated because of pornography and drugs. Over the last couple of years, however, the neighborhood has been in the process of redevelopment so that it can once again draw tourists.

Broome Street Broome Street in lower Manhattan commemorates John Broome, the first alderman of the city after the British had left and Lieutenant Governor of New York State in the early nineteenth century.

Bryant Park Located in midtown, it was named in honor of William Cullen Bryant, a writer from New England. He came to New York in the 1820's and practiced law for a while. Later he went into journalism and became editor and primary owner of a New York newspaper. Bryant Park is behind the New York Public Library, and for a long time people avoided it because of drug pushers. It has been cleaned up recently, and now attracts many individuals who would never have ventured there during the 1980's.

Canal Street There was a canal at this locality during the first decade of the nineteenth century which drained a pond into the Hudson River. Both the canal and the pond had to be filled in because of the insect pests. Canal Street presently connects the Manhattan Bridge to the Holland Tunnel. It is a large street with heavy traffic and crowds of people. Inexpensive stores attract thousands of shoppers.

Carl Schurz Park Schurz was a nineteenth-century German immigrant who served as an American diplomat, a Union general during the Civil War, a United States Senator, and a Secretary of the Interior as well as an editor of a newspaper. The park is located on a rocky cliff overlooking the East River.

Chambers Street The street was named to honor John Chambers, a lawyer who worked for the English colonial government of

New York as an alderman and judge. Chambers Street is in a crowded and busy commercial area of Manhattan.

Chelsea This neighborhood on the west side was originally the property of Captain Thomas Clarke, a soldier during the French and Indian War. Clarke called his property Chelsea, and after he died Mrs. Clarke built a large house there and named it Chelsea House. The name was significant because there was a Royal Chelsea Hospital for old soldiers in England. Chelsea Square took the name of Chelsea House and eventually the entire area was known as Chelsea. It extends from 14th to 30th Street west of Fifth Avenue and part of it has been "gentrified." The Chelsea Hotel, a local residential hotel, has been the home of many talented people, including Thomas Wolfe and Arthur Miller.

Christopher Street On the lower west side, Christopher Street was at one time Skinner Road in memory of Colonel William Skinner, a relative of the owner of this part of Manhattan during the eighteenth century. Later on, Charles Christopher Amos became owner of the land and the street was renamed for him.

Convent Avenue The Convent of the Sacred Heart stood here during the nineteenth century until it burned down in 1888.

Cooper Square Peter Cooper, for whom the square was named, was a nineteenth-century industrialist, inventor, and philanthropist. Cooper is known for building the first steam locomotive in this country and for improving the manufacture of iron. He even ran for president when he was eighty-five years old.

Corlear's Hook This piece of land on the East River was named for Jacob van Corlear, an early Dutch settler in New Amsterdam. In 1636 he bought a tract of land from the Indians which probably included Corlear's Hook.

Delancey Street On the lower east side of Manhattan, Delancey Street was named for an important family of colonial New York. James Delancy (1703-60) was a judge and later New York Lieutenant-Governor. There was a second James Delancey (1732-1800), who served in the provincial assembly just before the American Revolution. Oliver Delancey (1718-1785) was a merchant, politician, and loyalist during the Revolution.

Duane Street This street in lower Manhattan was probably named for James Duane (1733-97). Duane was a member of the Continental Congress and Mayor of New York (1784-89). He also served as the first federal judge of the district of New York.

Dyckman Street The Dyckman family owned a large tract of land in upper Manhattan during the middle of the nineteenth century. The family was in New Amsterdam since the Dutch period, and some of its members were Revolutionary War soldiers.

Ellis Island Dutch settlers called it Oyster Island and used it for a picnic ground. Later on it was called Bucking Island. In 1765 the name was changed to Gibbet Island, after a pirate had been executed there. At the close of the eighteenth century Samuel Ellis, a merchant from Manhattan, purchased the island. New York State bought it from Ellis in 1808 and sold it to the United States government. Ellis Island is known for the role it played in introducing new immigrants to the United States, and it is now a museum drawing thousands of tourists.

Fort Tryon Park Fort Tryon in upper Manhattan was important to the British during the Revolution William Tryon was a British governor of New York (1771-78). At West 192nd Street, this park is the home of Cloisters Metropolitan Museum of Art medieval collection.

Gay Street There was an R. Gay who resided in lower Manhattan at the time of the Revolutionary War, and the street was probably named for him. Gay Street was mentioned for the first time in New York City records in 1827. During the era of Prohibition Gay Street was known for its "speakeasies." It is a small street with Federal-style homes.

Gold Street Gold Street in lower Manhattan was originally a small road that ran into a pasture known as Golden Hill because of its yellow flowers.

Gracie Mansion It was named in memory of Archibald Gracie who settled in New York City in the late eighteenth century. Gracie was a merchant, a banker, and a supporter of the public school. He purchased some land and built a mansion which later became the home of the mayors.

Gramercy Park The name is derived from the Dutch word *crommessie*, which means "crooked little knife." It refers to the shape of some physical features of the locality in the seventeenth century. *Crommessie* appears in a document of the colonial period. The park dates back to the nineteenth century. Gramercy Park is in a neighborhood of townhouses with European-looking iron balconies.

Greenwich Village This is simply "Green Village" from *wick*, the old English word for village. It was called a village due to its rural character during the eighteenth century. Greenwich Village is known for its cultural contribution as well as for its nineteenth-century houses. Tourists are attracted to its shops, its restaurants, and its history.

Hanover Square Close to Wall Street, Hanover Square commemorates the Hanover Dynasty, which ruled Britain from

1714. It is a large commercial center in the vicinity of Wall Street.

Harlem Peter Stuyvesant established this community in 1658 as an agricultural settlement. The name comes from an old city in the Netherlands, Haarlem. Harlem has three sections: (1) Central or Black Harlem, (2) Spanish Harlem which is east of Park Avenue and north of East 96th Street, and (3) what used to be Italian Harlem, an old Italian neighborhood on East 116th Street.

Herald Square The square was named after the Herald building, where *The New York Herald* was published before it merged with *The New York Times*.

Hester Street This street was named for Hester Rynders, daughter of Governor Jacob Leisler of colonial New York.

Holland Tunnel It was named for Clifford M. Holland, the Chief Engineer. The Holland Tunnel runs under the Hudson River, connecting the lower part of Manhattan to New Jersey.

Houston Street Houston Street was named in memory of William Houstoun, a Georgia delegate to the Continental Congress. "Houston" is just a misspelling of Houstoun, and Houstoun appears on documents of the early nineteenth century. This street, which traverses Greenwich Village, is the site of the Italian feast commemorating St. Anthony of Padua every June.

Lenox Avenue The name commemorates the prominent Lenox family of New York. Robert Lenox arrived in New York from Scotland before the Revolutionary War.

Lexington Avenue In the late 1830's Samuel Ruggles, a lawyer and developer, opened up Lexington Avenue across his land. The street was named for the Battle of Lexington. Lexington Avenue, running from north to south, is one of Manhattan's most well-known streets, highly commercial in character.

MacDougal Street MacDougal Street is in the Greenwich Village area, and was probably named for Alexander MacDougal (1732-86). He encouraged support for the colonies in New York City during the American Revolution. MacDougal served as colonel of the First New York Regiment and as a general during the war. He was a merchant and eventually became the first president of the Bank of New York. MacDougal Street is noted for the Provincetown Playhouse, Eugene O'Neill's theater.

Madison Avenue Madison Avenue, opened in 1836, was named in honor of James Madison, who died that same year. Another one of New York's notable streets, it also runs from north to south on the east side of Manhattan. It has been traditionally known for the advertising industry.

Madison Square Garden It was named after Madison Street and Madison Square which, in turn, were named for James Madison.

Maiden Lane Maiden Lane was at one time a small road running along a stream. In Dutch it was *Maagde Paetje* (Maiden Lane). The settlers chose the name because young girls used the stream for washing clothes. A large Federal Reserve Bank presently stands on this lower-Manhattan Street.

Mott Street Mott Street first appears on a 1776 map. The name honors Joseph Mott, a butcher who supplied the troops during the Revolution. Mott Street is in lower Manhattan's Little Italy," one of the original Italian neighborhoods of New York City. Its restaurants and pastry shops attract many tourists as well as New Yorkers.

Murray Hill This neighborhood on the east side of Manhattan was named for Robert Murray, a local merchant. Born in Scotland, he settled at first in Pennsylvania because of his Quaker background. In 1753 he came to New York City and went into business with his brother. Murray Hill in Manhattan was the name of their country home. It is now a residential area with brownstone houses, but it is not far from the commercial center of Midtown.

Nassau Street King William III of England, who came to the English throne in 1689, was a member of the Dutch dynasty of Orange-Nassau, hence Nassau Street. The Federal Hall National Memorial at Wall and Nassau Streets is a Greek Revival building, where the original Federal Hall used to stand. The Stamp Act Congress met there (1765), George Washington was inaugurated there (1789), and Congress convened at this spot for the first time (1789-90).

Randall's Island Thomas Delaville, a customs official, was the first proprietor of this island, and in 1772 Captain James Montressor bought it from Delaville and named it after himself. Twelve years later Jonathan Randal became the next owner of the island until New York City purchased it from him (1835). The title deed misspelled Randal's name by adding an extra letter (Randall), and the misspelled form was perpetuated.

Reade Street It was named for Joseph Reade, a warden of Trinity Church. There is a possibility that this was the same Joseph Reade who served in the colonial governor's council.

Rector Street This street in lower Manhattan was named in honor of the rectors of Trinity Church. Many of them lived on this street.

Riker's Island In 1664 the Duke of York granted this island to Abraham Rycken. The Rycken (later Riker) family owned it for several generations.

Rockefeller Center Rockefeller Center is composed of a group of buildings in midtown Manhattan which were built with the financial backing of the Rockefeller family.

Sheridan Square Sheridan Square commemorates Philip Henry Sheridan, a commander of the Union cavalry during the Civil War.

Sherman Square It was named to honor William Tecumseh Sherman, the well-known Civil War general who marched through Georgia to capture Atlanta. He had a house in New York City, in the vicinity of the square which bears his name.

Spring Street There was at one time a spring in the area that was used as a source of water by the local residents.

Thompkins Square Located on the east side of Manhattan, it was named in memory of Daniel D. Thompkins, a governor of New York State for four terms. Thompkins served as Vice President of the United States and as an officer during the War of 1812. He was also instrumental in abolishing slavery in New York State. Thompkins Square includes an area in which many homeless people have erected temporary shelters using cardboard boxes.

Times Square The square was named after the Times Building which was erected at the turn of the century. *The New York Times* was moved to this new building which was called the Times Tower. The square upon which the Times Tower stood was known as Longacre Square. In April of 1904 Longacre Square became

Times Square. Both New Yorkers and visitors have traditionally looked upon Times Square as one of the symbols of New York City and as one of the central attractions. Over the years, however, it has deteriorated as a result of drugs and pornography. There have been efforts in recent years to improve the neighborhood.

Union Square Originally Union Place, it became Union Square in the 1830's. The planners of the city chose "Union" because there were a number of streets connecting at that location. It is within a busy commercial area of Manhattan, but it has deteriorated to some extent during the 1980's. Since 1990, however, there have been improvements.

Varick Street Varick Street, running on the west side of Manhattan, was named for Richard Varick (1753-1831). Varick participated in the Revolutionary War and served as speaker of the New York State Assembly (1787-88). He was also New York State Attorney General (1788-89) and Mayor of New York City (1789-90).

Wall Street In 1653 the Dutch built a wall at this location to defend their settlement against the English. The wall had one entrance which was at Wall and Pearl Streets. At the end of the seventeenth century the wall was taken down. Wall Street, symbolic of New York City's role in the world of finance, is in the oldest part of the city, which was settled early in the seventeenth century.

Ward's Island Ward's Island lies in the East River between Manhattan and Queens. At the time of the American Revolution it was employed as a British military post. Its earlier names were Tenkenas, Buchanan's Island, and Great Barn Island. After the Revolution Jaspar and Bartholomew Ward purchased the island and farmed it. At first, it was called Ward's Island occasionally, but eventually the name became permanent.

Washington Heights In the summer of 1776 George Washington fortified both banks of the Hudson River. Fort Washington was constructed where the George Washington Bridge stands today. The neighborhood was known later on as Washington Heights. It is an ethnically diverse neighborhood with African-Americans, Hispanic, and Greek communities. Washington Heights is both residential and commercial, while Fort Tryon Park and the Cloisters attract tourists.

Washington Square Park In colonial times this area was a marsh which was turned into agricultural land. The New York State militia used it in the early part of the nineteenth century. The Washington Square Memorial Arch, which was originally constructed of wood, was put there in 1889. The arch and the square commemorated the centennial of the United States. The center of Greenwich Village and the site of New York University, it has always been one of lower Manhattan's tourist attractions.

Worth Street In lower Manhattan, this street was named for William Jenkins Worth, an officer during the Mexican War under Winfield Scott. (see Fort Worth, Texas).

Queens

Queens This is New York's largest borough, making up more than a third of the city's area. Queens was established as a county by the English on November 1, 1683, and was named in honor of Queen Catherine of Braganza (1638-1705). She was the daughter of John IV, Duke of Braganza, who became King of Portugal in 1640. Catherine married King Charles II of England in 1662. Queens is basically residential and much of it is suburban in character, with its private homes, garden apartments, and shopping centers.

Alley Pond Park This Queens park was named for Alley Pond. The pond and the stream that drained it used to block traffic, leaving a narrow passage or alley between the water and the hills.

Arverne Arverne is a section of Rockaway in Queens. It was settled in the 1820's, but rapid development came in the 1880's when Remington Vernam arrived. Vernam's wife called the community "Arverne," a combination of his first initial ("R") and his nickname ("Verne"), hence Arverne. The village of Arverne was incorporated in 1895.

Astoria Astoria was incorporated as a village in 1839 and named for John Jacob Astor who pledged to contribute money for the construction of a school for women. Astor (1763-1848) made a fortune in the fur trade and purchased a large amount of property in New York City. Modern Astoria is a neighborhood of small apartment houses and private homes. The Lasky Movie Studios were there during the 1920's, and the Kaufman Astoria Studios make movies and commercials there.

Baisley Pond Located in Baisley Park in Queens, it was owned by David Baisley who used it as a mill pond. During the 1850's the pond became a source of public water, and it was about this time that the skeleton of a prehistoric elephant was discovered in it.

Belle Harbor This beachside community in Rockaway started to develop at the turn of the century. The developers gave it the name to attract settlers. Belle Harbor's old mansions, the summer residences of wealthy New Yorkers, are still standing.

Berrian's Island An island in the East River, it is administratively part of Queens. It was named for Peter Berrien, one of the administrators of Queens County during the colonial period.

Bowne Street Bowne Street in Flushing was named for John Bowne (1627/8-1695), an English Quaker who settled in Flushing in 1653. This street is in an Asian neighborhood with one of the largest Hindu temples in North America. There is also the Bowne House Museum, the original home of John Bowne.

Cambria Heights This section of Queens was developed in the late 1920's. It was given the name "Cambria" because it was owned by the Cambria Title Savings and Trust Company of Cambria County, Pennsylvania. The area is elevated, hence "Heights."

College Point College Point is a section of northern Flushing. In 1827 an Episcopal priest, Reverend William A. Muhlenberg, visited Flushing and was asked to serve as rector of St. George's Episcopal Church. Several years later, Muhlenberg bought some land on Long Island Sound. He wanted to build St. Paul's College, an Episcopal Seminary, at this location, but the financial problems of the 1830's, which had weakened the United States economy, made it impossible for the seminary to be as large as he had first planned. The buildings were completed by 1840, but the seminary had to close ten years later. The neighborhood, however, continued to be called College Point. It became an industrial area in the 1850's, when Conrad Poppenhausen, a German immigrant, opened a factory for the manufacture of rubber knife handles. College Point is a residential community with the atmosphere of a small town. The Flushing Airport used to be there for private planes.

Corona Corona is a neighborhood in northern Queens to the west of Flushing, originally known as West Flushing. Benjamin W. Hitchcock started to develop the area in 1872, and renamed it

Corona because it was on the crown (*corona* in Latin) of a hill.
The theory is that Hitchcock was promoting his development with
this name, hoping that it would some day be the "crown village" of
Long Island. Corona is presently a heavily populated residential
neighborhood with Asian and South American immigrant
communities. Flushing Meadows, where two World's Fairs were
held, is within Corona.

Crocheron Park This park in the Bayside section of Queens was
named for Crocheron House, a hotel that was there at one time. It
was believed that Boss Tweed went there to hide after he had
escaped from jail in 1875.

Ditmars Boulevard Ditmars was a local family
whose members participated in the RevolutionarWar
in Queens County.

Douglaston Boulevard and Parkway They are located in the
Douglaston section of northeastern Queens. George Douglas
obtained land in this area in 1835, and his son, William, planned
the village of Marathon. Marathon was renamed Douglaston in
1872.

Edgemere This section of Far Rockaway was developed in the
1890's by Frederick J. Lancaster. At first it was called New Venice,
but before long, it was renamed Edgemere due to its location on the
edge of the ocean. The word "mere" is derived from the Latin word
for sea, *maris*.

Elmhurst In northern Queens, this neighborhood was first
settled by the English in 1652 and was called both Middleburg
and New Towne. When the English took New Netherlands
from the Dutch in 1664 the English king called the Queens
settlement Hastings, after Hastings in England where the

famous battle took place in 1066. In 1665 or 1666 the name went back to New Towne and was eventually shortened to Newtown. In 1898, when Queens became part of New York City, Newtown was changed to Elmhurst by the land developer, Cord Meyer. He picked the name because of the many elm trees in the area. Elmhurst is the home of Lefrak City, a large housing development built during the 1960's.

Flushing In the seventeenth century it was called Vlissingen by the Dutch, after a town in the Netherlands. The English, who were settling in Queens at this time, were calling it "Flushing," their way of pronouncing Vlissingen. After the English had taken New Netherlands in 1664, the English form, Flushing, became official. Flushing is a residential area with many shopping centers and small businesses, but much of it has retained its suburban atmosphere. It has attracted many new Chinest, Korean, Indian, and Japanese immigrants.

Forest Hills Forest Hills was originally known as Whitepot. There are two theories with regard to the origin of this name. According to one theory, the territory was purchased from the Indians for three clay pots. It is also possible that the name was actually Whiteput, a "put" being a pit or hollowed out ground. This would indicate a dried stream in the area. The name was changed to Forest Hills in 1906 by the land developers because it was close to Forest Park and was located on high rolling ground. In 1909 part of the area was developed as a model residential community and called Forest Hills Gardens. Forest Hills is known as the "lawn tennis capital of the western hemisphere," being the home of the West Side Tennis Club.

Fort Tilden This part of Rockaway was named for Samuel Jones Tilden (1814-1886) a lawyer and politician in New York City. He made money in mining and in the reorganizing and refinancing of railroads. He served as chairman of the New York State Democratic Committee and helped to eject the "Tweed Ring." He was governor of New York (1875-77) and ran for President of the United States against Hayes. Most of his money was left to New York City for its library. Fort Tilden is located at the western end of Jacob Riis Park.

Francis Lewis Boulevard This large Queens road was named in memory of Francis Lewis (1713-1802), a Welshman who settled in New York in 1746 and worked as a government contractor. Lewis was active in the events leading to the American Revolution, served as a delegate to the Continental Congress, and signed the Declaration of Independence.

Hallett's Cove It is part of the East River off the coast of Astoria, Queens. William Hallett, an Englishman from Dorsetshire, was granted by Peter Stuyvesant in 1652 all of what is now Astoria.

Hollis This Queens community was named for an early Long Island family. Colonial records mention a Robert Hollis of Brooklyn who was granted a permit to keep an inn and serve liquor. Hollis filed a complaint about keepers of inns who were working without any kind of authorization. There were apparently members of this family in Queens as well.

Howard Beach Howard Beach is a community in Queens, on Jamaica Bay. It was called Ramblersville early in this century, but in 1910 it was renamed after the Howard family, owner of a local hotel for boaters and fishermen. This family also helped to develop the neighborhood.

Jackson Heights Jackson Heights was named after Jackson Avenue which, in turn, was named in honor of a prominent local family. The land is elevated, hence "Heights." One member of this family, John C. Jackson, was president of the *Hunter's Point*, *Newtown*, and *Flushing Turnpike Company*, which was chartered in 1859 and built Jackson Avenue. The residential community started there in 1909.

Jamaica The name may be derived from the Algonquian word for beaver. There is no relation to the island of Jamaica in the West Indies. The name in Queens appears in the colonial sources as "*Jaimaica*," "*Jamaico*," "*Jamanica*," "*Jameca*," and "*Jameco*." It is possible that the name refers to a pond for beavers. During the 1950's Jamaica was one of the most important commercial districts in New York City. In the following decade, its economy began to deteriorate because shopping malls were being erected in other parts of Queens, thus taking commerce away from Jamaica.

Juniper Valley Park This Queens park is to the immediate west of Flushing. In the seventeenth century it was known as Juniper Swamp, for many juniper trees flourished there.

Kew Gardens Originally this Queens neighborhood was called Hopedale. It was renamed Maple Grove, after a local burial ground by that name. In 1869 this area was bought by the developer, Alban P. Man. It began to grow as a residential neighborhood after 1912 and was named Kew Gardens, after the English village of Kew, the home of the Royal Botanical Gardens.

Kissena Boulevard It was at first known as Kissena Road, named for Kissena Lake. The Indian word kissena means "it is cold."

Kosciusko Street This street was named for Tadeusz Kosciusko (1746-1817), who came to America in 1776, where he was commissioned as a Colonel of Engineers in the Continental Army. He contributed to the American

Revolution in a military as well as in an engineering capacity.

Lefferts Boulevard This street is named for the Lefferts family, an old family of Dutch origin and owner of agricultural land in Queens.

Maspeth The name of the Queens neighborhood may be derived from the Delaware Indian words *mech* (great) and *sepe* (brook). Another possibility is that it comes from the Delaware phrase *missiachpitschik*, which means "those who are scattered." Colonial documents show it with a variety of forms including "Marshpath," "Maspath," and "Mespacht." The local Indians called their village Matsepe (great brook). Europeans first arrived in the area during the 1640's. Maspeth today, is basically an industrial area with some residential communities that have been there for generations. Poles, Lithuanians, Italians, and Germans are the main ethnic groups living in Maspeth.

Merrick Boulevard The name comes from Merrikoke or Merric, a local Indian tribe that occupied part of the present-day Nassau county during the seventeenth century. They were an Algonquian-speaking group.

Newton Avenue Newtown was the name of the English settlement, also called Middleburg, that was established in Queens in 1652.

Ozone Park The developer, Benjamin W. Hitchcock, planned this community in the 1880's. He named it for the fresh air that came from the ocean. Originally Ozone Park was called South Woodhaven. This residential neighborhood was originally Italian and Polish, but Asians and Hispanics have settled there during the 1980's. Ozone Park is known, also, for Aqueduct Racetrack.

Parsons Boulevard This street in Jamaica, Queens, was at one time divided between South Parsons Avenue and North Parsons Avenue. It was probably named for a family that had property in the area. It is, today, a busy street with heavy traffic and many small businesses.

Powell's Cove Powell's Cove is the part of the Long Island Sound that is situated between College Point and Whitestone, in Queens. There was a Powell family that owned land in this vicinity during the nineteenth century. Most likely the cove was named after this family.

Rego Park The Rego Construction Company started to develop this area in 1923. The name of the construction company was derived from the initial letters of the words, "real good."

Richmond Hill The developer, Alban P. Man, bought a piece of land in 1869, which included this section of Queens. He and another developer, Edward Richmond, built up the neighborhood and called it Richmond Hill, both having claimed that they named it after a place in England called Richmond Hill, which Man had possibly visited. It is more likely, however, that it was named for Edward Richmond. Richmond Hill was incorporated as a village in 1894.

Rockaway It may mean sandy place in either the Algonquian or the Delaware language. Names related to Rockaway are found in other parts of the Middle Atlantic region which derive from the Native American word for sand. There were Native Americans in southeastern Queens and in southwestern Nassau County whose main settlement was Rechquaakie, probably a part of Far Rockaway. By the close of the seventeenth century the Indians of Rockaway had moved into present-day Nassau County. Rockaway has the largest city beach in the United States.

Skillman Avenue This Queens street was named for John Skillman, Sr., a local farmer during the nineteenth century.

St. Alban's The name of this neighborhood in southeastern Queens was taken from a railroad station by that name. The name of the station was chosen by a committee of local residents. They named it for the village of St. Albans in England. St. Alban's has been and still is primarily residential, with middle-class African-Americans.

Steinway Avenue Originally Tenth Avenue, this street in northern Queens became Steinway Avenue in 1905. The name commemorates the Steinway family which manufactured pianos during the nineteenth century. They purchased more than four hundred acres of land in the vicinity for a factory and they helped to develop the neighborhood.

Van Wyck Expressway This major Queens thoroughfare was named in honor of the Van Wyck family. Cornelius van Wyck had a son who died on a British prison ship during the American Revolution. His other son, however, was a loyalist. John F. Kennedy International Airport is located at the southern end of Van Wyck.

Whitestone Whitestone was first settled in the eighteenth century. There is a legend that it was named after a large white stone that was found near the shore of the Long Island Sound. In the early nineteenth century, when the popular DeWitt Clinton was governor, the residents voted to change the name of their community to Clintonville. The old name, Whitestone, endured by force of habit. When the Post Office was established there in 1854 Whitestone prevailed as the official name of the community. Whitestone was incorporated as a village in 1869.

Willett's Point Willet's Point is a piece of land that extends into the Long Island Sound from northern Queens. It is the home of Fort Totten, which was built to protect the Long Island Sound. The name commemorates Marinus Willett (1740-1830), a local merchant and Revolutionary War soldier. He was a leader of the patriots in New York City and was elected mayor in the first decade of the nineteenth century.

Winfield During the seventeenth century this section of Queens was called Smith's Meadow. In 1840 G. G. Andrews, a developer, started to divide the area into lots and named the new neighborhood after General Winfield Scott.

Woodhaven In Souhwestern Queens, Woodhaven was developed in the 1830's and called Woodville for the Wood family, residents of the area. On July 30, 1853 some of the local people held a public meeting in order to change the name of their community to Woodhaven so that the Post Office would establish itself there. There was already another Post Office in New York State Called Woodville.

Staten Island

Staten Island The name is derived from the Dutch word *staaten* (states). It is a reference to the Staaten (States General), the assembly that governed the Netherlands. Staten Island, with a population of about 400,000, is the smallest of the five boroughs with regard to the number of residents. The borough has become suburban over the last thirty years, but there are sections which still retain an almost rural character.

Arrochar This Staten Island community was established in 1880 by W. W. MacFarland. He named it after Arrochar, near Loch Lomond in Scotland.

Arthur Kill Arthur Kill is a waterway that separates the western shore of Staten Island from New Jersey. "Arthur" is derived from the Dutch word *achter* which means after, behind or beyond. "Kill" is a form of the Dutch word *kull* or *cull* which means stream, river, bay, or passage of water. Arthur Kill refers, therefore, to a waterway beyond the river or bay; it lies beyond the passage of water known as the Kill Van Kull. (see Kill Van Kull).

Bull's Head At the corner of Richmond Avenue and Victory Boulevard in northwestern Staten Island, this spot was named after a local tavern.

Castleton Corners It is located at the junction of Manor Road and Victory Boulevard. The name first appears in 1872. It was originally Castle Town, named after the Manor of Cassiltowne, the Staten island estate of Governor Dongan of colonial New York. Dongan named it after his home in Ireland.

Dongan Hill This section of Staten Island was named for Governor Thomas Dongan of New York (1683-88). Dongan Hill is, today, one of the wealthiest residential sections of Staten Island.

Egbertville Located in eastern Staten Island, it was named for the Egbert family. Govert Egbert arrived in America in 1660, but there is no evidence that he had ever lived on Staten Island. In 1698, however, Tunis Egbert purchased some land there. There were many descendants of Tunis Egbert living on Staten Island during the eighteenth century and on into the nineteenth.Egbertville is presently the site of the Greenbelt High Rock, a wooded park with trails, environmental programs, and workshops.

Emerson Hills This Staten Island community was named for Judge William Emerson who moved to Staten Island from New England in 1837. He was the brother of Ralph Waldo Emerson who used to come there to visit.

Fort Wadsworth Fort Wadsworth is located in eastern Staten Island, on the Narrows which flows into Upper New York Bay. There was a British fort at this spot during the Revolutionary War. The present fort, however, was erected in 1847. In 1865 it was named in honor of Brigadier General James S. Wadsworth who died during the Civil War.

Gryme's Hill This promontory in northeastern Staten Island looks over the communities of the eastern shore. It was developed as a residential neighborhood during the 1830's. The name commemorates a Madame Grymes who came there to live in 1836. Gryme's Hill has been the home of Wagner College since 1918.

Kill Van Kull This is the waterway that bounds Staten Island on the northwest. The Dutch word *Kill* means stream, river or passage of water. *Kull* (or *cull*) is also a reference to a body of water, hence a passage of water flowing from another body of water. The reference here is probably to the fact that the waterway to the north of Staten Island flows from Upper New York Bay in the direction of the Arthur Kill which flows to the west and separates Staten Island from New Jersey. (see Arthur Kill).

Latourette Park Located in central Staten Island, it was the home of David Latourette, a local farmer who built a mansion there in 1836. The Latourette family owned about five hundred acres of land which is at present Latourette Park. The mansion is now used as a clubhouse.

New Brighton This community in northern Staten Island was named after the resort of Brighton in England. Thomas E. Davis, a land speculator, started a summer resort for New Yorkers there in 1836.

Port Ivory Port Ivory is in northern Staten Island near Richmond Terrace. Since soap was manufactured there at one time, it was named after Ivory Soap.

Prall's Island This island is located on the western shore of Staten Island, in the Arthur Kill between Staten Island and New Jersey. It was named for the Prall family, one of the early Dutch families of Staten Island. Prall's Island was probably owned at one time by a member of this family.

Prince's Bay On the south shore of Staten Island, the name commemorates British royalty. During the nineteenth century it was known also as Lemon Creek, since the Lemon Creek Post Office is listed in the New York State Manual for 1859. In 1861 the Post Office name was changed to Prince's Bay.

Richmond Richmond was established as a county on November 1, 1683. It was named in honor of the Duke of Richmond. (see Staten Island).

Rossville Rossville is a section of southwestern Staten Island. It was named in memory of an army officer, Colonel William E. Ross.

St. George St. George is the civic center on the northern shore of Staten Island, and the Staten Island General Post Office is located there. It was most likely named for George Law, a prominent Staten Island engineer. St. George has a small commercial area and a terminal for all Staten Island public transportation as well as the Staten Island Ferry which brings crowds of people to and from Manhattan many times each day.

Stapleton This community in northern Staten Island was named for William J. Staples in 1836. Earlier names include New Ferry and Second Landing. Stapleton draws tourists to its park, its antique stores, and its restaurants.

Thompkinsville Originally this Staten Island neighborhood was the village of Thompkinsville, named for Daniel D. Thompkins, New York State Governor and later vice-president. He lived on Staten Island later on in his life.

Todt Hill The name refers to a group or chain of small hills in northern Staten Island, at one time a source of iron ore known as "iron hill." There are two theories for the name Todt Hill, its name since the nineteenth century. According to one theory, it was actually "Toad Hill" in the eighteenth century. There is a local legend that before the American Revolution there was a woman living there who had two boyfriends who wanted to marry her. She gave the one that she did not want to marry a hint to go away by playing a practical joke on him. She put some toads in his pocket which he later discovered. The joke became well-known and the place began to be called "Toad Hill." "Toad Hill" eventually became "Todt Hill" through mispronunciation.According to the other theory, during an Indian conflict of the seventeenth century a group of people had hidden there, but they were later found and killed. The spot was then called *doode bergh*, Dutch for "hill of the dead." Eventually it became "doode hill" and later Todt Hill ("death hill"), combining the Dutch and English words. The second explanation seems to be the more plausible one. Todt Hill is the highest point on the entire eastern coast of the United States between Maine and the Florida Keys.

Tottenville This community in southwestern Staten Island was originally Bentley Manor. In the 1860's it was renamed after Ephraim Totten, one of the local settlers. The community began to be developed after the 1860's. Tottenville, today, is a quiet, rather isolated, residential community which looks like a small town. Public transportation connects Tottenville to the rest of Staten Island.

Chapter 2. Geographical Names Within the United States

Abilene (Texas) The county seat of Taylor County, in northwestern Texas, received its name from the Kansas town of the same name. It is derived from the Hebrew word *abel* meaning a grassy plain or a meadow.

Adirondack Mountains Located in northern New York state, the Adirondacks has been a popular resort area for a long time. The exact meaning of the name is no longer known, but it is agreed that it comes from the name of an Algoquian Indian tribe whose members were called "tree-eaters" by their enemies.

Akron Akron, Ohio, situated at the top of a divide that separates two rivers has a Greek name meaning summit. The choice of a Greek name may be a reflection of an interest in classical words, an early American phenomenon.

Alabama Alabama or Aliamu is a Muskogean Indian word which may mean "medicine gatherers" or "thicket clearers." Muskogean was spoken by the Creek Indians of southern Alabama. Some experts, however, believe that the name is a combination of the words *alba* (thickets or plants) and amo (reapers), both from the Choctaw Indian Language.

Alaska The largest state with respect to area, having almost 600,000 square miles, it is one of the smallest in population. Alaska has the highest mountain in North America (Mount McKinley at 20,320 feet) and the largest United States national park (13,000,000 acres). The Aleuts applied the name to the Alaskan mainland in order to distinguish it from the Aleutian Islands. In 1867, when the United States government purchased Alaska from Russia, several names were suggested for it. The candidates were "Aleutia," "Oonalaska," "Sitka," "Yukon," "Walrussia," and "Alaska." The present name was selected because the designation "Alaska Peninsula" was already being used on maps of the region.

Albany (New York) This state capital now has the Governor Nelson A. Rockefeller Empire State Plaza, a government and culture center more than forty stories in height. Albany was originally a Dutch settlement called Fort Orange, named for the Dutch House of Orange. It was also known as *Beverwyck* (Dutch for "Beavertown"). In 1664, when the English captured New Netherlands from the Dutch, they changed the name to Albany in honor of the Duke of York who also had the title, Duke of Albany.

Albuquerque New Mexico's largest city is a center for ballooning enthusiasts because of its clear weather. Albuquerque was named for the Duke of Alburquerque, viceroy of Spanish America (New Spain) when the town was established (1706). The first *r* was dropped by the American settlers later on.

Aleutian Islands The chain of islands that runs in a southwesterly direction from the Alaskan mainland, it was the site of a nineteen-day battle between American and Japanese troops during World

War II. The name comes from Aleut, the people who live there, relatives of the Eskimos.

Allegheny Mountains The Allegheny Mountains make up the western part of the Appalachians, running from southwestern New York through Pennsylvania, West Virginia, and Kentucky. The first part of the name is an English form of the Algonquian work *welhik*, meaning most beautiful or best. The suffix *heny* is Algonquian for stream. In this instance the stream is the upper part of the Ohio River. The mountain chain took the name of the stream.

Allentown Along with Easton and Bethlehem, Allentown is part of Pennsylvania's Lehigh Valley, the state's third largest metropolitan area. The town was called Northampton at first, but the name was changed to honor William Allen, a landowner, jurist, and founder of the settlement.

Appalachian Mountains The Appalachians form the mountain system that includes the White Mountains in New Hampshire, the Green Mountains in Vermont, the Catskills in New York, the Alleghenies in Pennsylvania, the Blue Ridge Mountains in Virginia and North Carolina, and the Cumberland Mountains in Tennessee. They may be described as the "breastbone" of the North American continent. Cabeza da Vaca, an early Spanish explorer, recorded the Indian name Apalachen. The name was to appear on maps of the mountainous parts of southeastern North America. At a later date the English settlers changed the spelling and applied the name to the southern section of this mountain chain. By the late nineteenth century the name was used to designate the entire mountain range.

Arizona More than three million tourists flock to this state every year to see the Grand Canyon and a Navajo Indian reservation larger in area than the entire state of West Virginia. There are three possible explanations for the name: (1) The Pima or Papgo Indian words *ali* (small) and *shonak* (place of the spring); (2) the Spanish words, *arida* (dry) and *zona* (zone); (3) the Aztec work *arizuma* (silver-bearing). Some silver deposits have been discovered in the southern part of the state.

Arkansas The only diamonds to be found in North America are at the Crater of Diamonds State Park in Arkansas, where visitors can dig for them. The name of the state has its origin in *Alkansas* or *Akamsea*, a name that the French gave to the local Indian tribe later known as Quapaw. French explorers were in Arkansas in the seventeenth century, when it was a part of French North America.

Asbury Park This Monmouth County, New Jersey town is part of the Jersey Shore resort area which has attracted bathers every summer since the late nineteenth century. It is located about twenty miles to the south of the area that was hit hard by the hurricane of 1991. Francis Asbury (1745-1816), for whom the town was named, was the first bishop of the Methodist Episcopal Church in America. Asbury toured the United States in order to ordain ministers and organize the Methodist Church.

Ashtabula This small town in the northeastern corner of Ohio, near Lake Erie, derives its name from the Algonquian words meaning "there are enough moving," a possible reference to fish.

Atlanta As depicted in the film, *Gone with the Wind*, almost the entire city was in ruins at the close of the Civil War. Today it is the economic and cultural center of the deep South. J.E. Thomson, a railroad builder, named the city in 1845, when it was the terminus of the Western and Atlantic Railroad. Thomson chose the name Atlanta because he made the assumption that it was the feminine form of Atlantic. Also, it was customary for many town names to end with the letter *a*.

Augusta Augusta, Georgia is in the eastern part of the state, at the border with South Carolina. It was named in honor of the Princess of Wales, daughter-in-law of King George II.

Austin The capital city of Texas, Austin also has over two hundred and fifty high-tech companies. Its name comes from that of Stephen F. Austin, a leading figure in the struggle for Texan independence.

"Badlands" The "badlands" of North Dakota is made up of hills formed from clay and carved by wind and rain. South Dakota also has a "badlands," named by the Indians who found it difficult to cross. Today the North Dakota "badlands" has a national park in which the terrain is preserved so that it has the same appearance as it had during the early 1900's. Fort Buford, where Sitting Bull was imprisoned in 1866, still stands.

Bakersfield This town is in the livestock-raising area of southern California, about one hundred miles north of Los Angeles. One of the early residents of the town was Colonel Thomas Baker who fenced off his field in the vicinity.

Baltimore This large port city on Chesapeake Bay was named for Lord Baltimore, founder of the colony of Maryland in the 1630's. The city, incorporated in 1729, was called Baltimore City to distinguish it from Baltimore County. Later on it was called simply Baltimore as it is today.

Bangor Paul Bunyan, the legendary woodsman and logger, according to local folklore, was born here. There is a statue in town to honor him. Bangor is a large community and county seat in eastern Maine. The name comes from that of Bangor in Wales or Northern Ireland.

Baton Rouge Louisiana's capital was named Baton Rouge (red stick) by the French settlers. The local Indians were calling it "red stick" in their own language because they used a red stick to mark the boundary between tribal hunting grounds.

Bergen County One of New Jersey's suburban counties, it is located on the Hudson River, across from New York City. Bergen was established as a county by the English in 1683, but it was named by Dutch settlers after Bergen-op-zoom, a place in the Netherlands.

Beverly Hills Famous for decades as a community of movie stars, mansions, and fancy shops, when President Taft stopped there for a couple of days he stayed at a spot called Beverly Farms. Burton E. Green, president of the Rodeo Land and Water Company, decided to name the entire area "Beverly" when he read in the newspaper that President Taft had been there. In 1907, when a new post office was established, it was named Beverly. The present designation, Beverly Hills, came into use by 1911.

Billings Tourists visit every year because of the scenery and nearby Yellowstone National Park. Frederick K. Billings (1823-90) served as president of the Northern Pacific Railroad which founded the town in 1882.

Biloxi The French first settled Biloxi in 1699 across the bay from its present location. It was damaged by a hurricane in 1969. Many buildings, including a winter resort, were destroyed, but malls and restaurants were built to replace what had perished. The name Biloxi is a form of the Indian word which means first people.

Binghampton William Bingham (1752-1804) was a Philadelphia merchant and founder of the Bank of North America. He made a large amount of money as a speculator in land, and he promoted the building of turnpikes. Bingham was also involved in politics, representing Pennsylvania in the U.S. Senate (1795-1801). Binghampton, New York started as a settlement under his auspices. It is a large town in the southern part of the state, close to the Pennsylvania border.

Bismarck Bismarck, the capital of North Dakota, is located in the "wheat-belt." The railroad officials gave the town its name in 1873 in honor of the German chancellor, Bismarck (1815-98) as a way of paying their respect to the German bondholders who had lent their support to the railroad.

Boca Raton This beach community has Florida Atlantic University in addition to some IBM research laboratories. It is located about forty miles north of Miami, on the Atlantic coast. *Boca des Ratones* is Spanish for mouth (or bay) of painted rocks.

Bogalusa Also spelled Bogueloosa, it comes from the Choctaw Indian word meaning black stream. Bogalusa is a small settlement in southeastern Louisiana.

Boise Bird enthusiasts flock to Boise, Idaho to see the falcons and eagles at the World Center for Birds of Prey. The city took its name from the river known in French as *riviere boise* (wooded river).

Boscawen Boscawen, New Hampshire was named for a British admiral who also had an island in the South Pacific named for him. The island, however, was later on called Niuotobutabu.

Boston Boston, Massachusetts was named for Boston, England. There was a large concentration of Puritans in that part of England, and some of the New England settlers had their origins there.

Brattleboro William Brattle purchased some lands and inherited others on the New England frontier. In 1773 he became a Major General in the colonial army, under the command of the British General, Gage. The town of Brattleboro lies on the Connecticut River in southern Vermont.

Brownsville This Texas town is on the Rio Grande, very close to Matamores, Mexico. Its name is a memorial to Major Jacob Brown, who was killed there in 1846, during the Mexican War.

Bucks County Covered bridges, inns, and antique shops draw visitors to Bucks County, Pennsylvania every season. The county was established in 1682 and named for Buckinghamshire, England. William Penn and his family originally came from Buckinghamshire.

Buffalo The Anchor Bar, where the spicy chicken wings, "Buffalo wings," had their start is here. Buffalo, an industrial city on Lake Erie, is New York State's second largest city. There were never any buffalo or bison in the vicinity and, as a result, there has been some controversy over the origin of the name. The Indians called the region Beaver Creek. Some local residents discovered the bones of large animals at the spot and believed them to be buffalo, thus naming it Buffalo Creek. There is also the possibility that the name is a derivative of the French *beau fleuve* (beautiful river). French explorers visited the area in earlier times. According to a third theory, the city was named for a local individual, an Indian, by the name of Buffalo.

Butte Gold was discovered here in 1864, then silver, and later on, copper. Butte became the main supplier of copper in the United States. It was so named because of a geological feature in the immediate area known as a butte, a flat-topped isolated mountain or hill.

Cadillac Cadillac, Michigan bears the name of Antoine Cadillac (1658-1730), a French explorer of the Great Lakes region.

California Ninety percent of American wine is produced in this state. It also claims the world's tallest tree, 367.8 feet high in Redwood National Park. With respect to population, California is the largest of the fifty states. The name California was originally applied to Baja or Lower California when it was first discovered by the Spaniards in 1535. The expedition continued up the coast to Alta or Upper California. The Spanish explorer, Cortes, took the name from a Spanish story, *Las sergas de Esplandian* (*The Exploits of Esplandian*), written by Ordonez de Montalvo in 1510. In the story there is a passage which states that "on the right hand of the Indies there is an island called California, very near to the Terrestrial Paradise..." There are three possible explanations for the name California: (1) the Spanish word, *califa*, meaning succession; (2) *calif* meaning sovereign; (3) a combination of the words, *calida* and *forno*, meaning hot furnace.

Cape Canaveral The home of NASA Space Center, it is also known as Cape Kennedy. The name is Spanish for canebrake, a spot at which there is a heavy growth of cane. A Spanish explorer gave the place its name when he noticed the cane from his ship as he sailed near to the shore.

Cape Hatteras This projection of land on the Atlantic coast is separated from the North Carolina mainland by Pamlico Sound. It is on a long, thin island that runs along the coast. The cape was first noted by the English sailors in the 1580's. *Hatrask* or *Hatoraske*, probably an Indian tribal name, was the original spelling. Cape Hatteras claims the tallest lighthouse in the United States, 208 feet high.

Cape May Presidents Lincoln and Grant visited this New Jersey ocean resort in the nineteenth century, but it goes back to 1631 as a vacation spot. Cape May is a peninsula that runs south from New Jersey, thus separating Delaware from the Atlantic Ocean. Cornelius Jacobson May, for whom the cape was named, sailed down the eastern coast of North America (c. 1612-14) to explore the shoreline between Long Island and southern New Jersey.

Carson City Nevada's capital, one of the smallest state capitals in the United States, was named in memory of Christopher ("Kit") Carson (1809-68), a well-known and semi-legendary frontiersman and trapper. During the 1840's Carson guided military expeditions to the southwest, and several years later he served as an Indian agent.

Catskill Mountains Proximity to New York City has made the Catskill region a resort area with its many hotels, its outdoor activities, and its craft fairs. As early as 1656 the name *Kats Kill* appears on a Dutch map. This name has been taken as a reference to a wildcat, but the possessive form of the name indicates that *Kat* was the name of an individual, perhaps a Dutch nickname. The 1656 map reads *Landt van Kats Kill* and it refers to an area west of the mountains. Eventually the name was applied to the mountains, themselves. *Kill* is Dutch for a stream or river.

Charleston Anyone interested in the antebellum South and the Civil War would have plenty to see in Charleston, South Carolina. Old buildings with ironwork gates and ornate stone houses give the city its old Southern atmosphere. The Civil War broke out at Fort Sumter, in Charleston's harbor. It was originally Charles Town, named for Charles II, but through common usage it became "Charleston" in speech. By the 1780's it was being spelled that way as well.

Charlotte Dilworth, a suburb of Charlotte, became the first "streetcar" suburb in the United States back in 1893. The town was named for Charlotte Sophia, wife of King George III. Charlotte is a large town and county seat in western North Carolina.

Chattanooga The Passenger railroad with a grade of 72.7%, the steepest known, ascends Lookout Mountain in Chattanooga, Tennessee. Chattanooga means "rock rising to a point" in the Creek Indian tongue.

Chautauqua Chautauqua County, New York is at the western end of the state, on Lake Erie. The lake coast in Chautauqua is called the Wine Trail with its five wineries. There is also the Chautauqua Institution, a vacation spot going back to the nineteenth century, where guests can attend operas, concerts, plays, lectures, and courses on all subjects. Jamestown, the birthplace of Lucille Ball, is also in this county. The name was applied at first to a large lake within the county. The meaning of this Indian name is uncertain, but there are some theories. "Foggy place," "where the fish were taken out," "bag tied in the middle," "place where a child was washed away," "place of easy death," and "place where one was lost" are all candidates, though they have nothing in common except for the notion of a place. There is one clue, however, which points to the "place where one was lost." This theory is based upon an Indian legend while the others have no such backing.

Cherry Hill This New Jersey community is not far from Philadelphia. A local farm on a hill had a path that was lined with cherry trees, hence the name.

Chesapeake Bay At one time Chesapeake Bay had one of the most abundant oyster and blue crab supplies in the world, but partly due to the sedimentation the numbers are dwindling. The earliest English explorers wrote the name down as *Chesepiooc* and as *Chesapeake* (1608). Originally the name of an Algonquian village near the bay, it would later become the name of the bay, itself. *Che* means big in the Algonquian language, but linguists are uncertain about the rest of the name. Some experts believe that the name was *che-sipi-oc*, at the big river (actually, "big- river-at").

Chicago Chicago has the longest list of nicknames of any city. Among some of its titles are Carl Sandburg's "Hog Butcher for the World," "Crossroads of the Midwest," "the Second City," and "Windy City." The French explorers wrote the name down as *Chigagou*, meaning "onion place" in Algonquian. Wild onions or garlic had been growing there at the time. Settlers applied the name to a local river, but by 1830 the new town was also being called *Chigagou* (or Chicago).

Cincinnati During the 1850's Cincinnati was given the nickname "Porkopolis" because it had America's largest pork-packing industry. General Arthur St. Clair named the city Cincinnati in 1790 for the Society for the Cincinnati, an organization formed in honor of a military hero of ancient Rome by the name of Cincinnatus. Immediately after the American Revolution there was an interest among many Americans in the Roman Republic and its history.

Cleveland The birthplace of Paul Newman, Burgess Meredith, Phil Donahue, and Henry Mancini, the city was named for Moses Cleaveland (1754-1806) who fought under George Washington during the Revolutionary War. Cleaveland was a lawyer and a surveyor in the Northwest Territory, a region that included the future state of Ohio. Spelled Cleaveland at first, it later on changed to its present form.

Cocoa Beach This community on Florida's Atlantic coast is located on Merritt Island, not far to the south of Cape Canaveral.

The name comes from the coconut palms which grow there in abundance.

Colorado Colorado attracts thousands of campers every season with its thirteen national forests and eight national parks. The name is Spanish for colored red or colored reddish, and was given by Spanish explorers to a small stream known today as the Little Colorado. The water appeared reddish to these early visitors. Later on the name was applied to the main Colorado River, also because of its color. In 1861 the United States government organized the Colorado Territory and it eventually became a state.

Connecticut The lollipop and the pay telephone both had their beginning in this state. In Algonquian it means "at the long tidal river," a name that the early settlers gave to the river. The colony and, later, the state took the name.

Cook County Chicago and its suburbs occupy this county which was established on January 15, 1831. Daniel Pope Cook (1794-1827) was the first attorney general of Illinois and a representative from his state
(1819-27).

Corpus Christi Alonso Alvarez de Pineda named the bay in honor of Corpus Christi Day, and the town took the name of the bay. Corpus Christi is Latin for body of Christ. The town is located on the Texas Gulf Coast.

Council Bluffs This town in southwestern Iowa, not far from the Missouri River, was named in memory of a meeting that the explorers, Lewis and Clark, had at that spot with some of the local Indians back in 1804.

Cumberland Gap Westward migrants used this "national Road" during the early 1800's. Today it is a pass for U.S. 40 in Maryland. William Augustus, Duke of Cumberland (1721-65), for whom this pass was named, was the second son of King George II. The Duke's title came from Cumberland County, England.

Dade County The twenty-seven independent municipalities of Dade County, Florida are all part of metropolitan Miami. The Everglades forest is also within this county. Dade was established as a county on February 4, 1836 and named for Francis Langhorne Dade (1793-1835), an officer in the U.S. infantry who died in an ambush during the Seminole Indian conflict.

Dakota Both North and South Dakota entered the Union as states on the same day in 1889. It is not known which received statehood first, since President Benjamin Harrison covered up the names of the two states when he signed the document that declared their statehood. The name Dakota was that of a local Indian tribe, and it means "allies" in the Siouan language.

Dallas Associated, now, with the television series of the same now, Dallas is a large industrial city surrounded by agricultural and petroleum-producing land. Settlers first came to the area in 1841 and named the community for George Mifflin Dallas, Vice President of the United States.

Danbury Danbury, Connecticut used to be famous for the manufacture of hats, especially for the silk top hats made for United States presidents. Early settlers named the town after Danbury in Essex, England.

Dayton Wilbur and Orville Wright, the two pioneers in aviation, were born and practiced flying in this Ohio city. The name of the city honors Jonathan Dayton (1760-1824), a general during the

American Revolution, a delegate to the Constitutional Convention, and later on a United States senator. Dayton owned some land in Ohio, a frontier territory at the time.

Deal Deal is a small residential community on the Jersey Shore, not far south of the New York Metropolitan area. There is a town in England with the same name.

Delaware The first state to ratify the Constitution in 1787, and the first place in which chemists produced nylon in 1938, Delaware takes its name from Lord Thomas West De La Warr, the first English governor of Virginia. Captain Samuel Argall discovered Delaware Bay and named it for the Virginia governor. The river, the colony, and the state took the name of the bay. European settlers also applied the name to the local Indian tribe.

De Queen Originally the name of this Arkansas town was De Goeijen, named for a Dutchman who backed the Kansas City Southern Railway. De Queen is the county seat of Sevier County in southwestern Arkansas.

Decatur Stephen F. Decatur (1779-1820) was commodore of the U.S. Navy during the War of 1812, and he engaged the Barbary pirates off the North African coast. He died in a duel with another naval officer. Decatur is a large town in central Illinois, in the "corn-belt" of the Midwest.

Denver Known as the "mile-high city" because of its location high in the Rocky Mountains, Denver is Colorado's main population center. J.W. Denver was a governor of the Kansas Territory which included the eastern part of present-day Colorado.

Des Moines This Midwestern city is a center for insurance and for publishing. It was named the "All-American City" three times, but in the summer of 1993 it was a victim of the flood. French explorers, passing through as early as 1673, recorded a local tribal name as *Moingouena* and applied it to a river, *Riviere Des Moing*s. Eventually the name changed through mispronunciation to *Riviere Des Moine*s, river of the monks. During the nineteenth century the American settlers called it the Des Moins River, from which the city took its name.

Desmet Originally De Smet, this Idaho town was named for a Catholic missionary to a local Indian tribe.

Detroit Besides being the center of automobile production, Detroit was the home of Charles Lindbergh and the birthplace of the ice cream soda. The name of the city is a derivative of the French word for strait. Antoine Cadillac, a French explorer, founded the settlement between Lake Erie and St. Clair Lake. (see Cadillac).

Dodge City This Kansas town is legendary as a frontier town, associated with the television series, *Gunsmoke*. During the nineteenth century cowboys and buffalo hunters would come there to drink and gamble, giving it the reputation of a lawless town. It was originally called Fort Dodge, named for Colonel Henry I. Dodge.

Dubuque Dubuque, Iowa is a large town on the Mississippi River, where the Victorian homes of the river merchants still stand. The town was named for Julien Dubuque, a French Canadian, the first settler in the vicinity.

Duluth This city is the largest freshwater inland port in the world. Located on Lake Superior, in northern Minnesota, the region is rich in forests, iron ore, and dairy products. Daniel Greysolan De

Luth (or Du Lhut), a French explorer, visited the area late in the seventeenth century.

Egg Harbor Egg Harbor, New Jersey, is in Atlantic County, not far to the west of Atlantic City. Early in the seventeenth century a Dutch sailor gave the place its name when he took note of the abundance of gull eggs that could be found there.

El Dorado This town is in southern Arkansas, and it means golden in Spanish. It is the name of a legendary place, believed by the Spanish to have been somewhere in South America. As a geographical name it is usually a reference to any place with an attractive feature such as mineral wealth or good soil. Matthew F. Rainey, the area's first settler, may have given it the name in gratitude for having found a suitable place to live after having come from New Orleans.

El Paso Poncho Villa, whose raids in the early part of the twentieth century brought the last foreign invasion of the continental United States, died in battle at El Paso, Texas. Juan de Ornate passed through in 1598 and recorded that he had crossed the Rio Grande at a place called El Paso del Norte. In English it means a passage (or a crossing) to the North.

Elmira Mark Twain took vacations here and became a permanent resident when he died. Elmira was originally the name of a child. According to a local legend, the child's mother was in the habit of calling out loud for her. The people of the settlement were always able to hear it, and decided to give the name to their town. Elmira is located on New York State's Southern Tier, south of the Finger Lakes.

Essex County Essex County, New Jersey, established in 1683, includes Newark, the county seat. The early settlers named it for Essex County in England. Essex is a highly urbanized and heavily populated county, part of the New York City Metropolitan area.

Eureka Eureka is a port city on the coast of northern California, a town of fog and frame houses. The name is Greek and it means "I have found it," a phrase used in 1849 as the motto of California, a reference to the discovery of gold and good agricultural land. The town of Eureka adopted its name in 1850, and many other states have a Eureka, recommending the town as a good place to live.

Everglades (The) Florida's Everglades is the only tropical national park in the United States. Alligators, sea turtles, pumas, and flamingos are among the inhabitants of this wildlife preserve. The term, glade, refers to a piece of low-lying marshland, which the prefix "ever" has more than one possible explanation. According to one theory, the word describes an extensive tract of land. The geographical designation, Everglades, was recorded for the first time in 1822.

Fairfax County Fairfax County, Virginia, is a part of the Washington, D.C. Metropolitan area. Included within it are the suburban communities of Arlington, Alxandria, Vienna, and Falls Church, towns with large residential sections along with many government offices. The English government established the county in May, 1742 and named it for Lord Thomas Fairfax (1612- 71), a member of Oliver Cromwell's first parliament. Fairfax supported Charles II in regaining the throne.

Fargo Fargo is the largest city in North Dakota, and it is the home of the Roger Maris Baseball Museum. The name of the city is associated with W.G. Fargo, the founder of the Wells-Fargo Express and director of the Northern Pacific Railway.

Fayetteville Fort Bragg Army Base and Pope Air Force Base are both in the neighborhood of Fayetteville. This North Carolina town was named in honor of the Marquis de la Fayette, who helped George Washington during the Revolutionary War. His popularity rose among Americans after his visit to the United States in 1824.

Flagstaff Tourists, skiers, and nature enthusiasts come to Flagstaff, Arizona every year for its resorts, its woods, and its monuments. Flagstaff was originally the name of a local spring, but was later given to the town. Flagstaff Spring was so named because at one time a flag was flown at the spot from a pine tree that had its branches removed. Flagstaff is approximately one hundred miles southwest of Grand Canyon.

Flint On June 8, 1953 116 people died in a tornado, the largest number of deaths on record caused by a storm in the United States. This Michigan city took the name of a local river, a source of flint rock used by Indians to fashion arrowheads and by settlers to make gunflints.

Florida The lakes, rivers, and coastal waters of this state have more different species of fish than any other spot on Earth. It is the first place within the present United States to have been named by a European, as the Spanish had in 1513, at the time of the Ponce de Leon expedition. The name is a derivative of a Spanish word meaning flowered or flowery. According to a Spanish chronicler by the name of Herrera, de Leon chose the name because the land appeared to have an abundance of flowers

Florida Keys Thirty-one islands between the Atlantic Ocean and the Gulf of Mexico make up the Florida Keys. Along with the natural beauty, there are motels, malls, and U.S. 5, the Overseas Highway joining the keys to the mainland. The name has no association with the English word key, but is simply an Anglicized form of the

Spanish *cayo*, meaning an island. Most likely, the word key was just a mispronunciation of *cayo*.

Fort Lauderale Located on Florida's Atlantic Coast, Fort Lauderale is both a residential community and a tourist attraction. One unusual feature is its three hundred miles of canals. The name is a memorial to Major William Lauderale, leader of a military expedition against the Seminole Indians in 1838.

Fort Lee During the early stage of the American Revolution (summer, 1776) George Washington constructed some fortifications on both banks of the Hudson River. Joseph Phillips, commander of a battalion of New Jersey militia, built an artillery battery on the present site of Fort Lee, New Jersey. The Americans called it Fort Constitution until October 19, 1776, when they changed the name to Fort Lee in recognition of General Charles Lee, defender of New York City. Modern Fort Lee, at the western end of the George Washington Bridge, is a large suburb with its high residential towers overlooking the Hudson River. At one time it was the home of the Palisades Amusement Park.

Fort Myers Known for its beaches with large numbers of porpoises, Fort Myers, on Florida's Gulf Coast, was named for General Abraham Charles Myers (1811-89), the first quartermaster general of the Confederate army.

Fort Wayne Fort Wayne is a large northern indiana town, named in memory of General Anthony Wayne (1745-97), who had won a victory over the Indians at the "Fallen Timbers" in 1794. General Wayne erected a stockade after the battle and it eventually grew into a town There is, at present, in Fort Wayne, a reproduction of the historic fort, portraying life as it was during the early nineteenth century.

Fort Worth Ironically, Larry Hagman, who played "J.R." on the T.V. series, *"Dallas,"* came from Fort Worth. William Jenkins Worth (1794-1849) was a veteran of the War of 1812, the Seminole Indian Wars, and the Mexican War. Modern Fort Worth is a part of the Dallas-Fort Worth urban and industrial center.

Fredericksburg George Washington lived here as a child. The town bears the name of the prince of Wales, son of King George II.

Fresno The Central Pacific Railroad founded Fresno in 1872 as a depot for grain shipment. Today, it is in the heart of California's fruit and wine-producing region. Originally it was the name of a river, and it means ash tree in Spanish, since trees of this species were growing not far from the river. The county and city eventually took the name of the river.

Gainesville General E.P. Gaines, for whom this Florida community was named, played a major role during the Seminole Indian conflict. Gainesville produces wood, electrical, meat, and poultry products as well as tobacco and peanuts. There are also many lakes and mineral springs in the vicinity.

Galveston This large Gulf Coast city had Texas' first telephone system, first newspaper, first electric lights, first golf course, and first brewery. The Spanish government named Galveston Bay in 1785 to honor Count Bernardo de Galvez, viceroy of the colonies of New Spain. Americans, when they began to settle Texas in the 1830's, gave the name of the bay to the city, itself.

Gary Gary Indiana is southeast of Chicago, on Lake Michigan, and one of the main centers of steel-production in the world. Elbert H. Gary was a lawyer and a chairman of the board of directors of the United States Steel Corporation. It was this corporation that founded the town.

Genesee River In the Iroquoian language the name means beautiful valley. The river runs through the Southern Tier of New York State, and it has many small falls, but there are also some larger ones, two of which have a one hundred-foot drop.

Gettysburg Famous for the Civil War battle and for Lincoln's Gettysburg Address, the town has over thirteen hundred monuments and four hundred cannon in its twenty-five square mile park. The town planner was a man by the name of John Gettys.

Gloversville Gloversville, New York, in Fulton County, south of the Adirondack Mountains, is noted for its glove industry, started by the first settlers. At one time Gloversville was regarded as one of the most important glove-production centers in the world. Before taking its present name the town was called Stump City.

Gouveneur This town is in northeastern New York State, and it was named for Gouveneur Morris, who bought the land in 1798. The first permanent settlers arrived in 1805.

Grand Island Visitors come in march and April to this part of Nebraska to see thousands of Sandhill Cranes stop over on their migration north. The town of Grand Island was named for a large island in the Platte River.

Grand Teton Mountain This is the highest peak in the Teton Mountain Range at 13,770 feet, hence Grand. The Teton Range is a part of the Rockies, and it extends from northwestern Wyoming into Idaho. The name Teton is of French origin and it means teat. Apparently, the early French explorers were reminded of the female breasts by these mountain peaks. Grand Teton National Park draws many tourists every year.

Great Smokey Mountains Great Smokey Mountains National Park is the most popular reserve in the United States with over eight million tourists a year. The Great Smokey Mountains are a part of the Appalachian Mountain Range in the states of North Carolina and Tennessee. There is a haze present in these mountains that resembles smoke.

Greenwich Greenwich is a New York City suburb with a New England atmosphere. The name comes from that of a borough in London, England. Greenwich was known at one time as Elizabeth's Neck.

Hackensack This suburban community in Bergen County, New Jersey has a Delaware Indian name which may be a reference to the hooked shaped mouth of the lower Hackensack and Passaic River. The two words *hocquan* and *sauk* refer to a hook-shaped mouth of a river. Some names recorded in the seventeenth century include such variants as *Ahakinsack*, *Haconsacke*, *Hagen-Sack*, and *Yaccinsack*.

Harrisburg Three-Mile Island, where an accident took place at a nuclear power station, put this Pennsylvania capital in the news back in the 1970's. John Harris managed a ferry across the Susquehanna River during the 1700's and his son, John Harris, Jr., planned the town in 1785.

Hattiesburg The town is close to the Gulf Coast of Mississippi, in the "cotton-belt." Its name comes from Hattie Hardy, the wife of the town's founder.

Hawaii Of the 132 islands that make up this group, only seven are inhabited. Hawaii became our fiftieth state in 1959. The name is Polynesian and it denotes a homeland; *hawa* is a place of residence and *ii* is a suffix that can mean either smaller or new. English explorers visited these islands in the eighteenth century and called them the Sandwich Islands for the Earl of Sandwich, First Lord of the British Admiralty. The Hawaiian king, nevertheless, continued to use the original Polynesian name for each of the islands while he called the group as a whole the Island of the King of Hawaii.

Hempstead Hofstra University, founded in 1935, has its campus in this Long Island suburb. Dutch settlers named it Heemstede, the name of a town in the Netherlands. The English changed it to Hempstead, the name of a town in England.

Hoboken The first game of baseball may have been played in Hoboken on June 19, 1846. Some famous residents were Washington Irving, Stephen Foster, and John Jacob Astor. Located on the Hudson River, in New Jersey, the name may be a derivation of the word Hobocan, a reference to a tobacco pipe in the Delaware Indian tongue. There is, however, the possibility that the Dutch named it for the village of Hoboken in Flanders (northern Belgium), not far from the border with the Netherlands. The first explanation is feasible because there was a local quarry from which the settlers extracted stone for the manufacture of pipes. The second theory is probably the better of the two, since Hoboken was a Dutch settlement and it was spelled the same way as the town in Flanders had been.

Hollywood Horace H. Wilcox, who planned this community in the 1880's, also selected its name. According to the story, Wilcox's wife was on a trip back east where she came across a bush known as American holly. She liked the name and brought two of the bushes back to Los Angeles so that the name could be used for the new town that her husband was planning. The plants were not able to survive in their new environment, but the name took root and has become a household word.

Holyoke Holyoke, Massachusetts, is known for the manufacture of excellent stationery. Originally called Springfield, it was later named for either Rev. Edward Holyoke or Eliezur Holyoke. The first Holyoke served as presidentof Harvard University (1737-69); the second one explored and settled the Connecticut River.

Honolulu Six million tourists arrive at Honolulu airport each year. It is the state capital of Hawaii and its largest city. The name is Polynesian and it means safe harbor.

Huntington This suburban community on Long Island's North Shore was the home of Walt Whitman before he had moved to Brooklyn. There are two theories regarding the name: (1) it may have been Hunting Town due to its abundant supply of game throughout the colonial era; (2) the English may have named it for Huntington, England, the birthplace of Oliver Cromwell. The second possibility is the more likely one, since many Puritans, partisans of Cromwell, were migrating to Long Island from New England during the late seventeenth century.

Huntsville In northern Alabama, Huntsville has the NASA Space and Rocket Center, and the largest space museum worldwide. John Hunt, for whom the city was named, was one of the town's pioneers.

Hyannisport This Massachusetts resort area has been and still is closely associated with the Kennedy family. The suffix port was added to Hyannis, the name of a local Indian chief.

Idaho Ernest Hemingway and the poet, Ezra Pound, were both born here. The name is Native American and it denotes sun coming down the mountain or light on the mountains. The first element of the name, *ee*, conveys the notion of coming down. *Dah*, the second part of the name, can mean both sun and mountain. The last syllable, *ho*, is simply an exclamation with the force of the word behold.

Illinois This state is the original home of McDonald's. The McDonald's Corporate Headquarters is at Oak Brook, and the Hamburger University and McDonald's Museum are at Des Plaines. Illinois was at one time the name of the Algonquian Indian confederacy, part of which included northern Illinois during the seventeenth century. The name, itself, comes from *ilinewek*, the Algonquian word for man.

Indiana Indiana is within the corn-growing region of the Midwest, but there are industrial centers in the state's urban pockets. The name is an adaptation of the Latin or Spanish adjective meaning Indian. Originally this name was used by a group of land developers known as the Indiana Company. The Company named its tract of land Indiana, since it was inhabited by Indians at the time.

Iowa Ten percent of America's food is grown here, and nine-five percent of the state's land is agricultural. Iowa is a derivative of the name of a Siouan Indian tribe that lived in the eastern half of the state during the seventeenth century. The name means either sleepy ones or narrow, and the original pronunciation was *ayuhwa*.

Islip This suburban community is at the center of Long Island. Aircraft plants, shipping, and fish-packing are some local industries. The first settlers named it for Islip in Oxfordshire, England, birthplace of the first Englishman to arrive there.

Jacksonville Mayport Naval Base, in Jacksonville, Florida has two well-known aircraft carriers, U.S. S. Forrestal and U.S. S. Saratoga. President Monroe picked Andrew Jackson to act as provisional governor of Florida Territory, and to organize its civil administration.

Johnstown This Pennsylvania town is one of America's most flood-prone. Heavy flooding is on record for the years 1862, 1869, 1936, and 1977. The flood of 1889 killed 2,200 people and destroyed the town in ten minutes. Joseph Johns was a Swiss immigrant who owned land on the site of the future Johnston. Johns is an Anglicized form of the man's original name.

Juneau Alaska's state capital, Juneau is built on a mountainside beside a channel of salt water. Until World War II it was a gold mine town. At one time it was a summer fishing camp known to the natives as Flounder Creek. Early prospectors called it Pilzurg and Flip Town. In 1881 the U.S. Navy arrived to keep law and order, and named the settlement Rockwell, for their commander. During the same year the postal service opened its office and changed the name to Harrisburg. In December of that year the miners assembled for the purpose of voting on a permanent name. They decided upon Juneau in honor of Joseph Juneau who, together with Richard Harris, discovered Gold Creek, thus bringing the town into being.

Kalamazoo This large town in southwestern Michigan has an Algoquian name that denotes a giving off of smoke.

Kankakee Kankakee, Illinois is about sixty miles south of Chicago, in a county of the same name. The name of the town comes from that of the river. There were a number of spellings, the oldest one preserved being *Thea kiki*. It may be a reference to wolves, since some of the people living along the river were Mohicans, a name that pertains to these animals.

Kansas More wheat is grown here than in any of the other states. Kansas is in the heart of agricultural America, and within it lies the nation's geographical center. When the Spanish explored the region (c. 1600) they recorded the name of a local Native American tribe as *Escanasaque*. When the French explorers arrived, close to a hundred years later, they wrote down the name as *Kansa*. At first the name was used for the tribe, then for the local river, later on for the United States territory, and finally, for the state.

Kennebunkport President George Bush used to come to relax here at his summer home. Kennebunkport is on Maine's southern coast, and it was originally *Kennebunk* in the Algonquian language, which means long-out bank. The suffix port was added by European settlers.

Kentucky Lincoln's birthplace is near Sinking Spring, three miles south of Hodgenville, in the center of the state. The name is probably a form of the Iroquois word *Kentake*, meaning meadow-land. First applied to the river, and then to a county organized by Virginia in 1776, the name went to the new state when it came into being in 1792.

Knoxville The Tennessee Valley Authority (TVA) has its headquarters here. This agency controls hydroelectric dams, and lakes for recreation. General Henry Knox (1750-1806) participated in the American Revolution.

Kokomo Elwood Haynes built a gasoline-driven automobile here back in 1893. Kokomo is in north-central Indiana, a rural part of the state. The name comes from that of a native American who lived there at one time.

Lackawanna Lackawanna is a suburb of Buffalo, to the south, close to Lake Erie. Bethlehem Steel Corporation has its plant there. The name has its derivation in an Algonquian word meaning "at the fork stream." There was, in the early days, a fork in a major trail at that spot.

Lake Erie Buffalo, Erie (Pennsylvania), Cleveland, and Toledo are on its shore, making it one of the most industrialized parts of the country. An Iroquoian tribe by that name lived on the southern shore of the lake, from western New York State to Ohio. *Erie*, *erike*, or *eriga* may mean long tail, a reference to the wildcat, which had a totemic significance to this tribe. This group of Native Americans called itself the Cat Nation.

Lake George Vacationers come to this resort in northern New York State for the amusement parks, the shops, and the cruises. There is also Fort William Henry, rebuilt on the plan of a fort used during the eighteenth century. English colonists named the lake for King George II.

Lake Mead The lake came into existence when Hoover Dam was built to keep the Colorado River in check, and to generate electricity. It was constructed in the 1930's, twenty-five miles east of Las Vegas, Nevada. Lake Mead is the largest artificial lake in the Western Hemisphere. There was a Dr. Elwood Mead, reclamation commissioner and irrigation engineer, who worked for the federal government around the turn of the century, and promoted irrigation and water conservation in the West.

Lake Okeechobee One of the largest fresh-water lakes in the country, it is located in southern Florida, just north of the swampland. It is a Muskogean name and it means big water.

Lansing Lansing is the state capital of Michigan and a center for car and truck manufacturing. John Lansing (1754-1829) served during the Revolutionary War, and later on he held some offices in the New York State government. When New Yorkers moved farther west they named some of their new settlements after him.

Laramie The Overland Trail and the route of the Pony Express went through this town in southeastern Wyoming. Jacques Laramie was a French-Canadian trapper who visited the vicinity back in the early 1800's. Though honest, and respected by the local native Americans, he died at the hands of a band of Arapahoes near the river that would later bear his name. Laramie, Wyoming took the name of the La Ramee or La Ramie River.

Las Cruces This town in New Mexico is known as the crosses because a group of men killed by local Indians were buried there. The crosses marking the graves remained there long enough to give the place its name.

Las Vegas Since the 1930's Las Vegas has been a center for gambling, shows, and nightlife. The name was originally Nuestra Senora de los Dolores de Las Vegas, our Lady of Sorrows of the Meadows, shortened to Las Vegas. Pioneers used these meadows during the nineteenth century as campsites.

Lawrence Confederates burned this Kansas town during the Civil War for its antislavery stand. A.A. Lawrence was a prominent individual who helped to start the town.

Leavenworth The United States government has a strong presence here, with its federal prison and veterans hospital. The Kansas State Prison is also in Leavenworth. Back in the nineteenth century James B. (Wild Bill) Hickok and William F. (Buffalo Bill) Cody both lived there. The town was at first Cantonment Leavenworth, built by Colonel Henry H. Leavenworth in 1827.

Lima Lima is in northwestern Ohio and it produces industrial products such as car engines and machine tools. The town is on an oil pipeline and refining center, but the oil wells that were discovered here in 1885 have all gone dry. Exotic names were popular during the early 1800's, and the fact that the name of a Peruvian city was chosen may be indicative of Americans' approval of the Latin American Revolutions that were in progress at this time.

Long Branch This is a small town on the Jersey Shore, just south of the New York City Metropolitan area. A resort, one of the country's earliest, was built there in the eighteenth century, and seven United States presidents have spent time there. The settlers named it Long Branch because the longest branch of the Shrewsbury River runs through it.

Los Alamos Los Alamos is a community in New Mexico and the name is Spanish for poplars or cottonwoods. The trees at one time indicated a spot at which water could be found.

Los Angeles The world's largest freeway system was built here after 1950 to connect the several communities that make up this sprawling city. The people of Los Angeles are extremely individualistic and have the highest standard of living in the United States. Ironically this city, with all its materialistic values and its generation of all sorts of fads, has a name that means the angels. In fact the name is short for Nuestra *Senora (Reina) de los Angeles e la Porciuncula*, Spanish for Our Lady of the Angels (or Queen of the Angels) of the Little Portion. The Porciuncula is the name of a Franciscan shrine near Assisi, Italy. The Spaniards gave the town its name in 1769, when visiting the coast of southern California. At first they called the river *Porciuncula* and later the settlement. The present form, Los Angeles, came into immediate use.

Loudoun County To the west of Fairfax County, Virginia, Loudoun is around twenty miles from Washington, D.C. One can drive through and see beautiful scenery, horses, and fox-hunts. The county goes back to 1757 and takes its name from John Campbell, the fourth earl of Loudoun.

Louisiana There is great diversity in this state on the Gulf Coast, in the deep South. The southern part of Louisiana has a French heritage and cosmopolitan New Orleans. There are large plantation houses throughout the state that are now museums. Robert la Salle, a French explorer named it *Louisiane* for King Louis XIV. The Spaniards wrote it down as *Luisiana*, and later on the Americans began to use the present form. Originally Louisiana was an expansive territory which made up the entire central portion of the present United States. When the government carved up the territory into smaller ones, and eventually into states, it retained the name for the state of Louisiana.

Lubbock This Texas town has one of the last colonies of prairie dogs in the United States. Colonel T. S. Lubbock organized the Texas Rangers.

Lynchburg United States Senator, Carter Glass, also secretary of the treasury, and Senator John W. Daniel come from this town in the western part of Virginia. John Lynch, for whom the town was named, started a ferry service there in 1757.

Mackinaw The name is a form of Mackinac, a derivative of the Ojibway Indian word *michilimackinak*, meaning "island of the large turtle." Mackinaw is a city in Michigan.

Macon The poet, Sidney Lanier, was born here in 1842. Macon is a large town in the cotton- growing region of central Georgia. The town was named for a soldier in the Revolutionary War by the name of Nathaniel Macon (1758-1837).

Maine If one travels from north to south along the coast of Maine it is 228 miles, but if one were to measure all of the inlets and projections there would be 3,478 miles of coastline. The term main or maine was used in the seventeenth century to refer to the open sea or to a continent, and from this comes our word mainland. The early explorers of coastal North America had discovered a number of islands near northern New England and they used the designation main to distinguish between the islands and the continent. A charter written in 1620 refers to the "country of the Main Land," and another charter (1622) refers to the "Province of Main." There was no wide official use of the name, but there was popular use. In 1820 the state was established and the name Maine was adopted.

Manhasset The name of this Long Island suburban community was that of a local tribe of Native Americans, the Manhasset.

Manhattan (Kansas) The town of Manhattan is in northeastern Kansas, one of the most agricultural parts of the United States. It was named after the borough of Manhattan in New York City. Those who picked the name had hopes that some day it would grow into a large city.

Marietta Six Flags Over Georgia amusement park is not far from Marietta. The town is located in Cobb County, and it is believed that Marietta was the name of the wife of Thomas Willis Cobb, the man for whom the county was named.

Massachusetts This heavily industrialized state was one of the earliest of the thirteen original colonies, and it can take pride in having the first public school back in 1647. The name is Algonquian and it means "at the big hills," originally the name of an Indian village. English colonists applied the name to the entire tribe, and not long after they gave the name to the bay.

By 1780 the colony was called the Commonwealth of Massachusetts.

Massapequa Massapequa is a residential community on Long Island, but there has been some light manufacturing there in the past. The name may be a derivative of *massa-pe-auke*, a Mohegan phrase meaning "on the great river." *Massa* means great and *sepe*, river. Some forms of the name recorded in colonial days include Marospinc, Marsapege, and Marsepeak. The first recording of the name took place in 1639, when the chief of the local tribe entrusted a portion of Long Island to the Dutch, who agreed to protect it.

Memphis The first Holiday Inn opened here in 1952. Barbecue restaurants number one hundred in this city which was voted in four national polls the cleanest, most orderly, and most peaceful in the United States. The early inhabitants called it Memphis for an Egyptian city of the same name, since unusual and exotic names were in fashion at the time.

Mesabi The Mesabi is a section of northeastern Minnesota, north of Duluth and close to Lake Superior. It is a heavily forested region containing large deposits of iron ore. Also spelled Mesaba an Missabe, the name means giant in the Ojibway language, a reference to a figure in the tribal mythology. The mountain in the vicinity was eventually associated with this legendary giant.

Michigan Northern and southern Michigan differ from each other in basic character. The north has abundant forests and many state parks, while the south has large urban centers and industries. Early visitors noted the Algonquian name which denotes big lake, a reference to Lake Huron and Lake Michigan. When the government made Michigan a United State territory, they adopted the name. It was a common practice in the early United States to name new territories on the basis of a local geographical feature.

Milwaukee At one time the largest beer-brewing center in the United States, today its economy is more diverse. There are, however, three breweries remaining. The name is Algonquian and it most likely means good land. Many different spellings have been recorded.

Minnesota Water-skis and snowmobiles were invented in this scenic state. First written down as Menesota and Minnay Sotor, it means cloudy water in the local Native American language. The name was originally applied to the river, the St. Peter River, as the French called it. When Congress declared the region a territory (1847) the name, spelled as it is today, was adopted.

Mississippi In a number of Native American tongues it means great water, with *meeche* or *mescha* expressing the notion of great and *cebe*, water.

Missouri Mark Twain was born here early in the nineteenth century. Missouri is derived from the name of an Algonquian tribe dwelling at the mouth of the Missouri River. French explorers first recorded the name in 1673 and applied it to the river. The usual course of events took place when the name of the river began to refer to the region as a whole, later to the United States territory, and then to the new state.

Mobile Mobile is on Alabama's Gulf Coast, a port city with a shipbuilding industry and a festival similar to the Mardi Gras of New Orleans. Spanish explorers found a local tribe there which they knew by the name of *Mauvila*, and a century later the French wrote down the name as Mobile and adopted it for the local river.

Modesto The largest American winery is at Modesto, and a third of all California wine is produced in the area. In Spanish it means simply modest or modest man. According to local legend, the people of the settlement (c. 1870) wanted to name their town for a San Francisco financier, W.C. Ralston. Because he refused the honor, the townspeople were impressed by his modesty and decided to give the town a name that would preserve the memory of the man's virtue.

Mojave (or Mohave Dessert) Less than five inches of rain falls on this part of southern California every year, and gales of wind produce large sand dunes throughout. A direct translation from the Yuma Indian language is three mountains, the name of a tribe in western Arizona and southeastern California.

Monterey Monterey is located about midway down the California coast. A Spanish explorer reached Monterey Bay in 1542, and fifty years later another Spaniard arrived, naming it *San Pedro*. In 1602 a third visitor changed the name to *Puerto de Monterey* for Conde de Monterey, viceroy of New Spain. The Spanish established a mission there in 1770, and in 1850 the Americans named the newly formed county Monterey from which the town took its name.

Montgomery Maxwell Air Force Base, where the flight school of Wilbur and Orville Wright was located, is in Alabama's capital. General Richard Montgomery was a Revolutionary War hero, but there was also a Major L.P. Montgomery who died in a war with the Creek Indians whose memory may also have been considered by those who had picked the name.

Mount Shasta Volcanic in origin, but probably extinct, this peak is in California's Cascade Range, has five glaciers descending from its top, and stands over fourteen thousand feet high. The meaning of the name is uncertain, but it comes from that of a Hokan-speaking tribe.

Nantucket At one time it was a whaling town, but today it is a tourist center. The Algonquian name most likely means "at the narrow river," a reference to the channel separating it from a nearby island.

Nassau County Nassau County, Long Island, is a heavily-populated suburban area within the New York City Metropolitan region. Dutch rulers during the seventeenth century carried the title of Prince of Orange-Nassau. Nassau became a popular name in the New Netherland colony. Set up in 1898, the name of the county represented the revival of a local tradition.

Natchez This town in southwestern Mississippi is located on a river of the same name. The name comes from the Caddoan Indian word for woods or timber.

Nebraska Millions of bison used to roam the plains of Nebraska, but today there are millions of cows insead. Nebraska is a combination of two Siouan words *ni* (water) and *bthaska* (flat), a reference o a widely spread river with low banks.

Nevada The state government made gambling legal here in 1931. It was going on before this date, but the state wanted to be able to exercise some control over it and to raise tax revenue. Eventually it grew to be Nevada's main industry. The direct translation of the name from Spanish is snowy, a reference to its snow-covered mountains.

New Brunswick The home of Rutgers University, New Brunswick is about thirty-five miles southeast of Manhattan. The New Jersey community was named for King George III of England who was also Duke of Brunswick.

New Hampshire This scenic state draws thousands of tourists every year. It was named for Hampshire County, England. John Mason (1586-1635), a sea captain, served as a magistrate of Portsmouth, a town in this English county. Mason received a grant to a piece of land in what would become New Hampshire.

New Haven New Haven is a large city on Long Island Sound, famous for Yale University. English settlers either decided upon the name in 1640, when they had discovered a new harbor at that spot, or they named it for the port of New Haven on the English Channel.

Newark New Jersey's largest city, it is also the birthplace of the author, Stephen Crane. In 1666 the English named it for the town of Newark in Nottinghamshire, England.

Newport News This unusual name was originally New Port Newce. Newce was the family name of the Englishman who founded this Virginia town in 1621. Newce eventually became News through popular usage.

Niagara Falls Turbine engines, put into motion by the falls, are able to produce more than two million kilowatts of electricity. Niagara is the Iroquoian expression for a point of land that is divided into two, a description of the place at which the river flows into the lake.

Nome Saloons and other buildings preserve the atmosphere of the prospecting days, when many people come to Alaska for gold. Nome is on Norton Sound, not far from the Bering Sea, to the south of the Arctic Circle. Known at first as Anvil City, it was renamed in 1899 for a spot on Norton Sound called Nome by a British map-maker who had misinterpreted a map. The map had "?

Name" written on it and the map-maker took it for "Cape Nome." The Eskimo word for this cape was *Ayasayuk*, sheer cliff and the Russian name was *Mys Tolstoi*, broad cape.

Norfolk The U.S. Naval Base at Norfolk, Virginia has more than 125 ships as well as the burial place of Douglas MacArthur. English colonists named it in 1691 after Norfolk in England.

Normal Normal is a small town in north-central Illinois. The unusual name is an American geographical designation indicating that the town, at one time in its history, had a school for training teachers. Such schools were formerly called normal schools.

Norman This Oklahoma town, originally called Norman Switch, was named for Abner Norman, a surveyor for the Santa Fe Railroad.

Nyack Nyack is in Rockland County, New York, not far from New York City. The name may be a form of the local Native American word *naiag* or *neiak*, meaning point or corner.

Oakland Oakland is on the eastern side of San Francisco Bay, opposite San Francisco. Its port is even busier than San Francisco's. The Spanish called it *Encinal del Temescal*, meaning "oak grove by the sweat-house," since oak trees were growing there in abundance. The city was planned and renamed Oakland in 1850.

Ogdensburg The city of Ogdensburg lies on the St. Lawrence River in northern New York State, across from Ontario Province, Canada. Colonel Samuel Ogden (1746-1810) was a land speculator who owned a vast tract of land in the vicinity as well as an iron foundry.

Ohio This state has contributed to Air and Space Technology over the last century with the Wright Brothers, Neil Armstrong, and the Goodyear dirigible. French explorers adopted the Iroquoian word for "fine river" and applied it to the Ohio River. The territory and ultimately the state took the name.

Okefenokee Swamp In 1937 President Roosevelt made these seven hundred square miles of swampland in Georgia and Florida a wildlife refuge. The name is Muskogean and it means "water shaking," a possible reference to quicksand.

Omaha Nearby is Father Flanagan's Boys Town, a village founded in 1917 or children. In 1938 Hollywood made a movie about Boys Town with Spencer Tracy and Mickey Rooney. French explorers visited this part of eastern Nebraska in the 1670's and recorded the Native American name as *maha* and adding the French preposition, *aux*, thus forming *aux Mahas*, "to or at the *Mahas*." According to some experts, however, the Native American name was Omaha to begin with.

Orlando Visitors come to Orlando in droves to see EPCOT Center and Disney World. The name honors Orlando Reeves, a soldier who died there in 1835 during an Indian war.

Oshkosh Oshkosh started off as a trading post on Lake Winnebago, in eastern Wisconsin, back in 1836. It was originally the name of a Menominee Indian chief.

Oxnard Every year, in May, Oxnard, California has a Strawberry Festival with wine-tasting, crafts, and all kinds of strawberry products. Oxnard is a coastal town, north of Los Angeles. Henry T. Oxnard was part owner of a factory at which sugar was extracted from beets.

Ozark Mountains The Ozark Range has been thought of as mountains, but it is actually a plateau. It is an isolated and wooded region that includes a part of three states: Arkansas, Missouri, and Oklahoma. Due to the area's terrain, it used to be a hiding-place for outlaws. The name comes from the French *aux Arks*, which means "in the Arkansas Country."

Palm Springs Hollywood celebrities have been vacationing here since the 1930's. Palm Springs is famous for its resorts with year-round golf and tennis. Originally the name was Palmetto Spring because of the many palmetto trees that were growing there. The name was first written down in 1849. On an 1874 map, however, the name that appears is Big Palm Spring. For a time the local people called it *Aqua Caliente* because of the presence of hot springs. The government established a post office there in 1890 and the name Palm Springs was chosen, since *Agua Caliente* was already the name of a town in another California county.

Palo Alto Stanford University, with ten Nobel Prize-winners on its staff, is located here. *Palo* is Spanish for a stick or a log, but it can also mean a tree. Palo Alto in California means a tall tree, and the Spanish settlers chose the name because of a particularly high redwood tree in the neighborhood.

Panama City This town on Florida's "panhandle," known for its beaches, its fishing, and its sailing, is also the home of Tyndall Air Force Base. The man who was promoting the town named it for the Panama Canal with the intention of publicizing the idea that the town was situated on a straight line drawn on the map from Chicago down to the Canal Zone.

Paramus Paramus, in suburban New Jersey, is basically residential, but there are some manufacturing plants that produce electrical equipment. The name is Algonquian for "turkey river," the old name for the town of Saddle River.

Pasadena In 1875 the local people wanted to give the town a Native American name that would be descriptive of it. Since there were no Native Americans living in the area, the citizens asked a missionary to the Chippewas to suggest a name that would denote either "crown of the valley," or "key of the ranch." The missionary sent back a letter in which he had written four long words ending in *pa*, *sa*, *de*, and *na*. Dr. Elliott, who wrote the letter to the missionary, decided to use the four syllables which come at the end of the Native American words. Thus, Pa sa de na became the name of the town.

Pascagoula During the middle nineteenth century Pascagoula, east of Biloxi, Mississippi, was a summer resort. Later on it served as a port from which lumber and pecans were shipped. The name comes from that of a local Muskogean tribe living near a river named for the tribe, and it means "bread people."

Paterson Alexander Hamilton planned this New Jersey city, and later on, during the nineteenth century, it became a center for the manufacture of silk. William Paterson (1745-1806) was governor of the state when the townspeople were looking for a name.

Pecos River Farmers and ranchers use this tributary of the Rio Grande to irrigate their fields and to water their cattle. The name is Spanish in form, but Native American in origin. It was probably the name of a Native American village at one time and later became the name of the river, but the particular language that it stems from and its meaning are undetermined.

Peekskill Peekskill is in northern Westchester County, New York, on the Hudson River, in the neighborhood of Bear Mountain State Park and West Point Military Academy. Jan Peek was a Dutch trader who settled there in 1665, and *kill* is the Dutch word for river.

Pensacola Located in the western part of the Florida "panhandle," on the Gulf of Mexico, the town attracts both bathers and fishermen. The name is a derivative of the Choctaw Indian words *panshi* (hair) and *okla* (people), hence "long-haired people." This may have been the original tribal name.

Peoria This city in northern Illinois, in the "corn-belt," is the headquarters of the Caterpillar Tractor Company. *Peouarea* was the name of a Native American clan, as the French noted on their visit in the 1670's. *Peouarea* eventually became Peoria.

Perth Amboy In the early 1800's Perth Amboy, New Jersey, just across the Arthur Kill from Staten Island, was a summer resort. .Industrial development began in the 1850's, and today there is shipping and shipbuilding. The first part of the name, Perth, is a memorial to the Fourth Earl of Perth, Scotland (1648-1716), and the second part is an Algonquian derivative that denotes a valley or a depression.

Philadelphia The Declaration of Independence and the United States Constitution were both drafted at Independence Hall in Philadelphia. William Penn, the Quaker founder of Philadelphia, picked the name because it means brotherly love. He named it for a Greek city in western Asia Minor mentioned in the *New Testament*.

Phoenix According to Greek mythology, the phoenix was a bird that arose from the ashes. It is found quite frequently as a place-name. In the case of Phoenix in Arizona, it expressed a hope on the part of the early citizens that this former Native American village would someday become again a flourishing community.

Pierre The enormous Oahe Dam and Oahe Reservoir are here in the South Dakota capital. Formerly Fort Pierre, the name honors Pierre Choteau, Jr., a trader for the American Fur Company.

Pittsburgh Southwestern Pennsylvania's urban and industrial center was named for William Pitt (1708-78), First Earl of Chatham. Pitt was the statesman who helped England win the French and Indian War.

Pocatello Home of the Minidome, Idaho State University's football stadium, the first indoor football stadium built on a university campus. In 1882 the first settlers named their town for Chief Pocatello of the Shoshoni Indians. His name was originally Dono Oso (Buffalo Robe), but was later changed to Pocatello, from the words *po* (road), *ka* (not), and *tello* (follow). This may be rendered as "one who does not follow the road." There is no way of being sure, but the name may refer to the chief's habit of taking the less-frequented trails when traveling.

Pocono Mountains Tourists come to this part of northeastern Pennsylvania to ski, skate, and snowmobile in winter, and to boat, golf, and hike in summer. The closest translation from Algonquian is "stream between the mountains." At first it was the name of the stream and later on the mountains.

Potomac River Washington, D.C. is on this river and Mount Vernon, the home of George Washington, is close by. John Smith wrote the name down as *Patawomeck* back in 1608. Most likely it is an Algonquian name meaning "something brought," a reference to the trade carried on by the Native Americans. This theory has not been confirmed, but it is a possible candidate, since the Native Americans did use this waterway and, thereby, could have transported articles of commerce on it.

Poughkeepsie Poughkeepsie, known for Vassar College, is the county seat of Dutchess County, New York. The local Algonquian-speakers gave this name to a waterfall. It means "little rock at the water," a reference to the stones at the bottom of the waterfall. Europeans made the first record of the name in 1683.

Prescott W.H. Prescott (1796-1859) was a writer of historical literary epics. The two that are still read are *The Conquest of Peru* and *The Conquest of Mexico*. The Arizona town was named in his memory.

Prince William County This county in northern Virginia is approximately thirty miles from Washington, D.C. Prince William (1721-65) was Duke of Cumberland, son of King George II and Queen Caroline.

Puerto Rico The Spanish name of this United States territory means rich port. Columbus named the island when he landed there in 1493. Only the bay, at first, was so named. The island, itself, was called San Juan. Columbus named it San Juan because he arrived on June 24, Saint John's feast day.

Racine Racine is south of Milwaukee, on Lake Michigan. Racine means root in French, and it is the name of the river upon which the city was built.

Raritan River Seventy five miles long, it is the longest river that is entirely within the state of New Jersey. Documents of the seventeenth century have the river name as Raretanoos and

Raretany, possibly from the Native American *nayantukq-ut*, meaning "a point on a tidal river." A group of Delaware Indians, known as the Raritans, used to dwell in central New Jersey and on Staten Island.

Reading Frontiersman Daniel Boone had his homestead here. It is in southeastern Pennsylvania, and it was named for Reading, England.

Reno Like Las Vegas, Reno is a gambling center. It is in western Nevada, north of Lake Tahoe. There was a General J.L. Reno who died for the Union during the Civil War. When the railroad came to the area, shortly after Reno's death, the town was named. The name looks and sounds Spanish, but it is French.

Rhode Island Rhode Island is the smallest state in the Union being only 1,212 square miles in area. Giovanni de Verrazano sailed near its coast, mentioning that he had seen an island about the same size as the Greek Island of Rhodes. The Dutch, when they explored the region, noted a red island (the Dutch spelling being *rood* or *rode*). When under English rule, the colonial governor passed a law that the island of Aquethneck be called Isle of Rhodes or Rhode Island. Eventually the entire colony, known as Providence Plantation, took the name of Rhode Island and Providence.

Richmond During the Civil War Richmond served as the capital of the Confederacy, and it has been Virginia's capital since 1780. William Byrd named the place where the town would be built, Richmond, in 1733 because it appeared to him like country around Richmond in England.

Ridgewood Ridgewood, New Jersey, is a suburban community in Bergen County. The name comes from the wooded, hilly terrain that characterizes the area.

Rochester Eastman Kodak is based here, and the mansion of George Eastman still stands. It is western New York's second largest city. Nathaniel Rochester (1752-1831), for whom the city was named, was an army colonel who owned the plot of land that would later become this city. Colonel Rochester participated in the American Revolution before he purchased land in New York State.

Rome (Georgia) Rome was a popular name for American towns in the early 1800's. In the case of Rome, Georgia, the terrain was hilly, thus suggesting the seven hills of Rome. Rome is in the northwestern part of the state.

Rome (New York) Erie Canal Village, a replica of a mid-nineteenth century settlement, is located in Rome. The town is in Oneida County, part of the dairy country of central New York State. Originally named Fort Stanwix, it was renamed in 1819 because of the heroism demonstrated there during the American Revolution.

Sacramento The California Gold Rush of 1849 gave the town its start. Its name is Spanish for sacrament, commemorating the Holy Sacraments of the Catholic Church. The Spaniards gave the name to the local river early in the nineteenth century and the city took the name of the river. The exact association that the river had with religion, if any, is unknown.

San Diego This city has the United States navy Pacific headquarters, and it is famous for its zoo. The Spanish gave the name to the bay in 1602 to honor St. Didacus. The city took the name of the bay.

San Francisco There is a high degree of cultural diversity here and, as a result, a great deal of tolerance. San Francisco has produced a number of famous people such as Jack London, Robert Frost, William Randolph Hearst, Robert S. McNamara, and Clint Eastwood. In 1595 the Spanish named the general vicinity for St. Francis of Assisi. The name was also applied to a bay that has not been identified with certainty. In 1769 a Spanish expedition tried to find this bay, but gave the name to the bay that still bears it.. The mission established there in 1770 took the name, San Francisco, and in 1847 it passed to the new city.

San Luis Obispo Each year in the middle of the summer this town has a Mozart Festival with concerts, choirs, and recitals. The Spanish named it for Saint Luis, Bishop of Toulouse in France (1274-97), son of Charles II, King of Naples. It is the name of both the town and the county. Father Juipero Serra started a mission there in the eighteenth century and named it for San Luis Obispo de Tolosa (Saint Louis Bishop of Toulouse

Sandusky Sandusky, Ohio is a manufacturing city with some wineries to the north, on Lake Erie. The American Commodore, Oliver Perry, defeated the British in a battle near Sandusky in 1813, during the War of 1812. The name is a derivative of the Wyandot Indian word *ot-san- doos-ke*, meaning "a source of pure water."

Santa Barbara The county and city of Santa Barbara are north of Los Angeles, on the Pacific coast. Originally it was the name of a channel of water separating the mainland from some of the islands off the coast. On December 4, 1602, the feast day of St. Barbara, a Spanish explorer named the channel and one of the islands. On the mainland the Spaniards established a mission, also calling it Santa Barbara. When California achieved statehood Santa Barbara County was set up, and the city was founded that same year.

Santa Catalina This island is near the coast of southern California, in the Gulf of Santa Catalina. It is a recreation area for those who like bicycling and fishing, and in 1919 William Wrigley, Jr., the chewing gum magnate, bought it for himself. Sebastian Vizcaino named the island on November 25, 1602, the feast day of St. Catherine.

Santa Fe Santa Fe, New Mexico, is the only American state capital that does not permit commercial jets to land at its airport. The purpose of this policy is to keep intact Santa Fe's image as an old city. At first the city was called *La Villa Real de la Santa Fe de San Francisco* (The Royal City of the Holy Faith of St. Francis), named by the Spanish in 1609. It did not take long, however, for the people in the area to use the present shortened form.

Sarasota In 1927 John Ringling used this town as the winter quarters for Ringling Brothers and Barnum and Bailey Circus. Today it is a popular tourist spot and retirement community on Florida's Gulf Coast. At one time there was a Seminole Indian village near the present town, and in that language it means "point of rocks."

Saratoga Saratoga, New York has been a resort area since the nineteenth century. Horse racing and medicinal springs have been the main attractions. The name is possibly Mohawk and it may refer to springs from the hillside. One other alternative is a Mohican origin, and in this language the name would be a reference to beavers.

Sausalito Across the Golden Gate Bridge from San Francisco, Sausalito is a resort area with shops and art galleries. The name comes from the Spanish word meaning "a little grove of willows."

Savannah Savannah has many historical features that bring tourists. It is an old colonial city with historic homes and churches. The word *savannah* or *savanna* is Carib Indian in origin, but it was absorbed by the Spanish language. During the late 1600's it was assimilated into English.The reference is to a wet meadow with coarse grass. The city name comes directly from the river name which may have come from a local Native American tribal name. Most likely, it was the Spanish who gave this tribe its name.

Scarsdale This Westchester County community, north of New York City, was the site of activity during the American Revolution. The British general, William Howe, had his headquarters at Griffin House in 1776. Griffin House, along with some other eighteenth century buildings, still stands. Scarsdale was one of the great manors established in colonial Westchester, and its proprietor, Caleb Heathcote, named it for his home, Scarsdale in England.

Schenectady General Electric, starting off with Thomas Edison and his Machine Works, has its origin here. Schenectady is in east-central New York State, just west of the Hudson River. It is an Iroquoian name and it may mean "beyond pines."

Scranton Early in the twentieth century Scranton, in northeastern Pennsylvania, was one of the world's centers of Anthracite coal production. There was a family by the name of Scranton, owners of a local coal mine.

Seattle This major West Coast port city has the name of a local Native American chief, Sealth.

Seward Peninsula It is a piece of land extending two hundred miles westward from Alaska into the Bering Strait, the channel of water separating North America from Asia. Gold deposits are present here. Secretary of State Seward, for whom it was named, purchased Alaska from Russia in 1867. Earlier names included Kaviak, Sumner Peninsular, and Nome Peninsula. Rev. John Green Brady (a former Presbyterian missionary), who served as governor of the territory of Alaska (1897-1906), suggested that the peninsula be named in honor of Seward.

Shaker Heights This affluent Cleveland suburb had at one time a colony of Shakers.

Sheboygan Sheboygan, Wisconsin is one of America's largest cheese-producers as well as a center for sausage-making. It is on Lake Michigan, about fifty miles north of Milwaukee. The origin of the name is uncertain, but there are three theories. It may come from *Shab-wa-wa- going*, meaning "rumbling waters" in the Potawatami Indian tongue. Another Native American tribe, the Menominee, called it *Saw-be-wah-he-con*, meaning echoes. The third possibility is that the name is a result of a legend, according to which the early pioneers were having only male children, thus making them so anxious that someone would exclaim "she-boy-again" every time another boy was born.

Shenandoah The Shenandoah Valley, a scenic region of Virginia, includes Skyline Drive, a highway through the most picturesque parts of the area. In Algonquian the name *schind-han- dowi* means spruce stream.

Shreveport The last Confederate stronghold during the Civil War, today it has the headquarters of several of the nation's largest natural gas companies. H.M.. Shreve, for whom it was named, opened the Red River to navigation in the 1830's.

Sitka Sitka used to be Alaska's capital, but in 1906 the state government was moved to Juneau. St. Michael's Cathedral, a replica of the original Russian Church, was built there in 1844. The name is of native Tlingit Indian origin and it means "by the sea."

Sparks This small Nevada town is not far from Reno. John Sparks was state governor (1903-08).

Spartansburg In western South Carolina, it was named in memory of the Spartan Regiment, a local militia that had a role in the American Revolution.

Spokane Grand Coulee Dam, constructed during the Depression for irrigation and electrification, is close by, in the arid eastern section of Washington State. The name is Native American and it may be a form of *spokanee* (sun), or *Illim-spokanee* (chief of the sun), the name of a tribe.

Stamford Twenty-four of the Fortune 500 biggest corporations are located in this Connecticut suburb. Stamford takes its name from a town in England.

Suffolk County Suffolk is Long Island's easternmost county, a rapidly growing residential and resort area which includes the Hamptons. Established in 1683, it was named for Suffolk County in England.

Sullivan County Part of New York State's Catskill Mountain resort area, it was named for General John Sullivan (1740-95) of New Hampshire, who participated in the Revolutionary War. He later served in the continental Congress and as governor of New Hampshire.

Susquehana River This river rises in New York State, flows through Pennsylvania, and empties into Chesapeake Bay, but it can neither be navigated nor used for hydroelectric power. An Iroquois tribe, the Susquehana or Susquehannocks, lived along the river's banks. The name is descriptive of a river filled with mud and sediment.

Syracuse Syracuse, in upstate New York, had a salt industry during the 1780's, and its well-known university opened in 1870. In 1825 the postmaster, John Wilkinson, had been reading about the ancient Greek city in Sicily of the same name. He believed that it resembled the New York State town because of its proximity to a swamp and its salt springs. Also, as noted above, classical names were popular at this time.

Tacoma From here the Olympic Mountains to the northwest and Mt. Rainier to the east are both in view. Tacoma is one of Washington State's main cities, south of Seattle, in the humid and rainy western part of the state. The name is derived from the Native American words *tah-koma,* "mother of us all."

Tallahassee Among this Florida city's attractions are its gardens, its historic houses, and its plantations, many of which are pre-Civil War. It means old town in the Creek Indian tongue.

Tampa Tampa, because of its large Cuban settlement, produces more cigars than any other place in the nation, with a daily output of over three million. It is possible that the name comes from that of a Spanish city, but it may be a form of the Cree Indian word itimpi (meaning near it), or a Native American expression denoting wood split for fires.

Tennessee Originally it was the name of a Cherokee Indian village known to the Spanish as *Tanasqui* and, later on, to the British as *Tinnase*. The Cherokees had been using the name for a long time, but the meaning is unknown. There was a small stream near to the village, also called *Tinnase*, which broadened into a river. The name was given to a county in North Carolina with the current spelling in use. The new state of Tennessee came into being in 1796.

Terre Haute Paul Dresser, composer of *On the Banks of the Wabash*, the Indiana state song, was born here. The city is on a plateau, hence Terre Haute, French for high land.

Texas Before Alaska became a state, Texas was the largest in the Union in area. The region is very diverse, with mountains, coastline, forests, plains, and lakes. Tejas, from which the present name comes, was the Spanish name for the local Hasinai Indian tribes. In pre-Spanish times the tribes of eastern Texas used the term Hasinai as a greeting, meaning welcome or "hello friend." The word could also mean a friend or an ally.

Ticonderoga Many battles took place here among French, British, Native American, American, and Canadian troops. The French built a fort at this spot in 1755, but the British destroyed it in 1777, after it had been occupied by the American colonists just before the Revolution. Today this town in northern New York State is a summer resort area. Linguists believe that this Iroquoian name means "between lakes."

Toledo Morrison R. Waite, chief justice of the United States, Brand Whitlock, a mayor who became ambassador to Belgium, and the Republican Congressman who introduced the motion to impeach President Andrew Johnson were all from Toledo, a large industrial city on Lake Erie, in western Ohio. Residents named it for the city in Spain, since there was an interest in foreign or exotic names, especially Spanish names, at this time (1833).

Topeka The Kansas state capital, it was the home of Alfred M. Landon, the Republican presidential candidate of 1936. Topeka comes from a Siouan word meaning "good potato place," a reference to a spot at which the Native Americans were able to dig wild tubers out of the ground.

Tucson Tucson's climate is so dry that during the oil shortage of 1973 a number of airlines that were without fuel and could not fly parked at this city's airport where the planes would not rust. The name is Papago Indian and it means "black base," a description of a local mountain. Not far away there was a mission named for a saint, but after some time its name was replaced by the Papago name, Tucson.

Tulsa Tulsa started as a post office on the Pony Express mail route in 1879. The Creek Indians had to migrate from their original home to Oklahoma and establish a new settlement at Tulsa, which means old town in their language.

Tuscaloosa The town is located in the "cotton-belt" of west-central Alabama, and it was named for a Choctaw Indian chief, Tascalusa, meaning "black warrior."

Tuskegee In this Alabama town the Tuskegee Institute had its start in 1881 as an African- American educational institution headed by Booker T. Washington, an educator and social reformer until his death in 1915. It is Muskogean Indian name and it means warrior.

Urbana Urbana is in Illinois, and its name is the feminine form of the Latin adjective meaning citified or urban.

Utah Dinosaurs roamed here many millions of years ago, and Dinosaur National Monument along with redstone canyons, gorges, lakes, and pines bring visitors every year to this clean and natural part of the country. A Native American people called the Ute, also spelled Uta and Utah, had lived here. Pioneers began to call a lake and a river flowing from it by this Native American tribal name. During the 1850's, when the United States government was organizing the region as a new territory, the Mormon settlers had named it Deseret, but Congress decided to change the name to Utah, after the river.

Valdosta Valdosta is a part of Georgia's rich agricultural region. The name honors Governor G.M. Troup, who before the Civil War, gave this Italian
name to his estate.

Ventura This is a town on southern California's coast, just north of Los Angeles. The name is an abbreviated form of San Buenaventura (Saint Bonaventure), the saint for whom a local mission was named back in 1782. Ventura is also a Spanish word for happiness and luck.

Vermont The famous Ben and Jerry's ice cream is manufactured here. Tourists come in large numbers for the skiing and the scenery. Samuel Champlain, a French explorer, took note of the mountains of Vermont when he was there in 1609. The Green Mountains, as they are called today, appeared as the most prominent geographical feature to Champlain. At the time of the Revolutionary War Dr. Thomas Young of Philadelphia suggested that the region be called Vermont, from the French words for green mountain. Previously, the area was known as New Connecticut.

Vicksburg The Vicksburg National Military Park forms an arc around the city and it contains forts, earthworks, artillery batteries, monuments, and plaques related to the Civil War battle that took place there. General Grant besieged the city until it had to surrender. Vicksburg was named for a Mississippi pioneer and Methodist minister by the name of Newitt Vick.

Walla Walla The town with this unusual name is located in southeastern Washington state. It is also the name of the county, but originally it was the name of a river. It is derived from the Native American words meaning "little swift river."

Wappinger Falls Located in southeastern New York State, it comes from *wapinkw*, a Delaware Indian word for opossum. A tribe by this name at one time lived in Putnam, Dutchess, and Columbia counties, on the eastern shore of the Hudson River.

Warren Warren, Ohio keeps alive the name of Moses Warren, the man who surveyed the land. The town is about fifty miles southeast of Cleveland.

Watertown In 1878 Frank W. Woolworth opened the first "five-and-ten-cent" store in this town of northern New York State. The first settlers decided upon the name Watertown when they recognized the locality's potential as a source of water power.

Waukegan Waukegan is in Illinois, not far north of Chicago, on Lake Michigan. It means fort or trading-post in the Algonquian language. Originally it was the name of a stream which the Native Americans called old fort, but in 1849 the citizens of the town voted to adopt the name for their settlement.

Waycross Waycross is in the peanut-growing region of Georgia, in the southeastern part of the state. First called Yankee Town, the present name was chosen because of the many trails that crossed there.

Wilkes-Barre This town in northeastern Pennsylvania honors two English politicians, John Wilkes and Isaac Barre, who favored the colonists in their conflict with Britain.

Wilmington The largest city in Delaware, it is the home of the Winterthur Museum and Gardens with its mansion surrounded by a private park. Spencer Compton, for whom the city was named, was Earl of Wilmington, a member of the English king's Privy Council, and a colonial administrator.

Winston Salem Winston Salem, North Carolina, is the home of R.J. Reynolds tobacco factory, the producer of over 450 million cigarettes each day. Originally there were two towns; Winston named for Major Joseph Winston (1746-1815), an American Revolutionary officer and member of the North Carolina State Legislature, and Salem, which like many American towns of that name, comes from the Hebrew shalom (peace). It is a shortened form of Jerusalem, hence its popularity. (see Jerusalem).

Wisconsin German immigrants in the nineteenth century used local barley to make this state the nation's largest beer-producer. Wisconsin is also famed for its dairy industry. French explorers who were there in the seventeenth century noted the river name, Mescousing or Mesconsing. Ouisconsin was a third form, the one from which the settlers derived the current name. The language is Algonquian and it may denote a big river, but linguists are uncertain.

Wyoming Of all the fifty states, Wyoming is the smallest in population. On the map this state is a perfect square. It is mountainous, scenic, and has deposits of oil, coal, and Uranium. The name was first applied to the Wyoming Valley of Pennsylvania. Thomas Campbell (1777-1844), a British poet, wrote "Gertrude of Wyoming" in 1809, a poem about an Indian raid in Pennsylvania's Wyoming Valley The poem was popular and, as a result, settlers in many parts of the United States used Wyoming as a place-name. The Wyoming Territory was organized in 1868 with Rep. James M. Ashley of Ohio suggesting that the name be adopted.

Yonkers Yonkers is famous for St. Andrew's Golf Course, where the game was introduced to the United States. It is an urban community in Westchester County, New York, on the Hudson River, just north of New York City. During the Dutch period of colonial New York there was an Adriaen van der Donck who owned a farm where Yonkers would later be. In the Dutch language he was known as Jonk heer, a title equivalent to the English, Squire. When friends would visit him they would say that they were going to Jonk heer's, and eventually Jonk heer's became Yonkers.

Yosemite Yosemite National Park, a well-known California vacation spot, features Yosemite Falls, giant Sequoias, and El Capitan, the largest granite monolith in the world. The park derives its name from a local Native American word meaning grizzly bear, also the name of the tribe.

Youngstown This town in northeastern Ohio is one of the largest centers of steel manufacture in the United States. John Young, for whom the town was named, was one of its early pioneers.

Zanesville Zanesville, the birthplace of the novelist, Zane Grey and the architect, Cass Gilbert, is a town in eastern Ohio. Ebenezer

Zane, the founder of the town, called it Westbourne. Later on the citizens renamed it Zane's Town, but in 1800, with the establishment of the post office, they gave the town its present name.

Chapter 3. European Place Names

Aachen This city in northwestern Germany was Charlemagne's capital during the eight and ninth centuries. The name is a derivative of *aha*, an Old High German word meaning water. The Latin name was *Aquae Grani* or *Aquisgranum*, "Waters of *Granus*," *Granus* being, most likely, a Celtic deity.

Aberdeen A port of Scotland's eastern coast, Aberdeen is known as a horticultural center as well as a producer of whiskey. In Gaelic it is *Abair-Eahdhain*, meaning an estuary of the river Don.

Abruzzi Poor soil, mountains, and earthquakes have made the southeastern part of Italy a very sparsely populated region. Called *Bruttium* or *Regio Brutiorum* in ancient times, it was the territory of the Bruttii, a local Italian tribe.

Adriatic Sea Separating Italy from the former Yugoslavia, its coasts are famous for resorts and beautiful landscapes. The water, itself, is notably blue. Adria, for which the sea was named, was an Etruscan city on the Italian coast. It was a powerful city that mounted a defense against the Greek colonists during the middle of the first millennium B.C.

Aegean Sea The islands of the Aegean collectively make up 5,600 square miles of land. During the Bronze Age there were civilizations in the lands bordering the Aegean (c. 2800-1100

B.C.). The name comes from the early Greek word *aig*, meaning water or sea, an example of the common practice of applying a generic term to a specific geographical feature. In very early times the Greeks identified this sea with the general concept of a sea, since it happened to have been the one that they were most familiar with.

Ajaccio Corsica's main city, Ajaccio has a busy urban center as well as good beaches. On August 15 each year the townspeople celebrate the birthday of Napoleon Bonarparte. The name may be a form of *adjacium*, Latin for a stop or resting place. One alternative explanation is that it comes from *Ajax*, the name of a mythological hero of the ancient Greeks. The first theory is the better one, since the Latin word is closer linguistically to the name of the city than is the name of the Greek hero. The Latin ending (*um*) became the Italian ending (*o*), and it is reasonable that a settlement would be called a resting place, especially since ships made stops there on their way across the Mediterranean.

Albania Albania is a small nation to the southwest of the former Yugoslavia, on the Adriatic Sea. The terrain is mountainous, and the people are known for their custom of interfamily feuding. In ancient times Ptolemy, king of Egypt and geographer, recorded the name of the people in the region as *Albanoi*. The *Albanoi* were a tribe of Illyrians, one of the original inhabitants of the Balkans. The Illyrians were the ancestors of the modern Albanians (see Bosnia). There are three possible sources for the choice of *Albanoi* as a name: (1) the Celtic word, *alb*, meaning a hill (see Alps); (2) the early Indo-European root *albh*, meaning white; (3) the Illyrian *olba*, a word denoting colonization. The first of the above is the most likely because the geographical description is fitting and because some Celtic tribes had migrated through this area not long before Ptolemy's time. The final possibility sounds convincing also, since it is a local Illyrian word.

Algarve Portugal's southern coast, a resort area attracting vacationers from many European countries, is known as the Algarve. Originally it was *al-garb*, an Arabic term meaning the west, a logical designation for the farthest west region familiar to the Arabs.

Alps This mountain range has made Switzerland and parts of Austria famous for their ski resorts. Twelve hundred glaciers have been counted in the Alpine region. Originally the name was Ligurian, a very ancient language of southeastern France and northwestern Italy. When Celtic people settled the area they began to use the old Ligurian word which mean height, elevation, hill, or loftiness.

Alsace Alsace is the easternmost region of France, along the Rhine River which separates France from Germany. There is a strong German influence in Alsace, and large numbers of tourists come every year. *Alsatia* in Latin and *Elsas* in German, its origin is in the ancient Celtic *alisa*, meaning a cliff. The Gauls, a Celtic people, noted this geological feature in the locality as they migrated through. The other Celtic word that it may stem from is *aliso*, an elder tree.

Amiens Amiens has a Gothic Cathedral dating from the thirteenth century that remained untouched by the bombing that had taken place during World War I and World War II. In ancient times this village of Belgian Gaul was called *Samarobriva*, "bridge over the Somme".

Amsterdam This city of many museums is built around concentric canals. Amsterdam is one of Europe's main commercial centers and tourist attractions. The name means simply "dike (or dam) on the Amstel." In the old Germanic language of the region *ama* meant a river or stream and *stelle* meant a place or spot. The reference is to an artificial mound or knoll upon which flocks of sheep or herds of cattle had taken refuge from floods. The name

Amsterdam denotes, therefore, a man-made structure built on a stream for the protection of livestock. Apparently such construction had been in progress at the early settlement which would later on develop into modern Amsterdam as well as at a number of other locations along the Amstel River.

Ancona Ancona is on Italy's Adriatic coast, with the sea to the east and the mountains to the west. The city has several historic monuments which include a triumphal arch built by the Greek architect, Apollodorus, in 115 A.D., and a more recent one built by Luigi Vanvitelli in the early 1700's. Greek colonists founded the city in 380 B.C., and the name is a Latinized form of the Greek word for a curve or an elbow, a relative of *sakura*, a Greek word for an anchor. The town is located at a curvature on the Italian coast.

Andorra This small principality in the Pyrenees Mountains between France and Spain is a rugged land with seven mountain peaks close to ten thousand feet high. The country's name is probably related to the word *andurrial*, which in the local dialect, means a land covered by bushes.

Antwerp This Belgian port, the fifth largest port in the world, has had a long history in the commercial life of the region. The name is a combination of the two old Germanic words *anda* (house or home) and *werpum* (pier) thus, home pier. Possibly sailors or traders had a house at this spot at one time.

Appenine Mountains The *Appennini*, as they are called in Italian, run along the Italian peninsula from north to south. Towns in the area are built on hills in order to avoid flooding. Originally a Celtic name, the Italians adopted it in ancient times. *Penn* is a Celtic word for a summit, peak, or head.

Apulia The hilly and narrow plain on the eastern coast of Italy is basically farmland with some grazing for sheep and cattle. Apulia is simply the Latin form of the Italian *Puglia*. The Indo-European root of the Latin word is *ap* or *apa*, a derivative of *akw*, a word for water.

Aragon This part of northern Spain was originally one of the kingdoms that had united with Castile to form a unified Spain. *Aracone* was the name or a river, with the prefix *ar* being the Indo-European root for any word that denotes water. *Aracone* could be either Celtic or Latin in origin, since they are both Indo-European languages. Also, both Celts and Romans had settled in Spain in ancient times. The only alternative explanation would be a Basque origin for the name, since Basques were present in the region long before any Indo-Europeans had arrived, and since geographical names tend to be remnants of the earliest local languages. Basque was spoken in early times over a much wider area than it is at present. There is a likelihood, therefore, that the name of this part of Spain comes from the Basque word *ur*, also a reference to a river or water.

Ardennes Forest The Ardennes stretches from the Meuse River in southeastern Belgium in the direction of Luxembourg, farther to the southeast. Battles were fought here, and most notably, the Battle of the Bulge. The Celtic word *ard* (or *aird*) means high or height, and the whole name refers to a forested area with hills and valleys.

Arles Vincent van Gogh did some of his work there in 1888, and today "Vince" T-shirts are being sold to tourists. The town is on the Rhone River of southern France, approximately twenty miles from the Mediterranean. In ancient times it was known by the Latin name *Arelate*, possibly of pre-Indo-European origin, but most likely a derivative of the Celtic *are*, meaning house and *lait*, a word for marsh or swamp.

Armenia In northeastern Turkey, very close to Armenia, stands Mt. Ararat, where according to the Biblical narrative, Noah's ark landed after the flood. Armenia, in Russian, *Ermenistan* in Turkish, and *Armanestan* in Iranian, the origin of the name is uncertain, but it may come from *Armenak*, the name of a legendary ancestor of the Armenian people. The Armenians, themselves, call their country *Hayasdan* or *Hayastan*, with *Hay* being the name of the people. *Hayg* or *Hayk* was a legendary hero.

Athens In 1834, when Athens became the capital of modern Greece, there were only ten thousand people living there. Today there are over four million, a third of the entire Greek population. *Athenai* in ancient Greek, *Athenae* in Latin, and *Athena* in modern Greek, the name is that of an ancient Greek deity. This goddess' name is probably derived from *athantos*, Greek for immortal (the prefix *a* means without and *thantos* means death). One other possibility is *atithana* (without a mother), thus coming into being spontaneously.

Augsburg This city is in the mountains of Bavaria and is the ´ birthplace of playwright, Bertolt Brecht. It was originally the Roman colony, *Augusta Vindelicorum*, named for the emperor and the local people. Another name was *Colonia Augusta Raetorum* (colony of Augustus in the territory of the *Raetians*), a Celtic people of the Alpine region. Some ancient writers called it simply *Augusta*. When Germanic people settled Bavaria at the end of the Roman era, Augusta became Augsburg, city of Augustus.

Austria This Alpine country has nearly eight thousand miles of cross-country skiing trails. The original name of the region was *Marchia Austriaca* (Eastern March), having been a march or frontier zone of the German Empire. *Austro* is a form of the old German word meaning eastern or shining, both words being a reference to the rising of the sun. The German word comes from the Indo-European root *aus*, meaning down or east.

Avignon Located in southern France, on the Rhone River, Avignon is a university town as well as a host to film festivals. The Latin name was *Avennio*, derived from a root meaning a course of water.

Balearic Islands There are four main islands in this group. Mallorca, the largest, is the most frequented by tourists. Menorca is quiet with nice beaches and landscape. The island of Ibiza, by contrast, is a lively resort with "cross-dressers," "hippies," and other varieties of guests. Formentera appeals to visitors who enjoy the outdoors, with its beaches and hiking trails. The Romans called these western Mediterranean islands *Baleares Insulae*. There are three possible explanations for the name: (1) it may be based upon the pre-Indo-European word *bal*, meaning shining, bright, or white; (2) it may be the Indo-European *bhel*, to shine or to glitter; (3) it may be a derivative of a Phoenician word for "islands of the stone-throwers," since the natives used stones in their battles against invaders.

Baltic Sea The Baltic Sea separates Sweden from the Baltic states. In Russian it is *Baltiiskoie morie*, in Lithuanian, Baltijes jura, and in Swedish, *Osterjon*, sea of the east. Baltic and Balt (the Balts are people living on its eastern shore) may be of Lithuanian, Slavic, or Germanic origin. *Baltas* means white in Lithuanian, and *blato* means marsh in Slavic. Balt is possibly a form of this Slavic word. If the name is Germanic it could be a derivative of *baelte*, Danish for straight, or *Balthe*, the name of the royal Visigothic family which, according to legend, was descended from deities called *balthes*. The Visigoths were Scandinavians who had left their homeland in Sweden during the second century A.D. and migrated through Europe. They crossed the Baltic Sea, water that had been familiar to them for centuries. It is not unlikely, therefore, that their country, their gods, their royal family, and their sea would bear the same name. The fourth possibility, therefore, seems the most likely.

Barcelona The 1992 Olympics were held here, the second largest city in Spain. Its name may come from that of the Carthaginian general, Hamilcar Barca, who led a campaign in Spain during the Punic Wars against Rome. *Barka* is a Phoenician word related to the Arabic *barq*, meaning lightning or thunderbolt.

Bari This port city in southeastern Italy is an industrial and commercial center with flour mills, petroleum refineries, steel factories, and a university that gives only doctoral degrees. *Barium* in Latin and *Barion* in Greek, the name is a derivative of *bari*s, a reference in Greek to a small boat with oars or sails.

Bavaria Lederhosen, brass bands, beer gardens, and Oktoberfest have all originated in this mountainous region of southeastern Germany. *Bayern* is the modern German form, but *Baiwarioz* is the old Germanic name. *Bai*, the first part of the name, comes from *Boii*, the name of a Celtic people who lived there in ancient times, before the Germans had arrived. *Warioz* means defender in the old Germanic language, from the verb *warjan*, to defend.

Bay of Biscay This bay is actually a part of the Atlantic Ocean, the eastern end of it that washes the western coast of France and separates Spain from Brittany. Biscay experiences severe storms and has strong currents, but there is good fishing and some beach resorts. The name comes from the Basque word *Bizkaia*, a derivative of *bizkar*, meaning a neck or a narrow portion of a mountain. The word may also be applied to the top of a house. Biscay refers not only to the bay, but to the Basque province of Spain as well.

Belfast The capital of Northern Ireland, Belfast has been the scene of a conflict between the Irish Republican Army and the British government for many decades. It is a Gaelic reference to a place of crossing by a sandbank.

Belgium This small European nation is the second most densely populated country on Earth and the most industrialized. The Belgians produce 165 different cheeses. Flemish, a Germanic language akin to Dutch, is spoken in the north and French is used in the south. The Flemish name for the country. is *Belgie* and the French, *Belgique*. In ancient times it was a part of *Gallia Belgica* (Belgian Gaul), a Roman province. The name *Belgica* is probably Gallic, a Celtic language used by the natives of the region.. It may come from *volca*, a word for rapid or active, or it may stem from the Indo-European root *bhelg*, meaning "to fill with anger," a reference to the warlike character of the local people.

Belgrade Capital of the former Yugoslavia and capital of Serbia, Belgrade is a river port as well as an air and rail center. The Serbs call it *Beograd*, white town. This city existed in ancient times and was known as *Singidunum* and as *Taurunum*, both Celtic names. When Slavic peoples, including Serbs, settled the Balkans during the sixth and seventh centuries they changed the name to *Beograd*.

Belorussia One of the newly-formed nations of the former Soviet Union, Belorussia (*Belarus* in the Belorussian language and *Bielorussia* in Russian) has over ten million people. Its main products are dairy, potatoes, oats, potash, and salt. *Bely* means white in Belorussian, and there are three possible reasons why the name has been applied in this way. The color white is significant for Belorussians in three different contexts: (1) it is the color of their national costume; (2) it is the color of the sand or earth covering part of the land; (3) white may stand for freedom in the local culture, since the Belorussians had never paid tribute to the Tartars as had the Russians farther to the east.

Berlin Since unification Berlin has been the largest city in continental Europe. The name probably comes from *Barlein*, a German word for a little bear, especially considering that the city's coat of arms contains a representation of a bear. (see Bern).

Bern The Swiss capital and one of the country's most beautiful cities, Bern has little industry, but it hosts the headquarters of several international organizations. The German *bar* (bear) may explain the name, since the Helvetians, the ancient Celtic inhabitants who had been there previous to the arrival of the Germans, worshipped a bear as one of their gods. (see Berlin). There is another theory, however, that the name is from the Indo-European root *ber*, meaning a marshy place.

Bessarabia *Biessarabia* in Russian and *Bessarabia* in Roumanian, this part of the western Ukraine and Moldavia gets its name from that of a Roumanian dynasty that ruled the region at one time, the Basarab family.

Bialystok The flat roll known as a bialy is named after this town. *Bialystok* is the Polish spelling and *Bielostok* the Russian. Before World War I this city in the northeastern corner of Poland was part of Belorussia. Between the two world wars it went back and forth between Russia and Poland, and after World War II it was ceded to Poland. *Bialy* (Polish) or *bielo* (Russian) means white, and *stok* in both languages is a river or a junction of two rivers.

Birmingham This is a large English industrial city. Sources of the twelfth century record the name as *Brimigham* and as *Bremingeham*, Anglo-Saxon for "home of the *Beormingas*." *Beormingas* means sons of Beorn, the name of a king or an Anglo-Saxon tribal or clan chief who made a home there along with his followers during the Anglo-Saxon settlement of England.

Black Sea This body of water is bounded by the Ukraine, Turkey, the Caucasus, and the Balkans. It is Russia's main outlet for commerce and fishing, The Russian name is *Tchornoi morie*, the Roumanian is *Marea Neagra*, and the Turkish is *Kara deniz*, names which mean the same as the English. According to one theory, the name comes from the dark color of the water, the result of black sediments. Nevertheless, the water appears clearly blue when the sun shines directly onto it. The ancient Greeks called it *Pontus Euxine* (*Euxine* meaning hospitable and *Pontus*, sea).

Bohemia The western portion of the new Czech Republic, it includes Moravia. Plzen, where Pilsner Beer is brewed, is a Bohemian city. Bohemia was originally *Baihaimoz*, "home of the Boii," a Celtic tribe that resided there until they migrated on the arrival of the Germans in the first or second century A.D. The Slavic Czechs, the present inhabitants, made their home there in the sixth century and called the country *Cechy*. (see Bavaria).

Bologna Known for having the oldest university in the world, the word university has its origin herre. Since the eleventh century Bologna has had a reputation as a center for the study of law. The Celtic *Boii* were in northern Italy until their ejection by the Romans. They called their settlement *Bononia* which would eventually become Bologna. (see Bohemia).

Bonn The history of this German city goes back two thousand years. It is also the birthplace of Beethoven. The name comes from *bona*, an ancient Gallic reference to the foundation of a building or to a citadel. In Roman times the name of the city was *Ara Ubiorum*, Latin for "Altar of the *Ubii*," the *Ubii* having been a Germanic people living in the Rhineland at the time.

Bordeaux Bordeaux is the center of the world's largest wine-bottling region, where five hundred million bottles of wine are produced each year. In ancient times the name was *Burdegala* or

Burdigala, a combination of two words in the local language, *burd* and *gala*, the meanings of which are unknown.

Bosnia Conflict between Christian Serbs and Moslems has put this part of the former Yugoslavia into turmoil. Bosnia comes from Bosna, the name of a river, a derivative of the Indo- European root *bhog* (running water). The word was probably introduced by the Illyrians, an Indo-European-speaking people, ancestors of the Albanians who were in the Balkans since very early times.

Bosporus This is the channel of water that separates the Black Sea from the Sea of Marmara, and European from Asiatic Turkey. It is a linking of the two Greek words *bous* (cattle) and *poros* (passage). Herders probably shipped their cattle across this waterway in early times quite often, since a number of different tribes crossed over from the Balkans to Asia Minor with their livestock .The Bulgarians, Roumanians, and the Turks call it the *Bosfor*, but the Turks also refer to it as *Karadeniz Bogazi* (strait of the Black Sea) and *Bogazici* (interior of the strait).

Brandenburg This is a province of northeastern Germany, on the North German Plain, where Berlin is located. Until the eleventh and twelfth centuries it was home to Slavic people who began to move farther east when Germans from the west settled the area. *Bran*, the first part of the name, is a Slavic word for defense and *burg* is German for city or fortress.

Bremen Bremen, in the German province of Lower Saxony, is a port city on the Weser River which empties into the North Sea. There is a marketplace in the city that is surrounded by buildings that go back to the twelfth century. The name comes from the Germanic *brem*, a word for swampy coast.

Bristol The old forms of the name are *Bristou, Brycgstow*, and *Bristow. Brycgstow* is Old English for bridge place.

Britain (Great) The island of Great Britain includes England, Scotland, and Wales. It contains a varied topography ranging from plains in the south and east along the coast to mountains in northern England, in Scotland, and in Wales. Livestock, oats, barley, beets, and wheat are some of the island's agricultural products. Major industrial centers include London, Birmingham, Newcastle, Manchester, Liverpool, Cardiff, and Glasgow. English, Gaelic, and Welsh are Britain's three languages. The name is Celtic, but there are differences of opinion with regard to its origin and meaning. The Celtic root *pri*, for example, is a reference to clay or soil, one possibility. More likely is the name of a chief of a local Celtic tribe that lived there in ancient times, an individual called Brit or Brut. Two other words, *brizh* and *broden*, may also be considered. *Brizh* means multicolored and refers to the Celtic custom of painting the skin for battle, while *broden* means the land of humans. The Celtic people of Britain were known in ancient times as Britons. During the sixth century, when Anglo-Saxons were settling southern Britain, some of the native Britons left their home to take up residence in northwestern France, a region that would later be called Brittany, Little Britain. The island of Britain, where the overwhelming majority of the Celtic Britons were to remain, would become Great Britain in order to distinguish it from Brittany or Little Britain (see Brittany).

Brittany This part of northwestern France was named for the Britons who had migrated there in the sixth century. As noted above, Brittany means Little Britain. (see Britain) Brittany has resorts and beaches, but is known also for its rocky coastline, pink granite rocks, and circles of large stones like the one at Carnac which is made up of about three thousand stones and may have been the site of an ancient religious ritual.

Brno Classical architecture dominates this Moravian city, a center of industry during the eighteenth and nineteenth centuries. *Brn* means clay or castle of clay in the Czech language, and it is possible that the city's name is a form of this word. It may, however, come from the German *brunnen*, the word for a mine shaft, a pit, or a well.

Brussels The Belgian capital is one of that country's main industrial and population centers. A striking feature of Brussels is the presence of very modern architecture alongside of old cobbled streets. The French spelling is *Bruxelles*, a form of the Latin *Bruxellae*, a name derived from the Germanic words *broka* and *sali. Broka* means swamp or marsh and *sali*, room or building. Belgium was the Roman province of *Gallia Belgica*, where the local Celts and Germans adopted Latin forms for words in their own languages. (see Belgium)

Bucarest During the nineteenth century this city was famous for its boulevards, its parks, and its neoclassical architecture. There is a story, most likely legendary, about the name of the Roumanian capital. According to tradition, it was a shepard by the name of Bucar who founded the village in 1457. The name is probably older and derived from either the Roumanian infinitive *bucura*, meaning to rejoice, or from the Albanian *bukur*, a word for pretty, fine, or handsome.

Budapest Originally Budapest was the two towns of Buda and Pest, separated by the Danube River, and united under one administration in 1872. Buda may have been named for Buda (also called Bleda), the brother of Attila the Hun, it may be a form of the Slavic word for water, since it is located on a river, or it may be a form of the Hungarian word *bode*, a hut or a cabin. Pest comes from a Slavic word for a cave or a cavern.

Bulgaria Between Sofia and the Black Sea coast is a place called Valley of Roses, where the people manufacture rose-oil which, pound for pound, is more valuable than gold. The name of the country may be a derivative of *bulga*, an ancient Turkish word that means to mix, a reference to the fact that the Bulgars were mixture of different Turkish tribes. They came from north of the Black Sea and settled what is now Bulgaria in the seventh century A.D. The Bulgars gave their name to the nation, but were assimilated by the Slavic people who were already there, and who formed the overwhelming majority of the population.

Burgundy This part of France is known for its scenic countryside with vineyards and monumental Romanesque Cathedrals. Originally the Burgundians were a Germanic people who had immigrated to eastern France in the fifth century A.D. The name, itself, may stem from the Gothic *baurgjans*, meaning inhabitants of fortified places, an apparent reference to the manner in which the Burgundians had lived in early times, before they had arrived in France.

Cadiz This southern Spanish port city is ancient, but it is today a center for nightlife. The Romans called it *Gades*, a Latin form of *gadir*, a Phoenician word meaning a fort, a wall, or a rampart. Phoenician trading colonies existed in Spain through the first millennium B.C.

Calabria Geographically Calabria is a small peninsula extending from the southwestern end of Italy. It is a mountainous olive-growing region. *Kalabra* or *galabra* is the pre-Indo-European word from which it comes, and it refers to rock, a topographically descriptive term.

Calais Located on the Strait of Dover, a small channel of water between France and England, this small French city has what is possibly a pre-Celtic name. It may stem from *kales*, a word that refers to an object or to a place that is like stone.

Cambridge Cambridge, in southeastern England, is known for its university from which individuals such as Lord Byron and the physicist, Stephen Hawking rank among its alumni. *Cam*, which may have been *camb* originally, is a Celtic word denoting a crooked river. A Roman writer of the fourth century A.D. noted a place called *Camborico*, a possible reference to Cambridge. Alternatively the name may be a form of *Grantabrycge*, bridge on the *Granta*, with *Granta* having changed over the centuries to *cam*.

Cannes Nightlife and an annual Film Festival attract visitors to Cannes each year. Cannes comes from *Canua*, a pre-Indo-European word, most probably Liguarian. The prefix *kan* in this ancient language refers to height. Ligurian was spoken along the northwestern Italian and southern French coasts in very early times.

Canterbury Canterbury Cathedral, where King Henry II killed Thomas a Becket in 1170, has given this English city great historical significance. *Cant* refers to southeastern England, and may derive from *canto*, a Celtic word for a border or a coastal district. There is also the possibility that *cant* is a form of the local Celtic tribal name, *Cantii*, a people living there in ancient times whose name may mean hosts. *Bury* is simply the Anglo-Saxon *burh*, a fortified place, hence fort of the *Cantii*, or fort of the coast or border.

Capri In modern times Capri has been a popular resort area, attracting many vacationers, but in ancient times it may have been a refuge for wild goats, since *caper* is Latin for goat.

Cardiff Wales' capital and industrial center is also a city in which many flowers beautify the surroundings. Dcuments of the twelfth and thirteenth centuries mention *Cardif, Kardid, Kaerdif,* and *Kerdife* as alternative forms of the name. In modern Welsh it is *Caerdydd*, with *caer* meaning fort and *dydd* being a form of

Didius, the name of the Roman general who led battles against the Celtic Britons. Cardiff was originally a fort built by the Romans.

Catalonia This prosperous section of Spain became one of Europe's main centers of textile manufacture during the eighteenth century. *Catalunya* in the local dialect and *Cataluna* in Spanish, the name may come from that of the Celtic *Catalauni*, a group of tribes living there in ancient times, or it may come from *Goth-Alania*, two peoples who had crossed the region on their migration into Spain. The Goths had passed through in the late fifth century, and the Alans had been there a little less than a century earlier.

Caucasus Mountains The Caucasus forms a mountain chain between the Black and Caspian Seas, in the former Soviet Union. Corn, sheep, and mineral deposits are some of its natural resources. Many different ethnic groups share the region, including Georgians and other aboriginal Caucasian peoples, Turkic groups, and Iranian-related nationalities. The name may stem from the ancient Greek word *kauk*, meaning mountain. According to another theory, one suggested by the Roman writer, Pliny, it is a Scythian name meaning "white as snow." The Scythians lived in the Caucasus during the first millennium B.C. In Russian the name is *Kavkaz*, in Armenian *Govgas*, in Turkish, *Kafkasya*, and in Iranian, *Qafqaz*.

Chartres Famed for its twelfth-century cathedral, this French city takes its name from the Celtic tribes that were there in early times, the *Carnutes*, for whom the place was sacred. The Latin name for the city is *Carnutum*, *Carnotum*, or *Carnotis*. In ancient times it was called *Autricum*, after the Autura River.

Cologne The world's largest Gothic building, Cologne Cathedral, is here. *Koln* in German, the name was originally *Colonia Agrippina*, Colony of Agrippa. Other Roman names included *Colonia Claudia Augusta Agrippinensium* and *Colonia Agrippina Ubiorum,* Colony of Agrippa in the territory of the *Ubii.* The *Ubii* were a local Germanic people. Cologne and *Koln* are forms of the Latin *Colonia,* colony.

Connaught This part of western Ireland has attracted many poets and painters because of its scenic landscape. Also spelled Connacht, it is one of the four historic provinces of Ireland. Conn was an Irish chief who established the Kingdom of Connacht in the second century A.D. The name of this province may be a derivative of the chief's name, but there is also the possibility that it is a form of *connadh,* a Celtic word denoting a forest warming up.

Copenhagen The city is constructed on two islands connected by bridges. *Copen* is a variation of *kioben,* Danish for merchant and related to the German *kaufen,* to buy. *Havn* is haven, hence merchant's haven.

Cordoba Moorish influence is preserved well in this Spanish city, at one time the center of Islamic art, culture, and learning. *La Juderia,* remnants of the Jewish quarter, still stands.Maimonides, the Jewish scholar, philosopher, and theologian of the twelfth century was born and raised there. It is *Corduba* in Latin and it may be a form of *qorteb,* a Phoenician word meaning to press oil. Spain had large colonies of Phoenician traders all through the first millennium B.C., and Cordoba could have been the site of an early olive oil industry.

Corinth Remains of the old city-state that date back to the sixth century B.C., including some small temples, can still be explored by tourists and by archeologists. Corinth is a pre-Indo- European name as are other Greek toponyms ending in *inthos.* Native Mediterranean people living in the Aegean area spoke a non-Indo-

European tongue before the introduction of Greek by Indo-European speakers who had migrated south from the Balkans circum 2000 B.C. At first the name may have been used to describe the high peak known today as *Akrocorinthos*, with the possibility that *cor* means a summit or a rock.

Cork Cork is the largest Irish county, and it includes the scenic south coast and Bantry Bay, a natural harbor. The name is a shortened form of *Corcach-mor-Mumham*, Gaelic for "the great marsh of Munster."

Cornwall Fishing villages, beaches, and Iron Age sites are some of the features of this peninsula that extends into the Atlantic Ocean from southwestern England. Agriculture supports this region in which the original Celtic language of the ancient Britons survived until the eighteenth century. The British tribe living there in early times was known as *Cornovii*, meaning folk of the promontory. *Wall*, the second half of the name, is the Anglo-Saxon *walh*, a reference to foreigners, especially to Welshmen.

Corsica Corsica is a hilly, pastoral island in the western Mediterranean, a part of France, and Napoleon's birthplace. There is the chance, but there is no certainty, that Corsica is derived from *horsi*, a Phoenician word that describes a wooded place. Phoenicians visited the island and used its abundant supply of timber for the construction of their ships.

Cracow A university dating back to the fourteenth century has made Cracow one of Poland's main educational and cultural centers. The Polish spelling is *Krakow*, and it comes either from the name of a legendary founder of the city or from *kruk*, Polish for a raven or a crow.

Crete Ruins of the Minoan culture of the second millennium B.C. has made this island a place of great interest. Blue-gray mountains with deep gorges give Crete a natural beauty as well. The name may be attributed to the mythical ancestor of the people, but it most likely comes more directly from a tribal name. Cres was the name of the mythical ancestor from which the tribe had taken its name, and from the tribal name comes, probably, the island name.

Crimea Part of the Ukraine, it is located on the northern coast of the Black Sea, where wine, corn, and wheat are produced. *Krim* in Russian, *Krym* in Ukrainian, the origin of the name is the Turkish *Kirim*, a word that the Turks had adopted from the Greek. *Krimnos* is the Greek word for an escarpment, a reference to the terrain of the region with its mountains running parallel to the coast.

Croatia On January 15, 1992 the European Community recognized Croatia as an independent nation. A part of the former Yugoslavia, Croatia was settled by Slavs in the sixth century A.D. The name may be a form of *hrebet*, a Slavic word for a mountain chain.

Cumberland Cumberland, an agricultural region of northwestern England, had the first nuclear power plant for the generation of electricity. The *Cumbri* or *Cymry*, the Welsh name for the Welsh people, gave their name to the region. After the Anglo-Saxons had arrived in England they mingled with Celtic Britons, and eventually through intermarriage and through Anglo Saxon rule, most of the Celts became English-speaking. Pockets of British or Celtic-speaking people remained in parts of England, especially in the north and west. Cumberland represented one of these Celtic-speaking pockets. The Welsh or *Cymry* were, themselves, Britons and the Kingdom of Wales included at that time a large part of what is presently northwestern England.

Dalmatian Coast Vacationers come every year to the Adriatic coast of the former Yugoslavia for the scenery and the climate. Dalamatia comes from *dalmo*, a word that has come from the early Indo-European into the local Illyrian (Albanian-related) language. (see Bosnia) *Dalmo* means lamb, and the people of the region may have herded sheep in ancient times.

Danube River Passing through a number of climatic zones, the flow of the Danube is unpredictable, subject to serious flooding. Rising in the Black Forest of southwestern Germany, this waterway winds across central Europe, through the Balkans, emptying into the Black Sea at its delta on the Roumanian coast. *Danubius* in Latin and *Danoubios* in Greek, the name may have originally been the ancient Sarmatian name *danu-avi*, meaning river of sheep. The Sarmatians were an Indo-European-speaking people living in the Ukraine and in the Danube Valley during Roman times. *Danu* is also the Persian name for a river. *Avi*, a word for sheep, is related to the Latin, *ovis*, also meaning sheep. The name passed into Old High German as *Tuonowa*, into modern German as *Donau*, and into Hungarian as *Duna*.

Dardanelles This strait forms a division between the Aegean Sea and the Sea of Marmara. (see Aegean Sea and Sea of Marmara) The modern Greek name is *Dardanellia*, and in ancient Greek and in Latin, *Dardania*, from the name of a town in Asia Minor. Originally it comes from Dardanos, the first king of Troy. The king's name, in turn, is a tribal name. His tribe, the Dardanians, were the ancestors of the Trojans and were probably akin to the Illyrians, progenitors of the modern Albanians. There may be a connection, however, to *dardhe*, an Albanian word for a pear or a pear-shaped flask.

Denmark The Danish peninsula and five hundred islands make up this nation of five million people. Dane, the name of the people may be the word, *Tanne*, Germanic for a fir tree, a reference to the forest, since the early Danes were forest-dwellers. Some linguists believe that the original word was *tenar*, Germanic for sandbank, also descriptive of the people's habitat. There is a third theory, according to which the Danes are thought to be the Biblical tribe of Dan, but there is no historical basis for this assertion. *Mark* is a word for a field, but it can also mean a frontier region of a state and is sometimes called a march. The Germanic *marka* is a descendant of *marg*, an Indo-European root denoting an area away from a main population center, hence margin in English. During the early Middle Ages Denmark was a frontier in relation to Western Europe.

Derby Derby is in the English Midlands, a dairy region where Rolls-Royces are also manufactured. The original Scandinavian form is *Diurby*, a village where deer live, with *diur* meaning a deer and *by*, a village. When Danes were settling England they probably found the spot rich in deer.

Devon Devon is a scenic and rural section of southwestern England. It has a Celtic name which may descend from the Old Welsh *Dyvnaint*, a dark valley or a dark stream. On the other hand, it may be related to the tribal name *Dumnononii*, a Celtic people living there in ancient times. The Latin name for the region is *Dumnonia*, and this became Devon in Welsh.

Dieppe This city in northern France is on the English Channel, in Normandy. Sources of the eleventh century have it spelled *Dieppa*, from the Germanic *deop* (deep). Large numbers of Franks, a Germanic nation, settled northern France during the fourth and fifth centuries A.D. Dieppe (deep) refers to the mouth of the Arques, a local river.

Dijon Dijon is an industrial city in Burgundy with a large university and a wine-producing region extending south of the city. It was called *Divio* in ancient times, for an individual by the name of Divius. Records of the sixth century A.D. list it as *Locus Divionensis*, "the place of Divius," and in the ninth century the sources mention it as *Castrum Divionense*, "the camp of Divius." Dijon eventually evolved from *Divionense*.

Dover Tunnels built under the cliffs of Dover housed a command post during the Second World War. White chalky cliffs overlook the Strait of Dover, the narrowest body of water between Britain and the European continent. An early reference to Dover, from the fourth century A.D., mentions a place called *Portus Dubris* (Port of Dover). A river called Douver flows through this part of England, a Celtic name that is related to the Welsh *dwfr*, a word for stream.

Dnieper River The source of the Dnieper is in tnorthern Russia from which it flows south through the Ukraine and empties into the Black Sea. The Persians called it *Danu-apara*, with *Danu* meaning river and *apara*, posterior, hence posterior river. In Greeek it became *Danapris*.

Dniester River Flowing through the Ukraine and Moldavia, the name of this river also comes from the Persian word for river. The second part of the name is a derivative of *nazdyo*, Persian for nearby, giving us *Danu nazdyo*, "the river nearby." The Greeks made it *Danastris* and from this form comes Dniester.

Dresden Built, for the most part, during the late 1600's and early 1700's, it is a city of Baroque architecture. The names of Wagner and Schumann are both associated with Dresden. Its name is a form of the Slavic word for forest. Slavs lived in the area until German settlers from further west expelled them during the eleventh and twelfth centuries.

Dublin This city has been preserved as it was at the beginning of the twentieth century, when James Joyce wrote his Ulysses and gave it a place in literary history. *Dubhlinne* means a black pool in Gaelic and it was applied to a part of the Liffey River upon which the city was built.Originally the name for Dublin was *Ath-cliath*, Gaelic for "hurdle ford," probably a description of a wooden structure spanning the shallow part of the river.

Dubrovnik Tourists from all over Europe and from the United States come to this city on the Adriatic coast of the former Yugoslavia. It is an old city that has been preserved very well, the surrounding countryside is scenic, and the water is crystal clear. *Dombrava*, the Slavic word from which the name of this town comes, means "forest of oaks." The Italians called it Ragusa, from Lausa, the name of a small island near the shore.

Dundee This Scottish city is the original home of marmalade and it is still a center for the manufacture of fruit preserves. There are a number of forms of the name such as *Dunde*, *Dundo*, *Dundde*, and *Dunddho*. *Dun* is Gaelic for hill, while the second part of the name may be a form of *deagh*, a word for excellent. A more likely explanation, however, is that *dee* comes from the Gaelic *de*, the genitive case of *dia*, a possible reference to an ancient Celtic god.

Dunkerque From May 29 until June 2, 1940 Dunkerque, also spelled Dunkirk, was surrounded by Nazis, but 350,000 Allied troops were able to get over to England on warships as well as on fishing and pleasure boats. Dunkerque is in northern France, on the North Sea, close to the border with Belgium. The name simply means "church on a hill," from two words in Old Dutch. *Dunen* is a small hill and *kerke* is a church.

Dusseldorf Located on the Rhine River, in the German province of

Westphalia, it is part of one of Germany's major industrial regions, an area rich in deposits of coal. The people of Dusseldorf have an income twenty-five percent higher than the national average. *Dorf* is German for village and *dussel* is an old Germanic word originating in *dur* or *dor*, an Indo-European root that denotes running water. *Dussel* comes directly from the name of a local river.

Ebro River The Ebro rises in the mountains of northern Spain and empties into the Mediterranean south of Barcelona. The name may be a form of the word *Iberian*, the name of the indigenous people of Spain, or it may be the Celtic *iber*, a word for river. Celts migrated into Spain from the north and mingled with the Iberians, but the Iberians, having been the earlier group, most likely gave their name to the river.

Edinburgh Scotland's capital and one of its main industrial centers, it takes ts name from King Edwin of Northumbria (613-33) the Anglo-Saxon kingdom just south of Scotland, known today as Northumberland. *Burgh* is a modern English word, a descendant of the old Anglo-Saxon *burh*, meaning castle or hill.

Elbe River The Elbe crosses northeastern Germany, emptying into the North Sea. Its name is a form of the ancient Gothic *elf*, a word for river. This is an example of a generic word, in this case river, being used as a specific name.

England This nation took the name of the Germanic people, the Angles, who crossed the sea from southern Denmark and settled Britain along with the closely-related Saxons during the fifth and sixth centuries. Angle, itself, comes from Angeln, an area between the North Sea and the Baltic. There is a possibility that the name Angeln is a form of a local Germanic word for a fish- hook, since the people of the area lived by fishing.

Epirus Over four thousand years ago this mountainous region of northwestern Greece was fertile and it supported a population of shepherds and hunters, but over-use and erosion has made the land poor. The name simply means mainland.

Essex Approximately twenty percent of this county is occupied by Greater London. Essex means land of the East Saxons, the eastern part of Saxon territory, settled by this Germanic nation during the fifth and sixth centuries.

Estonia In the summer of 1992 Estonia was the first of the Baltic states to get a new constitution and its own currency. In the native language the country is called *Eesti* and the people, *Eestlane*. The origin of the name may be a word in the ancient Baltic language, *aveist*, a reference to a people living near to the coast. Another, but a less likely possibility, is a reference to a people living in the East.

Europe It is the second smallest of the seven continents in area, but in population it is the second largest, with 676,000,000 people. There are two theories on the origin of the name: (1) it may come from the Greek *Europa*, the name given to the lover of Zeus in the mythology, with *euros* meaning large and *op*, eye; (2) it may be a form of the Phoenician *ereb*, meaning the West. Europe was, in fact, west of the Phoenicians whose home was in Lebanon.

Exeter Having been rebuilt after the Nazi bombing of 1942, this English city is a mixture of the very old with the very new. The ancient name of the city was *Isca Dumnoniorum*, "Isca of the *Dumnones*," a local Celtic tribe. Sources of the ninth century call the town *Escanceaster* and *Exceastre*. A twelfth-century manuscript has *Civitas Aquarum*, "city of the waters." *Esk, usk*, and *ax* are Celtic words from which comes the "ex" in Exeter, and it is a reference to water or to a river. The Celtic word whiskey, also denoting water, is related to these same root words.

Faero Islands This group of islands in the North Atlantic, about midway between Norway and Iceland, is a Danish dependency, and has been visited and settled by Scandinavians for centuries. Eighteen of the islands in this group are inhabited, and most of the natives are fisherman. *Farr*, the Norse word for sheep, which are plentiful on these islands, is the root of the name.

Ferrara This is a city of northeastern Italy, on the Po River. In Roman times it was called *Forum Alieni*, marketplace of the foreigner, for it was probably a trading station at which Greeks had been present for centuries. It is possible that *Forum Alieni* had eventually become Ferrara.

Finland Between four and five million people live in this forested country with 187,888 lakes. Finland is the Swedish name for the country and it comes from the Germanic word, *finna* or *fenna*, meaning fish-scale. The Finnish people, themselves, call it *Suomi*, from *some*, a Finnish word for fish-scale. At first this name belonged to a clan which in ancient times dressed in clothing made from fish-skin. One alternative explanation, however, is that *Suomi* is a combination of *suo* (marsh) and *maa* (land or country).

Florence Florence is in the Apennine Mountains of Tuscany. Its beauty and its history attract large numbers of tourists each season. *Firenze* in Italian, the Latin name is *Colonia Florentia*, "colony of flowers."

France The Latin *Francia* (France) is a derivative of *Francus* (Frank), the name of a Germanic nation originating in what is today western Germany. Settling in northern and eastern parts of the Roman province of Gaul, they eventually ruled it. Frank may be a form of *franka*, meaning brave, or it may be a derivative of a Germannic word for free, since this people came from a part of Germany that had been free of Roman control. The name *Francia* was applied at first to a small district of northern France, the region around Paris. Later on the rest of the country took the name as the royal family gained sovereignty, little by little, over what is now France. (see Frankfurt) Before the present name came into usage, France was known as Gaul. Gaul (*Gallia* in Latin), the name used since ancient times, was also the name of a Celtic people that lived there for many centuries. Gaul, itself, may be a form of *gal* or *gala*, a Celtic word for brave or strong, or it may be a Celtic word for white, since these people tended to have a fair complexion. Gaul or *Gallia* is the name used in the early written sources.

Frankfurt Today Germany's financial capital, and a city of skyscrapers, it was bombed heavily during World War II. Frankfurt simply means "ford of the Franks," a shallow spot or ford on the Main River where a group of these people had established a settlement or village circa 100 A.D. (see France)

Galicia This part of Eastern Europe, on the northern slope of the Carpathian Mountains, is divided between Poland and the Ukraine. *Galicja* in Polish, *Galitsia* in Russian, and *Galicina* in Ukrainian, it may have developed from the Polish *hala*, meaning mountain pasturage. There is a city in the region called Halicz, from this Polish word. Galicia would come directly from Halicz. The only other possibility would be that the Celtic Gauls who migrated across the area in ancient times left their name on the landscape. (see Gallicia in Spain)

Gallicia Spanish Gallicia is a mountainous region of the northwest, where there are plenty of sulphur springs, and where the language is very much like Portuguese. In the local dialect the name is *Galego* and it stems from *Gallaecia*, the Latin form. The Latin name comes from *Gallus* (Gaul), since Celtic Gauls moved into this part of Spain in ancient times. (see Galicia in Eastern Europe)

Galway Bay Galway Bay is on the west coast of Ireland, on the Atlantic Ocean, waters rich in Mackerel. According to one theory, the name comes from *Gaillimh*, Gaelic for a rocky river. Alternatively, *gal* may be a form of the Gaelic *ghoul* (fork), a reference to a spot between the prongs of two rivers, and *way* is probably the Gaelic form of the Scandinavian *vig* (bay).

Garonne River The Garonne of southwestern France rises in the Pyrenees Mountains and empties into the Gironde Estuary, which leads into the Bay of Biscay. The name of the river is of Celtic origin and it means rough stream or rough river. Etymologically related is the modern Welsh *garw* and the modern Gaelic *garbh*, words for rough or torrent.

Geneva The Red Cross and the League of Nations both had their start here. Today Geneva hosts the European headquarters of the United Nations. Located on Lake Geneva, in the French-speaking section of Switzerland, the city is a major tourist attraction. Geneva is a variant of the Celtic *Genava* and, according to some linguists, the first half of the name, *gan*, is an Indo- European root word for the mouth of a river. Others, however, maintain that the origin of the name is the Ligurian *gen*, denoting a curvature of an angle and related to the French word for knee (*genou*). *Eva*, the second half of the name, indicates water, hence the bend or curvature in the shore of a lake, a fitting geographical description.

Genoa For centuries Genoa was one of Italy's wealthy and powerful maritime republics, and it is famous as the birthplace of Christopher Columbus. Genova in Italian and *Genua* in Latin, the name comes from *gen*, the Indo-European root meaning angle or curve, a reference to the shape of the coastline. (see Geneva)

Georgia This republic of the former Soviet Union is in the southern Caucasus, near to the Turkish border. The economy is based upon cotton, sheep, and minerals. Georgians speak a non-Indo-European language, and have lived in their homeland since very early times. The Latin name for the country is *Georgi* and the Greek is *Georgoi*, from *Gurz*, the name of the people in their own language. The meaning of this word is unknown, but the Georgians also refer to themselves as *Kartveli* or *Kartuli* and to their country as *Sakartvelo*. Colchis, another name for Georgia, is found in the ancient Roman writings. Some people believe that the country took its name from St. George, the nation's patron saint.

Germany There are three theories with respect to the name's origin: (1) it may stem from the Celtic *gair*, a word denoting a neighboring people, since *gair* is Irish for neighbor and *maon* means a people; (2) it is possible that the name is Germanic and comes from g*er* or *gari* (lance) and *man* (man), hence man with a lance; (3) it could be *ger-man*, Germanic for chief or head of men. Each of these theories has merit. The first one should be considered because the Celts and Germans were living in proximity in ancient times and the Celts may have simply called the Germans neighbors, hence *gair*. The second alternative is sound because it is descriptive of Germanic warfare, thus making it a likely name for the people to give themselves. Number three refers both to their method of warfare and to their clan or tribal government, with *ger-man* signifying a man carrying a lance as well as a chief of a clan or tribe. The name passed into Latin as Germania and into English as Germany. The French call the country *Allemagne*, from the name of a Germanic people living in southwestern Germany from Roman times, a people called *Allemans*, meaning "all the men. *Deutschland*, the German name for the nation, is a form of Teuton, hence land of the Teutons. Teuton, in turn, is a general name for the Germanic people of Northern Europe and has developed from the old Germanic *theud*, a word for people.

Gibraltar Thirty thousand people live in this British outpost at the southern tip of Spain, an area of 2.28 square miles. The monetary unit is the English pound sterling, and English is spoken along with Spanish. Even today barbary apes still survive there. The name comes from the Arabic *jabal Tariq*, "mountain of Tariq." Tariq was the North African Berber leader who crossed over into Spain in the year 711 to initiate the Moslem conquest. In ancient times Gibraltar was known as *Herculis Collumnae*, "pillars of Hercules" and as *Ostium Oceani*, "Entrance of the ocean."

Glasgow During the nineteenth century Glasgow was the second largest and wealthiest city in the British Empire, second only to London. It is in the west of Scotland, in the country's main industrial region. Documents of the twelfth century have the name on record as *Glascu* and as *Cleschu*, forms of the Gaelic *glas* and *cau*, meaning green hollows.

Gorky This Russian city is west of the Ural Mountains, and was named in honor of Maksim Gorky (1868-1936). He was born there as Aleksei Maksimovitch Pechkov, but later on he adopted Gorky as his pen name. The city of his birth, originally called Nijni-Novgorod, was renamed Gorky in 1932, while the writer was still living. (see Novgorod)

Gotland At one time a Baltic commercial center, today Gotland is an island of cobblestone streets and wildlife sanctuaries. It is a Swedish possession in the Baltic Sea. Gotland or land of the Goths was visited and probably inhabited by these people in ancient times.

Granada The city is built on three hills under the high Sierra Nevada Mountains of southern Spain. Moslem influence is still evident in the city's architecture. Granada comes from *granatum*, a Latin word for pomegranate. Either this fruit was cultivated there in Roman days, or the name is descriptive of the city's division into four sections by the hills, reminding one of the inside of a pomegranate.

Graz An Austrian industrial town, its name is of Slavic origin. It is a Germanicization of the Slavic *grad*, a word for town.

Greece Greece is made up of the mainland or peninsula and the island of the Aegean Sea, Rhodes, and Crete. It is a mountainous country where the people herd sheep and goats, and grow olives and grapes. Tourism, also, is a major industry. According to one theory, *Graecia*, the Latin word, is a form of the Greek *Graicos*, a name originally applied to a tribe in Epirus and eventually used as a name for the entire Greek people. A second possibility is the Indo-European *gra*, meaning venerable. There is a third explanation according to which the Romans gave the country its name, taking it from the Latin *grex*, a flock or a herd of animals. From *grex* we get *Graecia*, and from this comes the English Greece. Greece was always a pastoral nation, and the presence of herds could have impressed the Romans enough for them to give the country a name descriptive of this activity. The Greek name for the country, *Hellas*, comes from Hellen, a mythical hero. Hellen, according to the story, was the ancestor of all Greeks.

Grenoble This French industrial city is also known for its scenery and its several museums. The Romans called it *Gratianopolis*, for the emperor Gratian established a bishopric there in the fourth century. *Polis* is the Greek word for city, a suffix used widely in the ancient word for the names of cities. Grenoble has developed from *Gratianopolis*.

Grodno Grodno is in Belarus, not far from the Polish border. Grodno is the White Russian form of the name, *Grodna* the Polish, and *Gardinas* the Lithuanian. It is simply a form of the Slavic *grad*, a word for town.

Guadalquivir River This river flows across southwestern Spain and empties into the Gulf of Cadiz. Seville and Cordoba are located on the Guadalquivir. The Moors gave the Arabic prefix *wadi* (a dry river bed) to some of the Spanish river names. Guadalquivir is the Arabic *wad-al- kebir*, "the great river."

Guernsey Island This is one of the islands in the English Channel. The name may be a form of *gransey*, Norwegian for green island, but there is also the chance that it is from the Breton *gwern*, alder tree, hence Alder Island.

Gulf of Bothnia This channel of water lies between Sweden and Finland. In Swedish it is *Bottniska Vitten*, from *botten* or bottom. There is a district in Sweden called Botten, and from this region the gulf takes its name.

Hamburg Hamburg is a city built on water, on the Elbe River and on the smaller Alster River. It is a city of many canals. A *burg* in German is a fortress, and *ham* or *hamma* is Germanic for gulf or bay. In this case, however, *ham* may be from the Germanic *heim* (home), hence home fortress.

Hannover Germany's main annual industrial fair is held here. *Hann* means high and *ufer* is a river bank, hence high river bank.

Hastings William the Conqueror built a castle here after the battle that took place nearby. The town is mentioned in a chronicle under the year 1011 and in a charter of 1191 as *Haestingas*. There was a Viking chief by the name of Hasten or Hasteng who arrived at the mouth of the Thames River in the year 893.

Heidelberg One of the earliest human fossils, a jawbone of Homo Heidelbergensis or Hedidelberg Man, is at a museum in this

German city, the first part of the name, *heide*, is a word for a health or a moor, and *berg* is
a mountain.

Helsinki The Finnish capital is built on peninsulas extending into the Baltic. There are many bays and islands offshore. Helsinki is the Finnish form of the old Norwegian name *Helsingfors*. *Helsingr* is probably the name of a local tribe and *fors* is a waterfall.

Hercegovina Part of the former Yugoslavia, it is a Moslem region included with Bosnia. Herceg is the title which Duke Stephen Vukcic took in 1448, when his own domain was separated from Bosnia. Duke Stephen's title is from the German *hercog*, probably a result of the growing influence of Austria in central European affairs. (see Bosnia)

Hesse Hesse is the region of western Germany in which the cities of Frankfurt and Wiesbaden are included. It was from Hesse that the troops commanded by Baron von Steuben came to participate in the American Revolution. *Hessen*, the German name for this area, comes from *Chatti* or *Hatti*, a Germanic people living there in ancient times. *Hatti* is a form of the Germanic *huota* (hat), a reference to the way in which the members of the tribe wore their hair.

Holland There are more works of art per square mile here than in any other nation in the world. Strictly speaking, Holland is a section of the Netherlands, North Holland and South Holland, on the shore of the North Sea. The name, however, has been applied popularly to the entire Netherlands. The terrain is low-lying with many rivers, so the name may come from the Germanic *hol*, a word for shallow or hollow land. Holland could also be a derivative of *Holtland*, a country of forests, *holt* being a reference to woods in the old Germanic languages of the region.

Hull The name used to be a Kingston-on-Hull, Hull being the name of a small river. Its origin is probably in the old English *hol*, meaning hollow or "lying in a hollow."

Hungary The Huns, an Asiaic people who settled there in the fifth century, gave the country its name. Hun, itself, is a form of the Mongolian word for a man or a human being. Hungarians call their country *Magyarorszag*, land of the Magyars. Magyar, or *Megyer* in old Hungarian, may come from *magy*, the name of a particular clan. The suffix *er* may denote a man or a human being. There is a connection with the Finnish *mies*, a word for a man or a male. Finnish is a Ural- Altaic language related to Hungarian and, more specifically, it is Uralic, also known as Finno- Ugrian, the same language family in which Hungarian is included. The Voguls, a Finno-Ugrian people living north of the Ural Mountains, a people closely related to the Hungarians, call themselves *Mansi*, a name which also means a man or a human being. The huns, themselves, were also people closely akin to the Finns and Magyars.

Innsbruck This Austrian town hosted the Winter Olympics in 1964 and again in 1976. Inn is the name of a river, and it is a Germanic form of *enos*, a Celtic word for water. Celtic people had lived there before they moved farther west with the arrival of the Germans. *Brucke* is German for bridge, hence Inn Bridge.

Inverness Inverness is the largest county in Scotland and it includes the famous Loch Ness. *Inver* is a Gaelic term for the junction of two rivers, or a place at which a river empties into the ocean. *Ness* is Scandinavian, from the Norwegian *naes* (nose) meaning a headland. Inverness is, therefore, a topographical description of a spot at which two rivers converge, or at which a river runs into the sea.

Ionian Sea Tourists visit the islands of the Ionian Sea, such as Corfu which attracts European aristocrats. The name may come from *Ion*, a legendary Greek hero, the mythical progenitor of Ionian Greeks, or it may stem from the pre-Indo-European *ya wane*, denoting western.

Ireland The Irish Republic has been independent since 1921, and it has between three and four million people. Ancient Greeks called it *Albion* and *Terne*, and other classical writers have recorded the name as *Ivernia*, *Ibernia*, *Ire*, and *Eire*. It is a tribal name, but its meaning cannot be deciphered because it is a very early form of Gaelic. Historical sources also use Scot as a reference to the Irish. The suffix land was added later by the Vikings when they gained familiarity with the country.

Isle of Man This island is in the Irish Sea, between England and Ireland. There are cliffs on the coast, and valleys in the interior that support the island's pastoral economy. Transportation is by antique trains that run across the island. The native language of Man is Celtic, closely related to Welsh, and *Mannin* is the island's name in the local dialect. It means center, a description of its location in the middle of the Irish Sea.

Isle of Wight There is more sunshine here, on this English Channel island, than in any other part of Britain. Tourism, yacht-building, fishing, and farming support the island's economy. Roman authors called it *Vectis*, probably a Latinization of the Celtic *gueid* or *gueith*, a word denoting a division and related to the Welsh *gwth*, a word for a channel. This follows because the Isle of Wight is separated from the English mainland by a narrow body of water.

Istanbul Turkey's largest city overlooks the Sea of Marmara, and occupies both the European and Asiatic sides of the Bosporus, with the major portion on the European side. The city's history extends back to the ancient Greeks who founded it as a commercial colony.

Originally called Byzantium, the Roman Emperor, Constantine renamed it *Constantinopolis*, "city of Constantine," in the early fourth century, when he made it an imperial capital. Both names, Byzantium and Constantinople, were used up until 1453, when the Turks captured the city. Istanbul, the Turkish name, may be a derivative of the Greek *eis-tin polis* which means "to the city." There is also the possibility that the name is a form of *Islam-bul* "city of Islam." The Greek *polis* could have become *bul* in the Turkish pronunciation. The Iranians call it *Eslambol*, similar to Istanbul.

Istria Istria is a peninsula projecting south into the Adriatic Sea from the former Yugoslavia. It is Latin and it comes from *Ister* or *Hister*, the ancient name for the lower Danube River. The name may be related to that of a Germanic people, the *Istaevones*, recorded by the Roman historian, Tacitus, as living in the Danube valley.

Italy Sharp regional differences mark Italy's economy, way of life, language, and political history. A highly industrialized north and a more agricultural south is one of the more obvious regional variations. More than fifty-seven million people live in italy. In Latin the name of the country is *Italia*, a form of the early Latin *Vitelia*. In Oscan, one of the ancient Italic languages, a language closely akin to Latin, it was *Viteliu*. The name may have been applied at first to one of the early Italian tribes, the *Vitali*, a name derived from *vitulus*, a Latin word for calf. The tribal name Vitali may be descriptive of their pastoral mode of life.

Jersey Island One of the Channel Islands, it is famous for the Jersey dairy cattle. The Romans called it Caesarea in honor of Caesar, and records dating from the twelfth through the fourteenth century have it as *Gesui, Geresye, Gerese, Gersey*, and *Jersey*. It is possible that they are forms of *Caesarea*, but it is also a possibility that they are from the Old Norse *gers*, meaning an island covered with grass.

Jura Mountains This mountain chain runs through eastern France to the northeast of Lyons. Jura is a form of *iuris*, a word for a wooded or forested mountain in the Celtic language of ancient Gaul.

Kaliningrad Before 1946 Kaliningrad was Konigsberg, a German city. When it became a Russian city it was renamed for Mikhail Ivanovitch Kalinin (1875-1946), a Russian statesman. *Grad* is Russian for town or city. Kaliningrad is a port city on the Baltic Sea, where factories turn out large freighters.

Kent This English county on the Strait of Dover, in the far southeast of the country, was called *Cantium* in the time of Julius Caesar, probably a form of the Celtic *canto* (*cant* in Welsh) which means a rim, a border, or a coastal district. It is also possible that *cantium* comes from the tribal name of the local Celtic people, the *Cantii*, which may mean hosts. (see Canterbury) Modern Kent is known for its horticulture and its fruit production.

Kiev The Ukrainian capital has a long history, extending back to the fifth century A.D. It has always been the political, cultural, and educational hub of the nation. Kiev comes from Ki or Kii, the name of a chief of one of the local Slavic tribes who fortified the settlement in the Middle Ages.

Lake Balaton Central Europe's largest lake, it is a vacation spot for German, Austrian, and Hungarian tourists. Balaton is in the western part of Hungary and it is approximately fifty miles in length. The name may derive from *blato*, a Slavic word for marsh.

Lake Como Because of the lake's warm water, there are a number of resorts on its shore. Near the north end of it is the place where the Italians captured Benito Mussolini while he was trying to escape to Switzerland and executed him in April, 1945. When the Romans were bringing the north of Italy into their republic they called the lake *Comum*, a form of the original Celtic *cumba*, a word for valley. Celtic people were settled in this part of Italy until the Romans displaced them. *Larius Lacus* was another name that the Romans applied to Lake Como.

Lancaster The name of this English city means "camp on the River Lune," caster being the Anglo-Saxon *ceaster* (camp), a word borrowed from the Latin castra (camp).

Languedoc Languedoc is a region of southern France located in part along the Gulf of Lyons which leads into the Mediterranean. The coastal section which is at sea level produces wine, while the mountainous interior has a pastoral economy. During the Middle Ages Languedoc had a very distinct local culture, quite different from that of northern France. The name has developed from *lenga d'oc* (language or tongue of *oc*). *Oc*, the word for yes, was used in southern France during the Middle Ages instead of *oil*, the word in use farther north. For centuries these words were one of the features that made northern and southern French distinct. *Oc* (Old French for yes) is a descendant of the Latin *hoc* (the demonstrative pronoun meaning this), and *oil* is from the Latin *ille* (the demonstrative pronoun meaning *that*). From *oil* comes the modern French *oui*.

Latvia One of the Baltic States of the former Soviet Union, Latvia became an independent nation on August 21, 1991. The language is Lettish, a Baltic tongue akin to Old Prussian and Lithuanian. In the Latvian and Lithuanian languages the spelling is *Latvija*. The name may be an extension of that of a local river, the *Late*, a small river near the Lithuanian border. *Late* comes from an Indo-European root and may mean sediment or mud.

Lausanne Lausanne is on Lake Geneva, in the French-speaking region of Switzerland. It is a scenic area, attracting many visitors each year. Originally it was *Lausodunum*, from two Celtic words, *leusa* (flat rock) and *dunum* (fort). *Onna*, a Celtic word for river, was added to *leusa* to form *Leusonna* (rocky river), evolving into *Lausonna* and eventually into Lausanne.

Le Mans Just south of this French city the twenty-four-hour auto race of Le Mans takes place. The ancient Gallic or Celtic word from which it may come is *lemo*, a word for elm tree. Some linguists believe, however, that it is the Gallic *lem* or *lim*, a word for sediment or mud.

Leinster Leinster is one of the four historic provinces of Ieland. Located in the east, on the Irish Sea, it includes the city of Dublin. In Gaelic it is *Laighean*, a form of *laigh*, the word for a lance. The suffix *ster* is a variation of the Scandinavian *stadr*, a palace or province. *Laigh*, the Gaelic portion of the name, goes back to ancient times, when a battle took place there. The Scandinavian element (*ster*) was introduced later on, during the period of Viking colonization.

Leipzig This city is around eighty miles southwest of Berlin. The name is from the Slavic *lipa*, linden tree. Until the eleventh or twelfth century this part of Germany had a Slavic population. German settlers from further west displaced the Slavs and Germanicized the local Slavic place names. The Slavic *Lipsk*, derived from *lipa*, became the German Leipzig.

Lille Traditionally Lille has been a center of textile manufacture, being part of a large industrial region with its abundant deposits of coal. The name is descended from the Latin *insula* (island) and the Germanic form of the name is *Rijssel*. It was also known as

Castellania Ylensi because it was built originally at the foot of a castle.

Limoges Since the eighteenth century Limoges, in western France, has been famous for its porcelain. There was a Gallic tribe settled there in ancient times from which the city took its name. The tribal name was *Lemovices*, from *lemo*, Celtic for elm tree. The elm tree may have been a sacred symbol to these pre-Christian Celtic people. (see Le Mans)

Lincoln Visitors of this English city can see a cathedral that was built in the twelfth century as well as a castle of the same period. Called *Lindum* in ancient times, it was recorded as *Lindcylene* in Old English, and as *Lindcolne* and *Lincolne* in the sources of the eleventh century. *Lindum Colonia*, the Roman name, comes from the Celtic *lind* (water) and is related to the Welsh *llynn* (lake or pool), hence "colony by the lake" or "by the pool."

Lisbon During World War II Lisbon was the scene of espionage for both sides, and after the war some exiled royalty settled there or close by. Portugal's capital and largest city was built where the Tagus River empties into the Atlantic Ocean. *Lisboa* in Portuguese records of the thirteenth century refer to it as *Liixbona*, and those of the twelfth century call it *Olixbona* and *Ulyxbona*, from the Latin *Ulisipona*, *Olisipo*, and *Ulisippo*. According to legend, the Greek king of Ithaca at the time of the Trojan War, Ulysses, founded the city of Lisbon, but there is also the theory that the name is a Phoenician word, *alisubbo*, meaning peaceful bay.

Lithuania On March 11, 1990 the newly elected legislature declared Lithuanian independence. In the Lithuanian language the name of the country is *Lietuva* and in Russian it is *Litva*. *Lietuva* comes from *Lietava*, the name of a local river, a name derived from *lieti*, a Lithuanian verb meaning to run or to flow.

Liverpool Liverpool is a port city on the Irish Sea in one of England's most industrialized regions. The first half of the name, *liver*, is a form of the Old English *lifrig* and the Middle English *livered* (coagulated or clotted). *Pool* simply means a pool, a pond, or a pool in a river hence "pool or pond in a muddy river."

Lodz This city in central Poland has played a major part in the country's economy as a center of the textile industry. The Polish *lodzi* or *lodzia* is a word for a small boat, but it is not known why such a name was chosen for the city.

Loire River The Loire rises in the mountainous region of central France and empties into the Atlantic Ocean to the south of the Breton Peninsula. In the regional dialect the name is *Lei*, *Leira*, *Leger*, and *Letge*, from the Basque *liga*, a word for sediment or mud. In modern times the Loire flows far to the north of Basque territory, but in ancient times this people occupied a much larger area than they do at present.

London There are two divisions of this city: the eastern part is the hub of banking and commerce; the western section is the center of government. There are the two main areas of London in which most of the historic buildings are located. The city's history goes back over two thousand years, and due to its location on the Thames River and its proximity to the European continent, it has always had an important place in English economic life. When England was a Roman province the city was called *Londinium*, from the Celtic *lan* and *din*, meaning lake and fortress respectively, hence lake fortress.

Lorraine This province of northeastern France is ethnically French, but it has been under the rule of Germany (The Holy Roman Empire) for much of its history. The German name is *Lothringen*, from the Latin *Lotharingia*, originally *Regnum*

Lotharii (kingdom of Lothar), the kingdom granted to Lothar II (835-69), a grandson of Charlemagne. Lothar is a form of *Hlodar*, a Germanic name, a fusion of *hlod* (glory) and *hari* (armed).

Lucca In ancient times this Tuscan city was spelled *Luca*, a reference to a sacred grove (*Lucus*). There was probably such a place in the vicinity in early times at which the Ligurians, an ancient Italian people, used to worship.

Luxembourg Luxembourg is a country of only 999 square miles and a population of approximately 360,000. The language spoken are French, German, and a local dialect called Luxembourgeois or Letzeburgisch. This small land is bounded by France, Germany, and Belgium. The name is a combination of two Germanic words *luttila* (little) and *burg* (fortress).

Lvov In the local Ukranianian language it is *Lviv*. Lvov is the Russian spelling and *Lwow* the Polish. Lvov was founded by Daniel, Prince of Volynia back in 1250 as a trading center. Daniel named the new city for his son, Leon, or *Liev* in Russian.

Lyon Lyon is the home of Bernachon, considered the best manufacturer of chocolate in the world. The city is on the Rhone River, in one of France's industrial regions. In Roman times it was called *Lugdunum*, a Celtic name. *Lug* was the name of a Celtic god and *dun* is a fort, hence "fort of *Lug*.

Macedonia Macedonia or Macedon, as it was called in ancient times, was the birthplace of Alexander the Great. The name may stem from the mythical Makedon who, according to legend, was a son of Zeus. Some scholars believe, however, that the origin of the name may be in Illyrian *maketia*, a word for cattle or domesticated animals, a reference to the country's pastoral economy.

Madrid Madrid is Spain's capital and largest city in both area and population. Celtic people from what is now France migrated to Spain in ancient times and mingled with the native Iberians, the dominant group. Some Celtic names were introduced onto the Spanish landscape. According to linguists, the name of this city is derived from two Celtic words *mago* or *mageto* (big) and *rito* or *ritu* (ford or bridge), thus big ford, a name of a local river.

Magdeburg This industrial city near the Elbe River is in one of the country's most fertile regions. Three theories on the origin of the name have been suggested: (1) the land on which the city stands was owned by a woman named Magda; (2) the Celtic people who had lived there in very early times named it for *Mogon*, one of their deities; (3) the name comes from a Germanic god.

Main River Rising in Bavaria, the Main joins the Rhine not far from Mainz. Its name is of Celtic origin and it means slow water (from *Moinas*) (see Mainz)

Mainz This city in Germany's Rhineland Palatinate has a history that goes back to ancient times. The city's name may have been taken directly from the river name, but there is an alternative explanation. The old name of the city was *Moguntiacum*, the Latin form of *Moguntiacu*, from the Celtic deity, *Mogon*. *Monguntiacum* was eventually shortened and Germanicized to Mainz. (see Main River)

Malta This Mediterranean island, located between Sicily and North Africa, is a former British possession. Approximately 350,000 people live on the island where both Maltese and English are spoken. Tourism is Malta's main industry. *Melita* in Latin, the name may descend from the pre- Indo-European root word, *mel*, an adjective denoting high or tall, a possible reference to the island's cliffs. Since, however, the Hebrew name for Malta is *meliti* and the

Syriac name is *militi*, it is possible that *Melita* has its origin in the Semitic *malat*, a word for a refuge or a port, related to the Hebrew infinitive *malot* (to take flight). Malta was known to the Phoenicians, a people whose language was very similar to Hebrew, and there is a chance that it was they who named the island. One other explanation points toward a Greek origin. The Greeks called it *Melitta*, a word for honey or bee (*melitta* in the Attic Greek, *melissa* in other Greek dialects), a reference to Malta's reputation as a producer of honey.

Manchester One of the largest municipal libraries in Europe is here. The Old English forms are *Mameceaster* and *Mamecestre*, from the Celtic *man* or *maen* (stone) and *chester* the English form of the Latin *castrum* (camp), hence stone camp.

Marne River Marne developed from *Matrona*, the designation used by the ancient Celts, the name of a female deity.

Marseilles This Mediterranean port, started as a Greek colony in ancient times, was called *Massalia* in the local language. Later on the Romans called the city *Massilia* and eventually it became Marseilles. The first part of the name, *mas*, means spring or fountain in the Ligurian language.

Mediterranean Sea Every year the Mediterranean lands attract roughly one hundred-million visitors. The name is a combination of the two Latin words *medius* (middle) and *terra* (land). The Romans thought of it as the center of their world, a sea surrounded by all of the lands that they knew. They called it *Mare internum* (interior sea) and *Mare nostrum* (our sea) as well as *Mediterraneum Mare* which became *Mediterraneo* in Italian and passed into English as Mediterranean. In modern Greek it is *Mesogeios* ("of the middle of the Earth"), in Arabic, *al- bahr al-mutawassit* (central sea) and *a-bahr ar-rum* (sea of Rome), and in modern Hebrew it is *yam hattihon* (interior sea).

Meuse River The Meuse is shared by France, Belgium, and the Netherlands. In Dutch, Flemish, and German it is *Maas*, from *Mosa*, the ancient Germanic name, a derivative of mos, a word for marsh or swamp.

Milan The northern city of Milan is Italy's main industrial center. In Roman times the name was *Mediolanum* or *Mediolanium*, from the Latin *medius* (middle) and *planus* (plain). There is the possibility, however, that the second half of the name comes from *lanu*, a Celtic word for plain, since Celtic people did live in the area before the Romans conquered it in the second century B.C.

Minsk Minsk is the capital and largest city of Belarus, with a population of over one million. The name is a form of *Menesk*, *Men* being the name of a river and *sk* denoting the presence of a town. Minsk has a long history, having been made the capital of Minsk Principality in the year 1101. It was one of the principalities of the Kievan period of Russian history, the era previous to the Mongol conquest.

Moldavia Divided between the Republic of Moldava and Roumania, it took the name of a Roumanian river which may be rooted in the Indo-European word *mel*, meaning dark or colored.

Monaco This tiny country, about one half the size or Central Park, has the smallest area and the largest population density of any nation in the world. The Principality of Monaco has 368 square acres of land and 25,000 people. There are three theories on the origin of the name: (1) according to popular etymology, it comes from the name of an ancient Greek temple to *Hercules Monoecus*, an edifice dating from c. 600 B.C., when the Greeks were establishing colonies in southern France (*Monoecus* means solitary and was the surname of Hercules); (2) some linguists link the name Monaco to the Ligurian *monegu* (rock or cliff); (3) it may be a form of the Basque *muno*, a word for mountain. There are no longer any Basques in the vicinity, but millennia ago this people occupied a much larger territory in southern France before they relocated to the southwest as a result of Celtic migrations into their country.

Montenegro Part of the former Yugoslavia, Montenegro is a mountainous land overlooking the Adriatic Sea. It means black mountain in Italian, which in Serbian is *Crna Gora*, a name that may be explained by the dark appearance of the forests that cover the region.

Moravia Moravia is the central part of the former Czechoslovakia, a Czech-speaking area between Bohemia to the west and Slovakia to the east. It takes its name from the *Morava*, a local river. *Morava*, in turn, stems from an Indo-European word for marshy river.

Moscow *Moskva* or *Moskova* in Russian, the city takes the name of a local river. Scholars offer five possible explanations for the origin of the name: (1) it may be a form of *mazgoti*, Lithuanian for to wash or to bathe; (2) it could simply be the Slavic *moskva* (swampy); (3) another Slavic candidate is *most-kva* ("water of the bridge"); (4) there are the Finnish *moska* (calf) and *va* (river or water) which denote a ford for bringing livestock across a river; (5) there is also the chance that the name is a combination of the Finnish *mos* (to render dark) and *ka* (water), hence dark water.

Munich Munich is Bavaria's main urban center. In modern German it is *Munchen*, from either *Munih* or *Monch*, both words meaning monk in Old High German. Monks founded the city in the twelfth century, a time during which monasteries in parts of Europe were involved in clearing forests and draining swamps. Munich's pioneers are likely to have been engaged in this kind of endeavor.

Nantes Nantes is a town on the Loire River of northwestern France, not far from the Atlantic Ocean. Most likely the name comes from *Namnetes* or *Nannetes*, one of the Celtic tribes of ancient Gaul, but it may stem from *nanto*, a Celtic word for valley or ravine.

Naples Mount Vesuvius, Pompeii, and Herculaneum are sites not far from Naples, the largest Italian city south of Rome. The Italian form is *Napoli*, from *Neapolis*, Greek for new city. Greek colonists established the city in the fifth century B.C., constructing it on a checkerboard pattern, a novel method of city-planning, hence new city.

Nice This French city has for decades attracted tourists from all over Europe as well as from the United States. During the first millennium B.C. Greeks were setting up colonies on the Mediterranean coast of France, and Nice was originally the Greek *Nikaia*, meaning "giver of victory," from *nike* (victory). The colonists decided upon the name because they had dedicated the city to a female deity that presided over victory.

Norfolk Some of Charles Dickens' story, *David Copperfield*, takes place here. Norfolk is a part of southeastern England and the name simply means north folk, a reference to the north Anglian tribe that settled there during the fifth and sixth centuries. (see Suffolk)

Novgorod This city of northern Russia is known for its wooden churches that date from the eleventh century. The name means new town (*novyi gorod*).

Nuremberg Throughout the 1930's Nuremberg was a center for the Nazi Party and it was heavily bombed during World War II. After the war it was the scene of the International War Crimes

Trials. The German is *Nurnberg*. *Berg* means mountain, but there are two theories about the origin of the first half of the name. *Nurn* may be a reference to *Nornes*, an ancient German deity, or it may be a contraction of *Neu-Rom*, new Rome, a likely explanation, since it would be commemorating the establishment of the Holy Roman Empire, which the Germans considered to have been the successor to Rome.

Oder River The Oder (Odra) flows from the Sudeten Mountains of Moravia, in the former Czechoslovakia, through part of Poland, where it forms a section of the Polish-German border and eventually empties into the Baltic Sea near the Polish city of Szczecin. Oder is the German form, *Odra* is the Slavic. The name may come directly from the Slavic *voda* (water), or it may be a descendant of the Indo-European *adu*, a word for stream.

Odessa This Russian port city is on the Black Sea. It is a relatively new city, founded in 1795 by Catherine the Great, Empress of Russia (1762-96). The Russians named it for *Odessos*, an ancient Greek colony.

Orkney Islands The Orkneys are north of Scotland, not far from the shore. Livestock and lobsters are the islands' main products. Orkney is a derivative of *Orcinnis*, "islands of the whales."

Orleans Orleans is on the Loire River, about sixty miles south of Paris, in one of the wine- producing regions. The Romans called it *Aurelianum* in honor of the Emperor Aurelian.

Oslo Oslo is an unusual city in that there are hiking trails, woods, and lakes within its limits, and that it has a subway system reaching these places of outdoor recreation. Oslo is also known as

Aslo. Os may be the Latin word for an estuary or the mouth of a
river, since the city is at such a spot. It is also possible that it is a
form of *Ase*, the name of an ancient Scandinavian deity. The
second theory sounds more likely, since Norway had never been
within the Roman Empire and had not been under the influence of
Mediterranean culture. The second half of the name (*lo*) is a form
of the old name for a local river. For a long time the Norwegians
had called the city Christiania (1624-1924), but in 1925 the
original name, Oslo, was restored.

Oxford Famous as a university town since the thirteenth century,
documents of the tenth century mention it as *Oksnaforda* and
Orsnaforda, a possible reference to shallow water through which
horses were able to cross. *Oxonaforda*, *Oxenafordscire*, and
Oxenefordia appear in the sources of the eleventh and twelfth
centuries. The original meaning may be in the Anglo-Saxon *oxena
ford*, a ford through which oxen cross. Alternatively, however,
ox could be a form of the Celtic *ax*, *ex*, or *usk*, a word for water,
thus arriving at water ford.

Padua In Roman times Padua was *Patavium*, a name that
probably came into Latin from the Celtic *padi*, pine or pine tree.
Padua is in northeastern Italy, a region that had a Celtic
population before the arrival of Italian settlers in late Roman
Republican times.

Palermo According to the accepted theory, Palermo (*Panormos* in
ancient Greek sources) means all harbor, and was adopted as a
name by the Romans when they annexed Sicily in 264 B.C., after
the first Punic War. This same toponym appears at many places in
the Greek world. The name indicates the presence of a good harbor,
one of the main criteria for the choice of a particular spot for
settlement. *Panormos* over time became Palermo.

Pamplona This town of northern Spain is in the Pyrenees Mountains, not far from the French border. Each year at a certain time the townspeople let bulls run through the streets, a local tradition. The Latin name for Pamplona is *Pampelona*, from *Pompeiopolis*, city of Pompey, with *polis* the Greek word for city. The Roman, Pompey, founded the town in 68 B.C. In the local Basque language the name is *Iruna*.

Paris Paris' history reaches back two thousand years. It was known as *Lutetia*, the Latin form of the Celtic *lut*, a word for marsh. As an island in the Seine River, it was easily flooded. *Lutetia Parisianorum* was the full name, and *Parisii* was the name of a local Celtic tribe, hence "marsh of the Parisians." In everyday speech it was shortened to *Pariis* and later onto Paris.

Peloponnesus This is the southern part of Greece, a mountainous region with a pastoral economy. Even though the name means "island of Pelops," it is actually a peninsula attached to the rest of the country. *Nesos* is island in Greek and Pelops is a character from Greek mythology, the son of the legendary king of Asia Minor, Tentalus. During the Middle Ages the Peloponnesus was also called *Morea*, meaning mulberry, a reference to its shape.

Perugia Perugia is a town in the Apennine Mountains of central Italy. The Latin form is *Perusia* or *Aperusia*, possibly a descendant of *phaersu*, an Etruscan name for the spirit that carried souls of the dead to the underworld, according to mythology.

Pisa Pisa's famous Leaning Tower, the bell tower of Pisa Cathedral, was started in 1174 by an unknown architect. The origin of the name is Etruscan and it may refer to an estuary.

Plymouth This English town is well-known as the port from which the Pilgrims sailed when they left their country for America is 1620. The early sources record different forms of the name but they all indicate that the town took the name of the River Plym, a Welsh name which may mean lead. Some linguistic authorities, however, claim that in this instance it simply denotes a river.

Poitiers Notre Dame la Grande, one of the finest Romanesque buildings in France, is here. Poitiers is an old city in an agricultural region of western France. The Romans called the city *Pictavis* or *Pictavium*, from the Celtic *Pictavi* or *Pictones*, a local tribe that had taken its name from a word meaning picture or figure, because of their custom of wear tatoos.

Poland The Polish name is *Polska*, from *pole*, a word for field, open space, or plain, a reference to the country's topography.

Portugal The ancients called it *Lusitania*. A form of its present name first appears in the records of a Church Council held at Toledo, Spain in 633. The bishops called it *Portucalensis*, possibly a form of *Portus Cale* (warm port), *Cale* having been the name of the town. There is also the chance that the name is a form of *Portus Galos* (port of *Galos*), *Galos* having been the name of a local tribe.

Poznan This city is one of Poland's centers of higher education, publishing, and scientific research. The name comes from that of a nobleman who owned land in the area.

Prague Mozart, Dvorak, and Kafka had each lived in this European capital. It is spelled *Praha* in both Czech and Slovak and it is possibly a form of the Czech *prah*, a word for threshold, entrance, or shelf. Similar versions of this word have the same meaning in other Slavic languages.

Provence This is one of France's historic regions, located in the far southeast, on the Italian frontier. Painters van Gogh and Cezanne have made Provence famous. The Romans called it *Provincia* the Latin word for province. It became a Roman province at the end of the second century B.C. with the official name of *Provincia Narbonensis*. The Latin word *provincia* is a combination of pro (before, in front) and *vincere* (to conquer, to subdue).

Ravenna Some of the best Byzantine mosaics can be found in this Italian city along with the Basilica of San Vitale, one of the finest examples of Byzantine architecture. The name is of Etruscan origin, but its meaning is unknown.

Reims At the map room in the College Moderne General Eisenhower had won unconditional surrender from the Germans on May 7, 1945. Reims is a northern French city, and its name comes from *Remi*, a Gallic tribe that had lived there in ancient times. The tribal name *Remi* is derived from a Celtic word that denotes a people who dominate. Before the fourth century A.D. Reims was known as *Durocortorum*.

Rekavik Rekavik is the capital of Iceland and it is at the southwestern tip of the island. In Icelandic the spelling is *Reykjavik*. *Reykja* means to smoke and *vik* is a bay, hence smoking bay, a reference to the warm springs in the vicinity that release water vapor.

Rhine River The Rhine varies throughout its course more than any other European river. It flows from the mountainous Black Forest region in southwestern Germany until it empties into the North Sea. Mainz, Frankfurt, Wiesbaden, Bonn, and Cologne are some of the cities of the Rhine. In ancient times a Celtic tribe known as the *Rheni* dwelt on the banks of the river. This tribal name comes from a Celtic word *ren* (or *rin*), a reference to water or to the sea.

Rhone River From Lake Geneva the Rhone passes Lyon and travels on until it empties into the Mediterranean near Arles. Along its banks is the wine region known as *Cotes du Rhone*. Originally the name was *Rodanos*, a Greek form introduced by colonists who were present as early as the sixth century B.C. (see Marseilles) The native Celtic people probably called the river *rhuit-an*, rapid water. It is related to the Gaelic *ruith* or *ruth* (to run or to race). *Rhuit-an* could easily have been Rodanos to the Greeks, and from Rodanos comes the modern form.

Riga Riga is the capital and largest city of Latvia, one of the Baltic states. It is the main center of industry and has over 900,000 people. The name comes from either *ringa*, Lithuanian word for a curve or bend, or from the Lettish (Latvian) *ridzina*, a stream or brook. *Ringa* is a likely choice because the city is at a spot on which the coastline curves to the south of the Gulf of Riga.

Rome The city, according to ancient legend, was founded in 753 B.C., but settlement at the site may go back to an earlier date. As the capital of an empire and later on as the seat of the Papacy, Rome's past could almost be thought of as a cross-section of the history of Western Civilization. The cityis on the Tiber River, half way down the peninsula, thus dividing Italy into north and south. Three explanations exist for the origin of the name. First, there is an early designation of the Tiber River, *Ruma* or *Rumon*, a name that is most likely of Etruscan origin. Another candidate is the ancient Greek *rem*, a word for force or strength. A third theory, and the one most widely accepted, is that the city was named for Romulus, one of its legendary founders.

Rotterdam The port of Rotterdam handles a volume of freight that exceeds the amount handled by any other port in the world. *Rotte* is the name of a small river or stream in the vicinity and *dam* is Dutch for a dyke or dam.

Roumania This country's name comes from *Romanus*, Latin for Roman. Originally the people, called Dacians in ancient times, spoke a native Balkan language related to Thracian. The Dacians learned Latin from the conquering Romans, and over the centuries the spoken Latin evolved into Roumanian. Slavic people settled in the area and introduced some Slavic words into the language, but it remained a basically Romance tongue. Parts of Roumania were under Turkish rule while other sections were Austrian until the nineteenth century, when the Turkish provinces gained independence. The creation of an autonomous Roumanian state in 1859 was sanctioned at the Congress of Berlin in 1878, when Roumania was officially adopted as a name. After World War I the Roumanian-speaking lands of the former Austro-Hungarian Empire were united with the original Roumanian state.

Russia *Rossia* in Russian and *Rosia* in Ukrainian, the name is of Finnish origin. The Finnish Rus was a name that was applied to the Varangians, Swedish merchants who sailed the Russian rivers to trade with the Slavs and with the Byzantine Empire.

Salerno The old part of the city slopes from the top of a hill which has a Roman fort. Salerno also had a well-known medical school that was founded in the eleventh century. In Latin the name is *Salernum*, possibly a derivative of the pre-IndoEuropean *sala*, a current of water. It is equally possible, however, that it is related to the Latin word for salt (*sal*), a reference to salt water.

Salzburg Salzburg is a small city in the Austrian Alps, a major vacation spot. For millennia the area has been rich in salt mines, hence the name, salt fortress or salt castle.

Saone River The Saone rises in Lorraine, in northeastern France, and joins the Rhone at Lyon. The ancients called it *Souconna, Souconna*, and *Sagonna. Onna*, the suffix, means river, but there is no certainty regarding the first part of the name. It may, however, come from the name of a Celtic deity.

Saragossa This city is on the Ebro River, in a valley between the Pyrenees and the Iberian mountains of Spain. Originally the name was *Caesaraugusta*, a Roman colony mentioned by Greek and Roman authors.

Sarajevo Sarajevo is the capital of Bosnia and Hercegovina, a division of the former Yugoslavia. The city has a Moslem population, and it has been the scene of religious conflict between Moselm and Christian Serbs. The name comes from the Turkish *saray*, a word for palace. Turks founded the city in the fifteenth century, as they were completing their conquests in the Balkans. The Turkish name was *Bosna-Saray* and the Slavic name is Sarajevo.

Sardinia Prehistoric monuments including tombs and underground chambers make this island in the western Mediterranean an interesting place to explore. There are also towers shaped like cones, thousands of which still stand. Sardinia is an Italian possession with a mountainous topography and a basically pastoral economy. Ancient Phoenicians called the island *Sardan*, and this could have been a form of *Sardus Pater*, the name of a North African deity. At this time Phoenician were colonizing North Africa and becoming familiar with the native Berber culture. There is also the chance that the name comes from that of a tribe living on the island. The Greeks called it *Sandliothin* because it has the shape of a sandal.

Scandinavia Scandinavia, as a geographical term, applies to Norway, Sweden, and Denmark. The name derives from

Scania, originally a reference to a portion of southern Sweden. *Scania* may come from an old Swedish word for island.

Schleswig Schleswig is the northernmost part of Germany, a bridge of land separating the North Sea from the Baltic, bordering Denmark. The local economy is based upon fishing and farming. *Scles* is a form of Schlie, the name of a German river. *Wig* is a form of the Scandinavian word for a bay or a place at the mouth of a river, hence a bay formed by the Schlie River.

Scotland Scotland is geographically divided between the southern Lowlands and the mountainous Highlands farther north. There are hills and lochs, deep lakes created by glaciers, throughout the country, and there are 186 inhabited coastal islands. Glasgow and Edinburgh are the two major industrial centers, while the rest of the country is agricultural and pastoral. In the fifth century A.D. large numbers of Irish, known as Gaels and as Scots, were crossing over from Ireland and settling the northwestern coast of Britain. (see Ireland) Their leaders founded a new kingdom in what would later be known as Scotland. These Scots from Ireland united with Picts, the aboriginal people of the land and kinsmen of the Celtic Scots, in the year 848 the Scottish King, Kenneth MacAlpine, began to rule over both the Scots and the Picts, and by the year 1000 his descendants were kings over most of present-day Scotland. They were beginning to use the current name for their kingdom.

Sea of Marmora This body of water lies between the Bosporus and the Dardanelles, and it separates European from Asiatic Turkey (see Bosporus and Dardanelles) *Marmoros*, the word from which the name is derived, is Greek for marble. A small group of islands in this sea, the Marmara Islands, at one time was a source of a very famous marble. One of these islands in particular, Proconnessus, had an abundance of this marble in ancient times.

Seine River The Seine rises in the mountainous part of northeastern France and empties into the English Channel. The Romans called it *Sequana*, possibly a form of the Celtic *soghan*, meaning calm. From *Sequana*, the name evolved over time to *Siguna*, *Signe*, and Seine.

Serbia Serbia is the largest republic of the former Yugoslavia, and includes Montenegro and Kosovo province in the southwest. Serbia became a kingdom in the nineteenth century once it had gained independence from the Turkish Empire. Serbs settled the Balkans during the sixth and seventh centuries A.D.; the name is Slavic, but was adopted from one of the Caucasian languages and means "man."

Seville Seville is the largest city of southwestern Spain. Moslem influence is evident throughout the city. The Romans called it *Hispalis*, but the modern name may have originated from *sefela*, Phoenician for a plain or a valley.

Sicily This triangular island is mountainous and produces citrus fruits, wheat, pastoral products, and sulphur. Sicilians are for the most part descendants of ancient Italian peoples who had arrived there in early times and Greek colonists who came in large numbers after 700 B.C., but the island has had many different rulers throughout its history: Greeks, Romans, Vandals, Byzantines, Moslems, Normans, Angevins, Spaniards, French, and with the unification of Italy in the nineteenth century, Italians. The name comes from *Sicel*, one of the ancient peoples of the island. According to the sources, there were three ethnic groups in Sicily: The *Sicels* in the east, the *Sicans* in the west-central portion, and the *Elymians* in the far western corner. The *Sicels*, a people of Italian origin, gave their name to the island.

Smolensk One of Russia's oldest cities, Smolensk has been rebuilt after having been almost entirely ruined by Nazi invaders. *Smola*, a Russian word, means resin, pitch, or tar. Smolensk is on the Dnieper River and in early times it participated in the Baltic-Black Sea trade. There were large amounts of resin in the area and the material may have been used in the construction of boats.

Sofia Turkish conquerors gave this Bulgarian city its name in the fourteenth century. They named it for the Church of Saint Sophia (*Sophia* is Greek for wisdom) in Constantinople, a church that the Turks converted into a mosque after their conquest of the city. The city of Sofia has its origin as early as the eighth or seventh century B.C. and was known as *Serdica*. *Serdica* comes from *Serd*, the name of a local Thracian or native Balkan tribe. In the first century A.D. it was called *Ulpia Serdica* by the conquering Romans for Marcus Ulpius Trajanus (emperor from 98-117 A.D.). Slavs, who had settled Bulgaria in the sixth century A.D., renamed the city *Sredets* (center) in the ninth century.

Spain The name comes from the Latin *Hispania*, as the Romans had called it. There are three theories regarding the origin of this Latin name: (1) it may have been derived from *ezpain* or *ezpan*, a native Iberian or Basque word for a beach or a shore; (2) it is possibly a form of the Carthagian or Phoenician *span*, meaning rabbit; (3) the name could also have come from the Greek *esperia*, "region of the settling sun" (the west). The first theory seems to be the most valid, since Basques were the natives of the country and were, thereby, the most likely to have named it. Also, a name that denotes a beach or a shore would be appropriate because of the country's long coastline.

Stockholm *Stoc*, the first half of the name, refers to a place protected by a stockade or surrounded by wooden piles or stocks. *Holm* is Scandinavian for island. The Swedish city, therefore, started out as an island settlement fortified by a wooden stockade.

Strasbourg One of Europe's largest inland ports, Strasbourg is a commercial, industrial, and cultural center. It is a French city on the Rhine River, in Alsace. In the second century A.D. it was known as *Argentoratum*, but in the sixth century the Germanic Franks renamed it *Strateburgo* from the Frankish *straza* (route) and *burg* (fortress). Note how similar the Frankish *straza* is to the English street. The Franks built their fortress adjacent to the original Gallo-Roman city of *Argentoratum*.

Suffolk Artists John Constable and Thomas Gainsborough made this part of the English countryside the subject of their paintings. A section of East Anglia, in southeastern England, it means south folk, the southern branch of the East Angles who settled the region in the fifth and sixth centuries A.D.

Sussex This part of southern England is agricultural, but many tourists come to see its Roman ruins and Norman castles, and to stay at its resorts. Sussex is the land of the South Saxons who began to arrive there at the close of the fifth century A.D. (see Esse)

Sweden More than one hundred-thousand lakes in addition to its rivers make up about one third of the nation's area, while forests cover about one half the land. In the Swedish language *Svensk* means Swedish and *Sverige*, Sweden. *Sve* is from *sweba*, a word for free in the ancient Scandinavian language, and *rike* means kingdom, hence free kingdom. The Scandinavian *rike* is related to the German *reich*.

Switzerland There are four languages in this small Alpine region. Seventy percent of the people speak German, nineteen percent use French, ten percent, Italian, and one percent, Romansch. The country is mountainous with several peaks over fourteen thousand feet. The German name for Switzerland is *Schweiz* and the French is *Suisse*. It is form of the older German name *Schwyz*, one of the three cantons or administrative districts that united in the year 1291 and established the core of what would later become modern Switzerland. *Schwyz* may have its root in the Germanic *suedan*, meaning to burn, a possible reference to a place at which people would burn trees in order to make a clearing in the woods.

Szeged The home of Josef Attila University since 1921, this Hungarian city is also a center for the manufacture of cotton textiles. Szeged may derive from *szeg* or *szog*, Hungarian for angle, a reference to the large curve formed by the Tisza River at that spot.

Tallin The Estonian capital has close to a half million people. The name was at one time *Tan- linn*, Estonian for "Danish fortress." *Tan* or *Taani* means Danish and *linn* is a fortress, castle, or palace. During the thirteenth century Tallin was under the rule of King Valdemar of Denmark. Another name for the city was *Reval*, a derivative of the Danish *rev*, the word for "a little sand bank."

Thames River Boat races between Oxford and Cambridge Universities take place along the Thames. The river flows from the Cotswold Hills of the southwest to the North Sea, where it empties just east of London. Roman sources mention the *Tameses* or *Tamesa* River, a name derived from a Celtic word for still, quiet, or silent.

The Hague Beside the Dutch government, The Hague has the Permanent Court of International Justice and The Hague Court. The Hague Court has been in session since World War II, but it is ready to handle cases whenever necessary. The Hague Conference established this court in 1899 to codify international law and to arbitrate in international disputes. The Germanic word *hag* or *hagen* refers to an enclosure or to a place surrounded by a hedge.

Thrace Thrace lies in the Balkans, to the northeast of Greece, and it includes the European portion of Turkey. The name is a form of the Greek *trachus* rough land.

Tiber River The Tiber rises in the Apennine Mountains of central Italy and empties into the Mediterranean west of Rome. It was named in honor of Tiberinus, one of the ancient Etruscan kings. (see Tuscany)

Tiflis This is the capital and largest city of Georgia, one of the Transcaucasian republics of the former Soviet Union. Tiflis is an older version of Tbilisi, the modern name. *Tbili* is the Georgian word for warm, possibly a reference to the warm sulphur springs not far away. Tiflis goes back to the fourth century A.D.

Toledo The Spanish city is elevated with narrow streets which end up at the Tagus River, and its long history gives it the feeling of a museum. Toledo existed in Roman times, and it served as a political and religious center through the centuries prior to the Moslem conquest of 711 A.D. The Romans called it *Toletum* or *Toletus* from *tol*, a Celtic word for mountain or height. (see Toulouse)

Toulouse This ancient city is today a center of the French aerospace industry as well as other areas of scientific research. The Latin form is *Tolosa* and it may have been adopted from the Celtic *tol*, meaning mountain or height. (see Toledo) There is also the chance that the name is of Ligurian or Iberian (Basque) origin and is, therefore, pre-Indo-European. According to a legend, however, the city was named for Tolus, a son of the Biblical Japheth, its founder. One other explanation suggests that it is the form of the Greek *tholos*, the word for a vault or an arched construction.

Transylvania The Dracula legend, based upon the historical Count Vlad who ruled the land during the fifteen century, has made Transylvania famous. Previous to World War I it was a part of the Austro-Hungarian Empire, but it is now western Roumania. *Trans* is Latin for across and *silva* is forest, hence "across the forest." This is how the Romans described the region when they annexed it to their empire.

Trier Trier (Treves in French) is a city of the Rhenish Palatinate, north of the Saar industrial region. It is rich in historic buildings, including an amphitheater and two imperial baths dating from Roman times. The old name was *Treviris* and it served as the cantonal center of the *Trevires*, a local Celtic tribe. *Tre* (across) and *wer* (a river crossing) are the two Celtic words that form this tribal name. The ford or crossing in this case is on the Moselle River. The emperor Augustus founded Trier in 15 B.C. and called it *Augusta Treverorum*.

Trieste This Italian city is at the head of the Adriatic Sea, not far from the border with Slovenia. *Tergeste*, the Latin name, ultimately stems from the Illyrian *terga*, a word for commerce. The Adriatic Sea had an active commercial life in ancient times.

Trondheim Trondheim (Trondhjem before 1931) is on Norway's Atlantic coast, on the Trondr fjord. Combined with *heim* (or *heimr*) it means "Trondr home."

Turin This is the home of the Fiat plant, a center of automobile production. Turin is the main city of the Piedmont section of northern Italy. In Italian it is *Torino* and it comes from the Latin *Augusta Tavrinorum*, *Augusta* of the *Taurini*, a local people living there in ancient times. They were possibly a Celtic people and their name may have been a derivative of *tauro*, Celtic for mountain. The region is mountainous and it did have a Celtic population before the Roman conquest and the arrival of Italian settlers.

Tuscany This is a region of northwestern Italy that includes the well-known cities of Florence, Siena, Pisa, Lucca, and Leghorn. Its name comes from *Tuscani*, Latin for Etruscans, a people who ruled the area in ancient times, before the rise of Rome.

Tyrol The Tyrol is an Alpine region that is politically divided between Austria, Italy, and Switzerland. The Romans called it *Castrum Terolis*, Camp of *Terioli*, with *Terioli* a possible derivative of the Celtic *tir*, a word for country.

Tyrrhenian Sea A section of the western Mediterranean, it separates Italy from the islands of Sardinia and Corsica. The Etruscans of ancient times were also known as Tyrrhenians.

Ukraine Ukraine is one of the new nations of the former Soviet Union. It has been a part of Russia since the eighteenth century, except for the westernmost part which was under Austrian rule before World War I. Previous to the eighteen century the Ukraine was governed by Poles, Lithuanians, and Mongols at different times in its history. Before the Mongol conquest of 1240, Ukraine was under the Grand Dukes of Kiev, descendants of the founders of the first Russian Christian state. The land has always been fertile and high in cereal production. There are rich mineral deposits as well. *Ukraina* is both the Russian and the Ukrainian spelling. It is a form of the word *oukraina*, Russian for a border region, as it was regarded during the period of Mongol rule. *Oukraina* has the prefix *ou* (near to) and the element *krai* (region), hence "region that is near." *Krai* is found in other Slavic languages in which it also means region, border, or country. An older name for Ukraine is Little Russia (*Malorussia* from *Malaia Rossia*)

Uppsala This Swedish city is about fifty miles north of Stockholm. *Upsalr* is Swedish for high hall or high dwelling (*up* means high and *salr*, hall or dwelling). The Germanic *sall* or *zaal* can refer to a stone house or to a one-roomed dwelling. The name of the city may be a reference to a building that stood there in ancient times, at the beginning of the settlement's history. It may have been a royal or noble residence considering the fact that the town was named for it.

Ural Mountains This mountain chain runs from north to south across Russia, separating Europe from Asia. The Ural region is rich in minerals such as iron ore, manganese, nickel, zinc, silver, and gold as well as in coal, oil, and natural gas. Ural is a word in the Tartar or Mongol language and it means girdle or belt.

Utrecht Canals run below street level throughout this Dutch city. *Drecht* in the early German dialect refers to a meadow or pasture. The Romans recorded the name as *Trajectus*, the full name having been *Trajectus-ad-Rhenum* ("meadow" or "pasture in the Rhine"). The land to the north of it was *Ultra-trajectum* ("beyond the pasture" or "meadow"). *Ultra-trajectum* evolved into Utrecht in the local Germanic dialect.

Valencia Valencia is a large Spanish port on the Mediterranean, in a region productive of oranges, grapes, and rice. *Valentia Edetanorum*, fortress of the *Edetani*, was the name of the Roman settlement. The *Edetani* were a local Iberian or native Spanish tribe. In 138 B.C., at the time of the Roman conquest, a military colony was established there. The Latin word *valentia* means strength or courage.

Venice This Italian city is famous for its canals as well as for its historic role as one of Europe's leading commercial cities. Before the thirteenth century the city had the name *Rivoalto*, raised bank, beach, or shore. *Rialto*, the name of a bridge and of a section of

Venice, comes from *Rivoalto*. Venice is a name derived from *Veneti*, an ancient Celtic people. *Veneti* in turn, comes from *vindo*, a Celtic word for white, and it is akin to the Breton *gwenn* and to the Cornish *gwyn*, both meaning white.

Vienna For three centuries this Austrian city was one of Europe's cultural centers. In German the name is Wien, but the Romans called it *Vindobona*, from the Celtic *vindo* (white) and *bona* (*citadel*). (see Bonn) Celts lived in present-day Austria before the Germans had arrived. *Wien*, the German name, refers to the river which joins the Danube at that spot. *Vedunia* or *Vedunis*, Celtic for tree, was the ancient name of this river.

Vilnius Vilnius is the capital of Lithuania, and the name comes from *Vilnia*, the name of a river. *Vilnia* is a form of *vilnis*, a word for wave, water, or sea, from the Indo-European root *wel* (to roll). Note the relation to the Latin *volvere* (to roll).

Vistula River This major Polish river winds north from the Carpathian Mountains through Warsaw, where it turns eastward through the center of the country, flowing north again into the Baltic Sea to the east of Gdansk. In Polish it is *Wisla*, a form of the Slavic *Veisla*, a possible derivative of the Indo-European *veik*, meaning to run or to flow. It may, therefore, be a distant relative of the Sanskrit *vis*, also meaning to run or to flow.

Volga River The Volga rises between St. Petersburg and Moscow, and flows south until it empties into the Caspian sea. The name probably comes from one of two Slavic words, *vlaga* (humidity) or *velik* (great). There is also the possibility that the origin is Finnish or the closely- related Estonian. *Valkea* and *valge* mean white in Finnish and Estonian, respectively.

Vosges This mountainous region of eastern France is in Alsace. The Gallic or Celtic *vosego* or *vosago* comes from *vos*, a word for a peak or summit. This is one possible explanation, but it may also be a combination of the two Celtic words *vo* (under) and *sego* (height), hence "under a high place."

Wales Tourists come to Wales to see its scenery, its rocky coasts, its sandy beaches, its mountains, and its castles. The country's name comes from the Anglo-Saxon *walas*, a word for foreigner. The Welsh call themselves *Cymri*, an old Celtic word for compatriots or brothers, and they refer to their nation as *Cymru*. The English continued to call the Welsh *walas* which eventually became Wales. (see Cumberland)

Warsaw The city appears in the records for the first time in the year 1224. *Warszawa*, the Polish spelling, may have taken its name from a village called Warsz. Warsz was the name of the village's founder and it is a form of the Polish *warchol*, a word meaning aggressive. This is one possible explanation. According to another theory, Warsaw is a combination of War and Sawa, the names of two Slavic tribal leaders. Some believe, however, that Warsaw has its root in Warsew, the name of the wealthy Czech family that had established the city.

Waterloo This is the site of Napoleon's defeat at the hands of the British under Wellington. *Loh* and *loo* are from the German and the Dutch, respectively and can refer to a meadow, a thicket, or a marsh, hence a watery meadow or a watery marsh.

Wurzburg The Bavarian city of Wurzburg has a 312-room palace, built during the eighteenth century in the Baroque style for the local bishop. Wuzburg is a combination of *wurzel* (root) and *burg* (fortress).

York This city of northern England is of ancient origin. Its old name was *Eboracum*, Celtic for marshy place. The Anglo-Saxons called it *Eoforwic*, *Eurvich*, and *Eferwic*. *Wic* is the Anglo- Saxon suffix that means a town or dwelling. York comes from the Danish pronunciation, *Jorvik*.

Yugoslavia The former Yugoslavia was originally a number of kingdoms that arose many centuries ago. For a long time the country was divided between the Austrian and the Turkish Empires, but in the nineteenth century Serbia, the largest of the Yugoslav nations, gained independence from Turkey. Following World War I the Kingdom of Yugoslavia came into being, and after World War II it became a republic under Tito. Today there are the new nations of Serbia (also called Yugoslavia), Croatia, Slovenia, Bosnia-Hercegovina, and Macedonia. Ethnically the people of all these new states are Slavic, but the Serbs of Montenegro, Kosovo, and Macedonia are partially descended from the Thraco-Illyrian or native Balkan people who have lived there for millennia. Large numbers of Albanians are also living in Kosovo. Yugoslavia means land of the Southern Slavs, *yugo* meaning south or southern in Serbo- Croatian. During the sixth and seventh centuries A.D. Slavs from the north and east moved into the Balkans and as they left their original homes for lands to the south they became known as South Slavs (Yugoslavs) as they are called today. The remainder of the Slavs stayed in their original abodes where they would later on be known as East Slavs (Great Russians, Ukrainians, and White Russians) and West Slavs (Poles, Czechs, and Slovaks).

Zagreb Zagreb is the capital and largest city of Croatia, with a population of approximately 680,000. The name is made up of two Croatian words, *za* (behind) and *breg* (mountain), hence "behind the mountain."

Zurich Surrounded by forested hills on the Lake of Zurich, the Alps can be seen in the distance. In prehistoric times the Swiss lake-dwellers built their houses on this lake. The name is a German form of the Latin Turicum, originally the Celtic *Turicu*, from *dur*, a word for water.

Chapter 4.
Place-Names of the
World

Afghanistan This Islamic nation is sandwiched between Iran and West Pakistan. The land is diverse with regard to its topography, with its highest mountain peak at twenty-five thousand feet and its lowest point at nine hundred feet below sea level. Afghan is the name of the people and it comes from *afghana*, a Persian word of unknown origin, though it may be the name of a tribal ancestor. *Stan* is the Iranian or Persian word for country. (see Kazakh)

Africa The African continent extends from the Mediterranean to south of the Tropic of Capricorn, and it separates the Atlantic Ocean from the Red Sea and the Indian Ocean. As you travel from one region to another you will find a great deal of diversity in terrain, economy, ethnicity, language, religion, and history. The name comes directly from the Latin name Africa, but in ancient times it was applied only to what is now Tunisia. Its origin may be in *Afer* (pl. *Ifri*), the name of a Berber tribe that lived near the Mediterranean coast in ancient times. According to another theory, however, it is a form of the Hebrew *afar* (dust or powder), a reference to the desert. Some linguists offer a third explanation, suggesting that it is derived from *faraqa*, a Carthaginian word for colony.

Alberta One of Canada's western provinces, it is heavily forested with its national parks, hot springs, wild life, and a segment of the Rocky Mountains. The Marquis of Lorne, Governor- General of Canada, named the region after his wife, Princess Louise Caroline Alberta.

Algeria Much of Algeria's territory is a part of the Sahara Desert, but the coastal region produces wheat, wine, and various minerals. Most Algerians live within one hundred miles of the sea. There are seventeen million people and the languages are Arabic, Berber, and French. The people are basically Berbers, descendants of the aboriginal tribes of North Africa with an admixture of Arabs who settled there in the seventh century A.D. French colonists brought their language to Algeria in the nineteenth century, and it was the French who named the country Algeria after Algiers, the city that they had selected for a colonial capital. Algiers, itself, is a form of the Arabic *al-jaza'ir*, meaning the islands, a name chosen because of the four islands near the Algerian coast.

Amazon River The Amazon flows through northern Brazil and empties into the Atlantic Ocean. It cuts through a thick tropical forest, one of the most natural places in the world today. The Portuguese and the Spanish call it *Amazonas*, from the local Indian *amazun* or *amassunu*, "great wave," a reference to the tidal waves that occur on the river's course. There were battles between Spaniards and local Indians, and the natives reminded the Spaniards of the mythical Amazons of ancient times. The legendary Amazons are supposed to have been female warriors dwelling on the Black Sea coast, and the word itself, is of Iranian origin and may denote a society without males. It may also mean a lack of breasts a reference to the custom of removing the right breast to facilitate the firing of an arrow from a bow

Amman Jordan's capital was named for the Biblical Ammonites who took their name from Ammon, their tribal progenitor. According to *Second Samuel*, King David captured this city in the eleventh century B.C. In *Genesis* XIX:38 There is a mention of an individual by the name of Ben-Ammi, possibly another name for Ammon. Ben-Ammi is Hebrew for "son of my people."

Amur This river of southeastern Siberia forms a part of the Russo-Chinese border. It is important for shipping and it has ninety-nine types of fish. The name could be a form of *amar*, a Mongolian word for tranquillity, or it could come from *har moron*, Mongolian for black river. *Saghalien*, another name for the river, is from the Manchu *sahalian ula*, also meaning black river. The Chinese call it *heilong jiang*, "river of the black dragon."

Andaman Islands This group of islands is in the Bay of Bengal, between India and Malaysia. The aborigines, of which there are only a thousand left, still live in the Stone Age. The name has the same form in Hindi, Bengali, and Malaysian. It is a variant of the Sanskrit *Hanumant*, the name of a legendary king.

Andes Mountains This mountain chain runs over four thousand miles and has more than twenty peaks of twenty thousand feet and over. The name is *Quechua* Indian, but there is no certainty as to the exact word from which it stems. *Andi*, a word for high summit, pea, top, or ridge sounds logical. Some linguists have suggested that it derives from *anti*, a *Quechua* word for east, but this is not apt, since the Andes are in the western part of the South American continent. There is one additional theory, according to which the name comes from *anta*, a word for copper or brass, both local products.

Angola This former Portuguese colony in southwestern Africa has been the scene of regional conflict for years. Angola is the Portuguese form of *N'gola*, the name of a local king who was alive in the sixteenth century, the time of Portuguese colonization.

Antarctica The coldest part of the world, temperatures have gone down as far as -126.9° F and winds have gusted up to two hundred miles per hour. *Anti* (opposite), a Greek prefix, is added to Arctic. (see Arctic)

Antigua The name of the Caribbean island is a form of the Spanish *antiguo*, ancient or antique. Spaniards landed there in 1493 and named it for the Church of *Santa Maria la Antigua* ("Saint Mary the Ancient") in the Spanish city of Seville.

Antilles (Greater and Lesser) Geographers divide the Caribbean islands into two groups (1) the Greater Antilles which include the large islands of Cuba, Puerto Rico, Jamaica, and Hispaniola; (2) the Lesser Antilles or small islands which form a chain extending from Puerto Rico southeast to South America. *Antillas*, a Spanish word, was used for the first time by the cartographer, Paolo Toscanelli. He adopted the word from the works of Aristotle, who had theories about a large island in the Atlantic Ocean, a mythical land, which the Carthaginians called *Antilia*, possibly a form of *Atlantis*. (see Atlantic Ocean) According to another theory, *Antillas* could be the Latin *ante* (before) and the Spanish *illas* (islands), hence "islands which are in front," a possible reference to their location east of the Central American mainland.

Aral Sea The Aral Sea is a large inland body of water in the south of the former Soviet Union, in Central Asia. Its area is twenty-four thousand square miles. Aral means island in the local Turkic dialect, a probable reference to some small islands in this sea.

Arctic The Arctic is an ice-covered ocean. Ninety percent of it is frozen during the winter and seventy percent is ice all year. *Arcticus* is the Latin and *Arcticos* the Greek, form *Arctos*, Greek for a bear, a reference to the two constellations known as the Great Bear and the Little Bear. (see Antarctica)

Argentina Some of the best agricultural land in the world is on the Pampa or great plain of Argentina. Most of the country is known for livestock and ranching, but the northeast produces wheat and corn as well. There are over twenty-eight million people, most of them being either of Spanish or of Italian descent. The name of the country comes from *argento*, Spanish for silver. Upon visiting the area for the first time, the Spaniards were impressed by the silver ornaments that the Indians were wearing.

Asia The largest of the continents, Asia encompasses a great variety of climates, terrains, economies, and peoples. Extending from the Equator to the Arctic and from the Mediterranean to the Pacific, it has more diversity than any of the other continents. The name, according to some scholars, is from *asu*, an Assyrian word meaning to leave or to lift oneself up, perhaps a reference to the east and the rising sun. If its origin is the Sanskrit *usa*, a word for dawn or east, the same rationale would apply. Some linguists believe, however, that the Etruscan *aes* was adopted into the Latin to become Asia, but the meaning of this Etruscan word is unknown.

Atlantic Ocean *Atlantikos* in Greek, the name is most likely a form of *Atlantis*, the famous mythical land. According to Plato, it was beyond the Strait of Gibraltar, an island larger than Libya and Asia Minor. Even though *Atlantis* was legend, the tradition was influential enough to pass the name on to the Atlantic Ocean. (see Antilles)

Auckland Auckland, New Zealand is a city on the northern isthmus of the north island. It is the largest city and the main industrial center of the nation. The first governor of New Zealand named the city to honor Lord Auckland, Viceroy of India, for giving him command of *HMS Rattlesnake*.

Australia Tourists come to the southern continent to see the unusual mammals that lay eggs and carry their young in pouches, the deserts, the rain forests, the mountains, and the Great Barrier Reef. The Latin *australis* means eastern, and in ancient times there was a legend about the existence of a *Terra Australis Incognita* ("an unknown eastern land"), taken into consideration on one of Ptolemy's maps. Dutch sailors, the first Europeans to reach

Australia, called it New Holland, but in 1814 Matthew Flinders, an English explorer, renamed it *Terra Australis* which was later shortened to Australia.

Azores Islands This group of islands is in the North Atlantic, two thirds the way between North America and Europe. It is *Acores* in Portuguese, from acor, the name of a bird that Portuguese sailors found on the islands when they first arrived in 1427. The name of the bird, acor, is derived from the Latin word *auceptor* or *accipiter*, a form of the Greek *ukupteros*, to fly fast.

Baffin (Island and Bay) This island forms the northeastern most part of Canada and is separated from Greenland by the Davis Strait. The northern two thirds of Baffin Island extends north of the Arctic Circle. Baffin Bay is north of Davis Strait. William Baffin discovered both the island and the bay in 1616.

Baghdad Baghdad is in the Tigris-Euphrates Valley in what used to be called Mesopotamia. Today houses of various colors line the banks of the Tigris River as it flows through the city. Baghdad is Arabic and it denotes a divine gift. *Bagh* is a word suggesting divinity and *dad* comes from a root word meaning to give.

Bahama Islands In the early 1700's the Bahamas served as bases for pirates including Edward Teach, also known as "Blackbeard." There are two possible explanations for the name. If the origin of the name is Spanish it would probably have been *baja mar*, meaning lower sea. If the name is Native American it would most likely have come from *Guanahani*, a word of unknown meaning. Before the present name came into use, the islands were called *.Lucayes.*

Bangkok Bangkok, the Thai capital, is a city of four hundred Buddhist temples. The name means "region of olives" or "region of olive trees." The Thai people also call the city *Krung Thep*, "city of angels," and *Phra Nakhon*, "city of the master," a more honorific title. Because of its many canals, Bangkok is called the "Venice of the Orient."

Bangladesh This is one of the poorest and most crowded nations in the world with 750-2,000 people per square mile. Formerly East Pakistan, it is located at the head of the Bay of Bengal. The first part of the name comes from *Bengal*, the name of the original pre-Indo-European- speaking tribe of the region. *Desh* is a form of *desa*, Sanskrit for place or country. (see Bengal)

Barbados This Caribbean vacation spot is a former British possession. The name, however, is Spanish, a plural of *barbado*, the word for beard or bearded. The reference is to figs that grow on the island, the leaves of which resemble a beard.

Beirut This Lebanese city has been the scene of much turmoil over the years. "City of wells" is the translation from Arabic. *Bir*, Arabic for well, is akin to the Hebrew word *be'er*, also well.

Belem Belem, a city of northeastern Brazil, takes its name from a suburb of Lisbon, Portugal. It is a contraction of Bethlehem.

Belize Originally British Honduras, this small country on the eastern coast of Central America was renamed Belize in 1973, after the river and the town. The only explanation for the name, one that may stretch the imagination a little, is that it is an altered form of Peter Wallace, the name of a British pirate who reached the area at the end of the seventeenth century.

Bengal The region is divided between India and Bangladesh. A tribe called Bengal had been living there from very early times.

Later on the name was applied to the entire region. (see Bangladesh)

Bethlehem This city is mentioned in the Bible as a place in which Ruth had lived, David had spent some of his youth, and Jesus had been born. Bethlehem is a Latin form of the Hebrew *bet- lehem,* "house of bread," *bet* meaning house and *lehem*, bread. Bread was a symbol of fertility in early times and apparently the city was built because of the good soil in the vicinity. Sources of the fourteenth century B.C. contain the earliest reference to Bethlehem. The Arabic name is *Bayt lahm.*

Bhutan Bhutan is a small country in the Himalaya Mountains, between India and Tibet. In 1962 some roads connecting Bhutan with India had been completed, but before that all travel was by foot or by horse. The name is a combination of Hindi and Nepalese, ultimately a derivative of the Sanskrit *Bhota* The first part of the name, *bod*, means Tibet and the second part, *anta*, refers to an extremity, hence "the end of Tibet." The Tibetans called Bhutan *Druk yul*, "the country of the dragon." (see Tibet)

Bogota The Colombian capital lies in a basin over 8,500 feet in the Andes Mountains. At first the name was Santa Fe, but later on it became Santa Fe de Bogota. Bogota, the name of a river, is a form of *Bagotta*, the name of a Native American ruler.

Bombay Bombay, on India's west coast, is the largest center of cotton textile manufacture in the country. *Bambai* is the Hindi spelling and it may have been *Mumbai* at one time, a form of *Mumbadevi*. Mumba was the name of an ancient female deity.

Borneo The island of Borneo is separated from the Asian mainland by the South China Sea. The four states on the island are Kalimantan, Sarawak, Sabah, and Brunei. Borneo is covered by heavy tropical forests, and it has no large cities. Rubber, spices, and rice are its main products. Portuguese explorers who arrived in the Far East at the end of the fifteenth century began to use the name Borneo, an alternative form of Brunei, a Hindi name that is probably related to the Sanskrit *bhumi*, meaning land or region.

Bougainville During World War II the Japanese occupied this Pacific island until the Australians took it from them in 1945. Two years later it became a part of the UN Trust Territory of New Guinea until 1975, when it went to the independent Papua. Bougainville is the largest of the Solomon Islands, in the west-central Pacific. The name honors Louis Antoine, Count of Bougainville (1729-1811), a French explorer, but the island was renamed North Solomon.

Brazil Brazil is a large country of 3,284,426 square miles and 119 million people. The cities are concentrated on the coast and the inland areas are sparsely populated. The heavily-forested north produces rubber, and various food products, while the southeast grows rice, coffee, tobacco, cotton, and livestock. The Portuguese spelling is *Brasil*, from braisil, the name of a tree that grows there in abundance. Braisil comes from *brasa*, a word for embers, due to its red color. Before Brazil had acquired its present name, it was called *Terra de Vera Cruz* ("Land of the True Cross") and *Terra de Santa Cruz* ("Land of the Holy Cross").

Brazzaville This city is the capital of Congo. It was named for Pierre Savorgnan de Brazza (1852-1905), an Italian who had explored the region for the French.

Brisbane Brisbane, on Australia's east coast, was established in 1824 as a penal colony. Because of its climate it has become more recently a haven for vacationers and retirees. Sir Thomas Macdougall Brisbane, for whom the city was named, served as governor of New South Wales during the 1820's. Originally the name was applied to a local river, but not to the penal colony. The colony was known as Edinglassie, but eventually the name was changed to Brisbane.

Buenos Aires More than one third of the Argentine population lives in this metropolitan area. The name is Spanish and means good breezes, a probable reference to the air from the South Atlantic.

Cairo The modern city lies on the east bank of the Nile, and east of the modern city is the old city. Old Cairo has the greatest number of buildings in the Islamic style than any other city worldwide. The name may have developed from *al-qahira*, an Arabic word for strong or victorious, a reference to Mars which was rising in the sky when construction of the city had started (July 6, 969). According to another theory, the new Fatimid Dynasty, conquerors of North Africa, Egypt, and other parts of the Middle East, named it for their military victories. *Al-qahira* was pronounced *Kahir* by the Turks and it came into Latin as *Cairus*, hence Cairo.

Calcutta This city was for a long time a commercial, administrative, and cultural center of British India. Many people died here with the Hindu-Moslem riot of 1946. Greater Calcutta is Indian's largest city. *Kalakata* in Hindi and *Kolikata* in Bengali, the name comes from the Sanskrit *Kali*, a female Hindu deity of death. The name of the deity, in turn, is derived from *kala*, Hindi for black.

Calgary Canada's highest city, Calgary is in southern Alberta. James Farquharson MacLeod, a colonel in the North-West Mouned Police, named the city after a town in Scotland, his place of origin. Calgary is a Gaelic name and it may denote clear running water.

Cambodia On September 21, 1993 Cambodia received a new constitution. The nation is a monarchy with Norodom Sihanouk as king. Rebels in the west and economic difficulties have caused the country some serious problems. The Cambodian name is *Kampopha*, from Kambu, the name of a mythological figure who had lived as a hermit. According to tradition, Kambu married the nymph Mera and their descendants are the Cambodian people.

Cameroon Cameroon is one of the states that had been carved out of Equatorial Africa. There are more than eight million people in Cameroon, and the languages spoken are French, English, and four African languages. The name comes from the *Portuguese Rio dos Camaroes* ("river of crabs"), a name given to the local river in the sixteenth century because of the abundance of these crustaceans.

Canada Extensive in size, much of Canada is water when taking into consideration Hudson Bay, the islands of the far north, and the many large lakes throughout the country. Most of the people live in the south, close to the United States border. Ottawa is the capital and Montreal, the largest city. There are a number of ideas on the origin of the name but the one that is most likely to be correct is the following: the name comes from the Iroquois *Kanata* or *Kanada*, a word for cabin or lodge, first recorded by Jacques Cartier, a French explorer, in 1535. It refers to the one section of the country that the Iroquois were describing, an area with many cabins, permanent Native American homes all clustered together. At the time of Cartier's visit there were Algonquins in the Lower St. Lawrence Valley, but the Iroquois were probably there earlier, leaving some of their geographical names.

Canary Islands This group of islands is not far from the North African coast. They belong to Spain and are called *Canarias* in Spanish. *Canarias* comes from the Latin *Canariae Insulae*, a name that pertains to dogs (*canis* in Latin). The Romans visited the islands and according to the writer, Pliny, they were inhabited by large dogs. In ancient times the Canary islands were also known as *Fortunatae Insulae* (Fortunate Islands). In the language of the indigenous people they are called *Tamaran*, "land of forts."

Canton This city is in southeastern China, and its name is a Europeanized form of the Chinese *guangdong*, a word that means "the vastness of the Orient," *guang* meaning vast and *dong*, Orient. The Chinese also call it *Guangzhou*, vast region.

Caracas The Venezuelen capital is a highly modern city surrounded by mountains. Many oil and steel companies have offices in Caracas, which has been attracting industries and experiencing rapid growth since the 1940's. When the Spanish founded the city in 1567 they named it *Santiago de Leon de Caracas* ("Saint James of Leon of Caracas"), but it was later shortened to its present form. Caracas was the name of a local native tribe.

Caroline Islands The Caroline Islands are in the western Pacific, not far north of the Equator. Spanish sailors reached the islands in 1528 and named them *Islas de los Barbudos* ("Islands of Barbus"). In 1542 they changed it to *Islas de los Jarines* ("Islands of Gardens"). The present name came into use in 1686, when the Spaniards decided to rename the islands out of respect to their king, Charles II. In Spanish it is *Islas Carolinas*.

Caribbean Sea The people who had lived on the islands of this sea, the Carib Indians, gave their name to it. Carib comes from *Caribale*, a form of the Native American *Kalinago* or *Kalino*, a name that these people called themselves, denoting brave men. The word cannibal also comes from *Caribale*.

Casablanca The city's old section has narrow streets and part of its original wall. The modern portion, built by the French, forms a semicircle around the older part. Casablanca is Spanish for white house. The original name given to it by the Portuguese was *Casa Branca*, also meaning white house.

Caspian Sea The Caspian is the world's largest inland sea, and it is a major source of sturgeon and caviar. According to Strabo, a Greek geographer of the first century B.C., the Caspian Sea took its name from the *Caspii*, a Persian or Iranian tribe dwelling at its southern end. Another early name for the Caspian was the Hyrcanian Sea, also an Iranian tribal name, but Caspian was the one that lasted.

Cayman Islands The three islands, Grand Cayman, Little Cayman, and Cayman Brac, are in the Caribbean, south of Cuba and west of Jamaica. There is a reptile known as a cayman which is abundant on these islands. Cayman is a short form of *acayuman*, a Carib Indian name for this reptile.

Celebes Islands This unusually shaped island is triangular with four "limbs" projecting from it. There are also small islands off shore which make up the island group. It is part of Indonesia and lies east of Borneo and northeast of Java. The name is a form of *celebres*, Portuguese for celebrated or famous. Originally the name was applied to the dangerous headlands or promontories on the island's northeast coast, but eventually it came to refer to the whole island.

Ceylon Now called Sri Lanka, Ceylon is an island nation near the southern tip of India. There are mountains and valleys, plenty of streams and waterfalls, and tea plantations. In Hindi the name is *Silon*, from the Sanskrit *simhala* (*simha* is Sanskrit for lion). The name for this island in a number of languages signifies lion, possible evidence for lions having existed there in early times. (see Sri Lanka)

Chad Chad is in north-central Africa, a very arid land that has severe famine as a result of its lack of water, especially back in 1982. Other names for the country are *Saghe*, *Sara*, *Tsade*, and *Tsad*. Ironically all of the names for this nation, including Chad, denote water in the local language and refer specifically to a lake of the same name.

Chile This long, narrow, and mountainous country extends from South America's west-central coast down to the southern tip of the continent. Chile averages only about 150 miles in width. Northern Chile is rich in minerals, but farther south agriculture and herding predominate. The far south is heavily forested. The name is Native American, and according to one theory, it denotes a place at which the land comes to an end, a reference to the southern tip of South America. Some linguists link the name to a Native American word for cold, a reference to its climate in certain sections. There is also the possibility that it stems from the name of a local bird.

China Mainland China, the most populous country on the globe, has almost one billion people. The Chinese are the main ethnic group, but there are also Uigurs, Kazakhs, Mongols, Tibetans, and other peoples. Taiwan, an island southeast of the mainland, has under seventeen million. Hong Kong, on the South China Sea, was a British outpost and Macau, east of Hong Kong, is Portuguese. In ancient times the Chinese would use the name of the ruling dynasty for their country. There was no name for the whole of what is now China. The Chin Dynasty (c. 200 B.C.) governed much of what is today China, and it was known as the Chin "Empire." When the Chin Dynasty ended foreigners, such as the Malays who traded with China, continued to call it the land of Chin. The Indians adopted it from the Malays and introduced it to the Greeks. The Greeks and Romans shifted the first letter of Chin to *s*, hence Sino as a reference to China (Sino- American). In India the original form, Chin, was kept in use and in the late fifteenth century the Portuguese adopted this form from the Indians and added the *a*, the Portuguese ending for geographical names. The Portuguese brought the name back to Europe, and China is the name still used by non-Chinese. The Chinese, themselves, have experimented with some names of their own.

Congo Once a part of French Equatorial Africa, French is spoken along with three African languages. *Kongo* is a Bantu word that signifies a mountain.

Costa Rica Costa Rica is one of the more stable and democratic countries of Latin America. The name is simply Spanish for rich coast.

Curacao The island of Curacao is a Dutch possession in the Caribbean. Its economy is based upon the refining of petroleum as well as upon tourism and hotel construction. The Spaniards named the island *Curacion*, from the Latin *curare*, to care for. Curacao is the Portuguese form of the name.

Cuzco This town in southern Peru was at one time the Inca capital and is now a major archeological site. The name comes from the Quechua Indian *Qosqo*, but its meaning is unknown.

Cyprus Conflict between Greeks and Turks has made this eastern Medierranean island a battleground throughout the twentieth century. Cyprus is a Greek name, but it has its origin in the ancient Sumerian *kabar* or *gabar*, meaning bronze. This word passed on into the Akkadian language of Mesopotamia in the form of *siparru* or *sipiru*, and it eventually entered the Greek language as Cyprus.

Dahomey Known today as Benin, Dahomey is the older name of this West African nation. The name comes from *Dan Home* and it means "built on the belly of Dan." This is a reference to a certain king, Aho, who constructed his palace on the spot where Dan, his rival, was buried.

Davis Strait John Davis (1554-1605) was an Arctic explorer who had discovered this body of water that separates Baffin Island from Greenland. Davis also discovered the Falkland Islands in the South Atlantic.

Delhi Delhi is the capital of the Republic of India. There is the old city of Delhi, New Delhi (the official capital since 1931), and Union Territory of Delhi which includes Old Delhi, New Delhi, and the surrounding areas. Delhi is mainly an administrative center. In Hindi it is *Dilli*, but there is no certainty as to the name's origin. It may be a form of Hindi *dehli*, meaning threshold, beginning, or entrance, from *dehali*, a Sanskrit word with the same meaning. This may be a geographical description, since Delhi is at the threshold between the Indus and Ganges Rivers.

Easter Island Over six hundred megalithic monuments have been found on this island in the southeastern Pacific Ocean, today a Chilean possession. Europeans first landed there on April 16, 1722, the day after Easter. The Dutch explorer, Jacob Roggeveen, named it *Paasch Eiland*, Easter Island. The natives called it *Mata-kite-rani*, "the eyes which look at the stars." The original inhabitants are Polynesian, and anthropologists believe that they arrived there c. 400 A.D. Other Polynesian names for the island are *Rapa Nui* and *Te Pito te Henua*, "the navel of the world."

Edmonton The capital city of the Canadian province of Alberta was founded in 1795 as Fort Edmonton, named after Edmonton, England, near London.

Egypt Egypt is on the African continent, but it is also a part of the Middle East both culturally and politically. The Nile River has made it possible for civilization to thrive in Egypt for many millennia. In ancient times Egyptians called their country *Kemet* (black) due to the color of the soil in the Nile Valley. Egypt, however, is a Greek name. *Aigyptos* appears in the *Iliad* and *Odyssey* of Homer, and was applied to the Nile as well as to the whole country. In the Greek language river names are usually masculine in gender, while countries tend to be feminine. The name of the country, *Aigyptos*, however, is masculine. What this suggests is that the name was given to the river before it was given to the country. *Aig* is the Greek prefix that denotes water, thus strengthening the position of scholars who say that *Aigyptos* was originally a name for the Nile. The second part of the name, *ypt*, may be from *hyptio*, a Greek adjective meaning flatness. *Hyptos* used in connection with a river may be a reference to low banks or to lack of current. After a while *Aigyptos* fell out of use as a river name, and continued to be applied only to the country. *Neilos* was adopted as the name of the river. (see Nile)

El Salvador This nation is the smallest in area and densest in population of all the countries of Central America. It has been the scene of bloody political turmoil in recent years. The name is Spanish for savior and it was originally the name of a fort that the Spaniards had built during the early years of their colonization. Eventually the name of the fort became that of the entire nation.

Ethiopia Africa's oldest independent country, it had a monarch until 1974, when the last emperor was ousted by a military coup. Ethiopia has a long history of civilization and cultural contact with the eastern Mediterranean to the north. Christianity, Islam, and Judaism, have come to Ethiopia from this source. In Latin it is *Aethiopia* and in Greek, *Aithiopis*, from the Greek *aitho*, to burn, a reference to the color of the people.

Euphrates River This river rises in the mountains of eastern Turkey and empties into the Persian Gulf. It runs alongside the Tigris River, thus forming Mesopotamia, "the land between the rivers," as it was called in ancient times. The Euphrates kept the land fertile and permitted agriculture and a settled mode of life to flourish. According to one theory, the name means "father of rivers," from the Akkadian *ur* (river) and *at* (farther). It may, however, be a combination of *u* (very) and *pratu* (large), also Akkadian. The second theory sounds better because *u pratu* could easily have become Euphrates in the Greek pronunciation.

Falkland Islands This island group is located in the South Atlantic, approximately four hundred miles from the southern tip of South America. The two major islands are West Falkland and East Falkland, separated by the Falkland Sound. They belong to Britain, but Argentina's claim to them brought on the military clash between the two nations in the early 1980's. Herding sheep and fishing for cod are the two main economic activities in the Falklands. John Davis, a British explorer, came upon these islands in 1590, but it was another explorer who named the islands. The British seaman named them twenty or thirty years later for the Earl of Falkland, the Minister of State under King Charles I. (see David Strait)

Fez Part of this Moroccan city is surrounded by what is left of its old walls and tower. In Arabic it is *Fas*, the origin of which is uncertain. It may be a form of *fa's*, Arabic for an ax or a battle ax.

Fiji Captain James Cook arrived in the southern islands of this archipelago back in 1774 and Captain William Bligh followed in 1789, after the mutiny on the *Bounty*, Bligh's ship. Fiji is the English and Malaysian name for these islands which the natives call *Viti*. One of the two main islands of the group is *Viti Levu*, a name of unknown meaning.

Formosa This is the old European name for Taiwan meaning beautiful in Portuguese. (see Taiwan)

Gabon Gabon, an exporter of petroleum is one of the wealthiest African nations. It is on the West African coast, and is rich in forests and various minerals. The name of the country was originally the name of a bay that the Portuguese had discovered and named *Gabao*, a word for hood, a probable reference to its shape. The Portuguese borrowed this word from the Arabic (*qaba*).

Galapagos Islands Charles Darwin visited these islands in 1835 and made a study of the local fauna. His observations strengthened his theories on evolution. Since 1959 the islands have been a national park and wildlife preserve. The Galapagos Islands are on the equator, in the Pacific, around eight hundred miles west of South America. Galapagos is Spanish and it means "islands of the water tortoises." The large tortoises of these islands have always fascinated both tourists and scientists.

Ganges River The Ganges rises in the Himalaya Mountains, flows across northern India, and empties into the Bay of Bengal. It is a holy river for Hindus. Ganges is the name used by the English and Portuguese, but in Hindi it is *Ganga* and in Bengali, *Gonga*. In Sanskrit *Ganga* means river or stream.

Gaspe Peninsula The peninsula takes the name of a county in the Canadian province of Quebec. There is no certainty about the name's origin, but it may be a form of the Micmac Indian word for extremity. Some people believe, however, that it was named for the Portuguese sailor, Gaspar Contereal, while others say that the name comes from Caspe, a Basque village.

Gaza Gaza used to be the land of the Biblical Philistines.
Following the Arab-Israeli War of 1947-9 it was a part of Egypt,
but it became an Israeli territory as a result of the War of 1967.
There is a city of Gaza in the Gaza Strip, the name of this Israeli
territory. A series of ancient Egyptian documents, the *Amarna
Letters*, refer to Gaza as *Hazati* or *Azzati*. *Gazza* in Arabic and
Azza in Hebrew, it comes from *az*, a Hebrew word for force.
Azoz is the Hebrew verb meaning to be strong. At one time the city
of Gaza was a fortress.

Ghana Ghana, a West African state with a population of over
eleven million, has seven African languages in addition to English.
Gana is an African word that the Arabs had adopted and it means
king or sovereign. Before the thirteenth century Ghana was part of
a large empire called *Aoukar*, an area much greater than that of the
modern nation. The English called the area Gold Coast, from the
Portuguese *Costa do Ouro*, because of the gold that had been
discovered there.

Granada This Caribbean island is very close to the Venezuelan
coast. In March, 1979 Grenada experienced a coup which disrupted
its parliamentary government, but United States intervention in
October, 1983 restored normalcy. The Spaniards originally named
the island Conception, but later renamed it after the Spanish city.

Guadalcanal This is one of the Solomon Islands in the west-
central Pacific. The battle that took place there during World War
II meant a big defeat for Japan. Alvaro de Mendana de Neira, a
Spanish explorer, discovered the island and named it after his
birthplace in Spain.

Guatemala Guatemala is south of Mexico, in Central America, a
heavily forested country with some agricultural regions. Its
Native American population is more than half. The name comes

from the Native American *Quauhtemellan*, "country of the
eagle." The eagle was a totemic animal for the local people.

Guinea Bissau This is a small country on the West African coast
where Portuguese and four African languages are in use. At one
time Europeans applied Guinea as the name for the piece of the
African coast running from Senegal to Gabon. Guinea comes from
aginaw, a Touareg or Berber word for the color of the people's
skin. *Aginaw* passed into Arabic as *giniya* and later on into
Portuguese as Guinea. (see New Guinea) Bissau, the name of the
capital, is the Portuguese form of *Bijuga* or *Bijago*, the name of the
local ethnic group.

Gulf of Tonkin In 1964 two United States destroyers were fired
upon by North Vietnamese torpedo boats. President Johnson
asked for the Tonkin Gulf Resolution, a constitutional means for
stepping up the war. Congress approved that the president take
any necessary action to push back attacks against American
troops, and to put a stop to aggression on the part of the North
Vietnamese. This gulf is formed by a curvature in North
Vietnam's coastline. The name is from *Dong-Kinh*, the
Vietnamese form of Tonkin, a part of North Vietnam. *Dong* is the
word for east and *kinh* means capital, hence "Capital of the East."

Haiti Haiti was the first nation in the Western Hemisphere,
after the United States, to win independence. It occupies
the western third of the island of Hispaniola, sharing it with
the Dominican Republic. Haiti is an Arawak Indian name
and it means mountainous land.

Halifax This city, the capital of Nova Scotia, is the easternmost
seaport in North America. It claims many "firsts" such as being the
first Canadian city to have a printing press, a newspaper, a printed
book, an elected government, a free public school, and a post
office. Halifax was founded in 1749 and named in honor of George

Montague Dunk, the second Earl of Halifax and president of the Board of Trade.

Hanoi The Vientamese capital today, it was the capital of French Indo-China, and then the capital of North Vietnam in 1954, after the French had left. Hanoi is an island city, on a river that empties into the Gulf of Tonkin. *Ha-Noi*, in fact, is Vietnamese for "interior of the rivers" (*ha* is river and *noi*, interior). The Chinese established Hanoi in the third century A.D., and it was known by other names throughout its history.

Havana Havana is the largest city in the West Indies, and before Castro it was the focus of governmental attention as well as a center for nightlife and entertainment. The name is Spanish for harbor, and it is the largest of many bays and harbors along the Cuban coastline.

Himalaya Mountains This range forms the northern border of India. Nepal, Bhutan, Tibet, and some Indian states share these mountains. Mount Everest, the highest peak on Earth at 29,028 feet, is in Nepal. According to some experts, the name comes from the Sanskrit *hima* (snow) and *alaya* (home or place). Others, however, believe that the name is from the Dravidian *malai*, a word for mountain. Dravidian was the language spoken by the pre-Indo-European aborigines of India.

Hindu Kush This range of high mountains spans northern Afghanistan and northern Pakistan. Nomadic and semi-nomadic people travel with their herds through its grasslands. In the Afghan language it means "killer of Indians" (*Hendu Xos*). In Hindi it becomes *Hindu Kus*. Originally it was the name of a hill at which some Indian slaves had died from exposure to the cold.

Hiroshima At the southern end of Japan's main island, this was the first city to have been destroyed by an atomic bomb. Having been rebuilt, it is now one of Japan's most modern cities. The name simply means large land, *hiro* denoting large and *shima*, an island.

Honduras This Central American nation has about 3,700,000 people, mostly engaged in agriculture. The country is mountainous and heavily forested. *Hondura* is Spanish for depth and was given to this nation because of the deep water near its coast. At first the name pertained only to the coastal area, but eventually the entire country was known as Honduras.

Hong Kong Hong Kong is made up of 234 islands and a piece of mainland China. The Chinese pronunciation is *xianggang*, *xiang* meaning perfume and *gang*, port, hence "port of perfume."

India Without Pakistan and Bangladesh, India is a triangular peninsula of 1,269,339 square miles. The people are basically a mixture of the aboriginal Dravidians and the Indo-European-speaking groups that came into the country between three and four thousand years ago. Sixteen different languages are spoken, with Hindi, Bengali, and English being the more well-known. Among India's religions are Hinduism, Islam, Christianity, Sikhism, Buddhism, Jainism, Zoroastrianism, Animism, and Judaism. The name of the country has developed from *Sindhuh*, a Sanskrit word for river which was applied to the river on the country's western border. In 500 B.C. the invading Persians continued to call this river Sindhuh, and later on the Greeks recorded Sindhuh as Indos and the country as India.

Iran This mountainous country produces livestock, cotton, rice, tobacco, cereals, and various minerals. Large oil deposits exist in the southwest. Tehran is the capital and largest city, but Tabriz in the far northwest and Isfahan in the center are also major urban areas. *Era* is the modern Persian or Parsi name for the country, and the ancient name is *Ayryanem*, country of the Aryans, the people from which the nation took its name. Aryan may come from *ar* or *har*, an Indo-European root denoting mountain.

Iraq Historically Iraq has been known as Mesopotamia and as Babylonia, and it was one of the places in which urban life had arisen in early times. The land between the Tigris and Euphrates Rivers, the "Fertile Crescent," supported agriculture and settled life, making it possible for advanced civilizations to flourish. *Al-'iraq* is an Arabic reference to the bank of a river. The rivers in question here are the Tigris and Euphrates. Mesopotamia is a Greek term and it refers to "the land between the two rivers."

Irkutsk Irkutsk is on the Trans-Siberian Railroad and it is the largest city in eastern Siberia. The word *irkut* refers to a large curve in a river.

Isfahan This Iranian city manufactures cotton textiles and has a number of examples of Islamic architecture. The ancient form, *esbahan*, comes from *esb* (horse) and *han* (place or country). The name is fitting, since Iranians have always been horse-breeders.

Israel The name has been used in several contexts: the Kingdom of Israel in the Bible, the modern state of Israel, the biblical Jacob, Jacob's family, the twelve tribes descended from his sons, the Hebrew inhabitants of Canaan, the first Christians, and the world Jewish community as a whole. The modern Israel takes its name from the biblical one which was used with reference to the patriarch, Jacob, after he had wrestled with the angel. Jacob's new name, Israel, denotes striving or struggling as he had done with the angel in the biblical account.

Jakarta Due to rapid growth over a short period of time, public services are still undeveloped. Many people have no water pipes and must buy their water from vendors. Jakarta is on the island of Java and is Indonesia's capital. Djakarta is an alternative spelling, but Jakarta is the one more commonly used. It is a Malaysian name and is a short form of *Jayakarta*, meaning "conquer and prosper," from *jaya* (victory) and *karta* (prosperity). The name was given to the city by Fatahillah, who had captured it in 1527 it's old name was Sunda Kelapa. The Dutch, who took over in 1619, called it Batavia.

Jamaica This Caribbean nation, a former British colony, has been independent since 1962. Bananas, sugarcane, and bauxite are its main products. Jamaica is a form of *xaymaca*, an Arawak India word meaning "rich in sources," or "country of sources."

Japan For two thousand years Japan has been a very homogenous nation as a result of its relative isolation. There are four main islands, but when one includes all the small islands, there are nearly four thousand. There are two theories with regard to the origin of the name, which apply also to the alternative form, Nippon. One possibility is that it comes from a Japanese word meaning "fireland." It may, however, be Chinese for "rising-sun-land," a fitting name, since Japan is to the east of China.

Java Java is one of Indonesia's main islands. Population growth has been high, jumping from five million in 1815 to sixty-five million in the late 1960's. *Jawa* or *Djawa* in Malaysian, it comes from the Sanskrit *yavadvipa*, meaning island of barley. *Yava* is a word for barley and *dvipa* means an island.

Jerusalem The Western Wall, the Church of the Holy Sepulchre, and the Dome of the Rock, holy places for Jews, Christians, and Moslems, respectively, are all in proximity. Egyptian texts mention the city c. 1900 B.C., and again c. 1400 B.C. as a Canaanite city-state. The Egyptian source, the *Amarna Letters*, refers to the city as *Urusalim*. *Ur* is a form of *ir*, Hebrew for city and *salim* is a form of *shalom*, peace.

Johannesburg This is the largest city in South Africa, and it sits in the region of the world's most abundant deposits of gold. According to the city's *Official Guide*, it was named for Johannes Meyer, Acting Mining Commissioner, who set up a mining camp at that spot. Other possibilities exist, however, such as Johannes Rissik, government surveyor. Johannesburg was founded near the gold fields in 1886.

Jordan Called Transjordan until 1949, the name was changed to Jordan. The country takes its name from the river. It is *Urdunn* in Arabic and *Yarden* in Hebrew, and it may be a variation of the Hebrew *yarod*, meaning to descend. Another possibility, however, is that it is a derivative of the Hebrew *Yeor-dan*, a loan word from the Indo-European *Yardan*, meaning "year river," a river that flows all year. The first explanation is probably correct, since it is more likely for the name to be Hebrew than Indo-European.

Kalahari Desert This desert in Botswana, just north of South Africa, has one of the largest expanses of sand on Earth. Kalahari comes from the African *karri-karri*, a word for desert.

Kamchatka One of the most volcanic areas in the world, it has 120 volcanoes of which twenty percent are active. Kamchatka is a peninsula extending south from eastern Siberia, bounded to the east by the Pacific Ocean. *Kamcadal*, the name of the local people, is a Koriak word, a form of *konchatchal*, an eastern Siberian term meaning "men of the extreme end." This is a reference to the geographical position of Kamchatka Peninsula.

Karachi The capital city of Pakistan, the name comes from *Kulachi*, a local tribe.

Kashmir Kashmir is politically divided between India, Pakistan, and China. It is a country of mountains, valleys, and plateaus. The name is a combination of the eastern Turkish *kash* (border) and the Persian *mir* (mountain), hence "border mountain." This mountainous region of India separates the lands of Central Asian Turks and Iranians from the Himalayas and the Far East.

Kazakh Kazakh or Kazakhstan was an important agricultural region of the former Soviet Union. It became an independent country on December 16, 1991. *Kazak* is a Turkish word for nomad and *stan* is a form of *ostan*, Iranian for land.

Kenya The earliest human fossil remains have been found in Kenya. Many African names are descriptive of topographical features such as rivers and mountains. Kenya is simply Swahili for mountain.

Khartoum Once the center of caravan traffic, the Sudanese capital is now a center for trucking. In Arabic it is *Al-hurtum*, a short form of *ra's al-hurtum*, "end of the elephant's trunk." There is a narrow tongue of land between the White and Blue Nile that has the shape of an elephant's trunk.

Korea Korea is a peninsula projecting south from China. The nation is divided politically between North and South Korea. In Japanese it is *Koryo* and in Chinese, *Korai. Hankuk* is the Korean name. The Japanese and Chinese names signify the idea of a land of the morning calm.

Labrador Only 34,000 people live in this coastal section east of Canada's Quebec Province. South Labrador has forests and the north has tundra with moose, caribou, bears, and wolves. Administratively Labrador is a part of Newfoundland. There are five theories on the origin of the name. According to one, the Portuguese named it for the farmers or laborers who had been granted a patent of land there from King Henry VII of England. It is also possible that the Basques named it after a place called Labour in southern France, near the Basque region. There are some linguists, however, who claim that Labrador comes from the Latin *laboratores terrae* ("workers of the land"), a reference to some Indians who had been captured and brought to Europe to be sold into slavery. Likewise, the Spanish *Tierra Labrador*, "land of the laborers" or "farmers," is another candidate. One other suggestion is that Labrador developed from the French *le bras d'or*, "arm of gold," a name expressing the hope of some explorers that the land would yield gold.

Lagos Lagos was the Nigerian capital during the years 1960-1991. It is the chief port city, and it hosts the headquarters of most of the European companies and banks in the country. The name is related to *Lkes* (lagune), many of which can be found along the Nigerian coast.

Lake Baykal This body of water is in southeastern Siberia and has an area of 12,150 square miles. It is the deepest freshwater lake in the world. The name is Mongolian and means rich sea, a possible reference to its abundance of fish and seals.

Lake Titicaca Titicaca is in the Andes Mountains and is divided between Peru and Bolivia. It is the largest South American lake, one hundred miles long, and it sits 12,500 feet above sea level. In the local Quechua language *titi* means lead and *kaka*, mountain chain, hence "lead mountain chain." However, the name may be in the Aymara language, and in that case it would mean "rock of a jaguar," a reference to the shape of the lake.

Laos This small southeast Asian country is basically a land of tropical forests with some herding and agriculture. Lao is the name of the main ethnic group, and it may be etymologically akin to the Sanskrit Lava or Lo, the name of a legendary individual. The nation's full name is *Pathedlao*, *Pathe* meaning land or country.

Lebanon This small land has been the site of religious, political, and military conflict for decades. The country takes its name from Mount Lebanon, *Jebel-Libnan* in Arabic, meaning white mountain. The mountain is covered with snow during most of the year.

Lesotho This small independent African nation is surrounded by the Republic of South Africa. Its economy is based, for the most part, upon subsistence agriculture. *Sotho* is the name of the people and *le* is simply a prefix used in the local language. *Sotho* may mean black or brown.

Liberia The oldest black African republic, it goes back to 1821, when American slaves began to settle there. In 1847 it became an independent state. The name simply means free land, from the Latin word for free.

Libya More than ninety percent of Libya is desert or semi-desert and consequently its economy depends entirely upon the export of oil. Money from oil exports goes into agriculture and industry. The people are basically Berber and have been there since time immemorial. Libya is a Latin form of *Libou*, the name of the local people. The *Lehabim of the Bible* may be a reference to the Libyans and *Loubim* or *Luvim*, also in the *Bible*, may have been a Libyan city. Egyptian texts reaching back to 2000 B.C. also mention Libya.

Lima Francisco Pizarro, the Spanish conqueror of Peru, named this new city Ciudad de los Reyes, "City of Kings." Lima, a name adopted later on, may come from either *Rimak* or *Rima*, Quechua Indian words. *Rimak* was the name of a deity and a temple, and *Rima* is a verb meaning to speak, a reference to the Inca priests who would speak to the worshippers.

Luzon Luzon is the largest of the Philippine Islands and it has almost half of the Philippine population. Manila, the Philippine capital, is on Luzon. The Spanish name is *Isla de los Losones*, *Losones* being a form of the native *losong*, a bucket to beat rice.

Macau Also spelled Macao, it is a Portuguese colony. In 1987 Portugal and China agreed that in 1999 Macau would become Chinese. The economy of Macau is based upon gold trading, gambling, and tourism. It is located not far west of Hong Kong, has an area of only six square miles, and has 270,000 people packed into this small space. The name comes from *Ama*, an ancient Chinese deity who was the patron of sailors. The rest of the name is from the Chinese word *ngao*, meaning bay or port. Macau is the name used by the Portuguese, but the Chinese call it *Aomen*, another word for port.

Madagascar One of the smallest mammals in the world, an insectivore called the geogale, less than three inches long, lives here. Madagascar, an island in the Indian Ocean, across a channel from Mozambique in southeastern Africa, produces rice, coffee, and vanilla. The languages are Malagasy and French, and the religions are African tribal as well as Christianity. Marco Polo mentioned Madagascar in the thirteenth century, but he was not speaking of this island, but rather of *Mogadishu* on the coast of Somalia. Diego Dias, a Portuguese explorer, discovered Madagascar for Europeans in 1500 and called it *Sao Lourenco* (St. Lawrence). Cartographers, however, decided to continue the use of Madagascar as a name even though the reference was to

Mogadishu, far to the north. Mogadishu (*Mogadiscio* in Italian) is from the Arabic *maqdasu*, a form of the word for saint or holy. Madagascar is presently called Malagasy Republic. (see Malagasy Republic)

Madeira Islands This group of islands is in the Atlantic Ocean, not far from the African coast. The name is Portuguese and it means wood, fitting for islands covered with trees. Madeira comes from the Latin *materia*, meaning wood for construction. The Phoenicians may have known of these islands, but the Genoese of the fourteenth century were certainly aware of them. John Goncalves Zarco, a Portuguese explorer, reached the islands in 1419 and claimed them for his country.

Maghreb This Arabic word means west, a reference to northwestern Africa, the region that includes Tunisia, Algeria, and Morocco.

Malagasy Republic This is the modern name for Madagascar. The name Malagasy comes from the Malagasy language, one of many languages spoken there, but also the most important one. Indonesian settlers brought this language to the island in the eleventh century. Previous to the introduction of Malagasy, the island was inhabited by Bantu-speaking Africans and Arab traders. (see Madagascar)

Mali Formerly a part of French West Africa, Mali became an independent nation in 1960. Drought is a major problem in this part of Africa. Four African languages are spoken along with French. Mali may come from *Malinke*, the name of a local tribe, or it may be a form of an African word for hippopotamus.

Malvinas Islands Also known as the Falkland Islands, they were discovered by the English explorer, John Davis, in 1590.

They were later called Malvinas because the Malouins, people from the French town of Saint Malo, colonized them in 1764. (see Falkland Islands)

Managua Nicaragua's capital, it was named after Lake Managua. Managua is a Guarani Indian name and it means "rain phantom" (*ama*, rain and *nagua*, phantom).

Manchuria The Japanese conquered the region in 1931 and occupied it until 1945. This portion of northeastern China is the home of the Manchus, an ethnic group. The Chinese called the area *Tung San Sheng*, "the Three Eastern Provinces." Manchu, itself, is a word for pure.

Manila Manila is the capital and largest city of the Philippine Islands, a city of high office buildings, hotels, embassies, and nightclubs. This is the name of the city in the English, Spanish, and Malaysian languages, but it is a derivative of the native Tagalog words, *may* and *nila* or *nilad*. *May* means "there was" and *nila* or *nilad* is the name of a local indigo bush.

Manitoba Seventy-five percent of this central Canadian province consists of public land that has been set aside for parks, forests, and reserves for Native Americans. Much of this land is not inhabited. Originally Manitoba was the name of a lake, and it is either Cree, Objibway, or Sioux. In Cree it would be a form of *manito-wapow*, and in Objibway it would be *manito-bau*, both meaning the "Strait of the Spirit," the strait being the narrows of the lake. If the name is Sioux it would be *mine-toba*, "Lake of the Prairie."

Marianas Islands This island group is in the west-central Pacific and is a part of Micronesia. The largest of the group, Guam, is a United States territory, but the other fourteen islands govern themselves. The Spanish named them *Islas Marianas* in 1668 after Queen Maria Anna of Austria, the wife of King Philip IV of Spain. Ferdinand Magellan first discovered the islands for Spain in 1521 and called them *Islas de los Ladrones*, "Islands of Thieves."

Marrakech The old city goes back to 1070, and parts of the original wall still stand. The name of this Moroccan city comes from the Arabic *marukus*, originally a derivative of a Berber word meaning fortified.

Marshall Islands Located in the western Pacific, the Marshalls are named in memory of a British captain who landed on one of the islands in 1788, after he had delivered the first group of convicts to Australia, a new penal colony.

Martinique This Caribbean island is an administrative district of France. There are 320,000 people living there who are mostly of African descent. It is a mountainous island with a volcano, Mount Pelee, which erupted in 1902 and destroyed the capital city. Martinique has become popular as a vacation spot. Early maps show that it was at one time called *Madanina*, a name of unknown meaning or significance. Later maps show it as *Martinino, Martinini*, and finally as Martinique. It may have been named for St. Martin.

Mauritius Island Mauritius is in the Indian Ocean, southeast of Africa. Its area is 790 square miles and its population is around 960,000. There is a large amount of linguistic and religious diversity on the island, especially considering its size. A variety of traders and settlers came to Mauritius over the centuries. English, French, French Creole, Hindi, and Urdu are spoken The Dutch called the island Mauritius in honor of Prince Maurice of Nassau. Portuguese sailors discovered the island, but the Dutch occupied it shortly thereafter.

Melanesia The Melanesian islands include the Solomon Islands, New Guinea, the Bismarck Islands, New Caledonia, and other islands in the western Pacific, just south of the Equator. These islands have a very rainy climate, some of them getting as much as three hundred inches each year. In some of the high valleys there are hundreds of species of birds. Melanesia means black islands, a name used by Europeans in the nineteenth century because the people of these islands were darker than those in other parts of the Pacific.

Melbourne This city started in 1835 as a place for grazing sheep. It is the main city of Australia's Victoria Province, at the southeastern corner of the continent. Melbourne became the first permanent settlement in Australia when John Batman purchased 600,000 acres of land there in 1835. Two years later Governor Bourke named the settlement for Lord Melbourne, the British Prime Minister.

Mexico *Mejico* in Spanish, the name comes from *Metztlixihtlico*, a word in the local *Nahuatl* Indian language signifying the center of the moon. There is a short form of this name, *Metzxihco*, from which the modern name directly stems. Aztec Indians founded the city in 1325 on an island in the lake and they named the island *Metzliatl* from *Metztli* (moon). *Atl* is a word denoting water, and according to the Aztec religion, the lake was consecrated to the moon. The Aztecs called the city *Tenochtitlan*, from *tetl* (rock) and *nuchtli* (fruit). Later on the full name of the city, as it was known to the Aztecs, was *Mexico-Tenochtitlan*. Therefore, the name Mexico was first applied to an island in the lake, then to the city of *Tenochtitlan*, and eventually to the entire country. In pre-Spanish times the region that would later be called Mexico was known as *Anahuac* or *Anawak*, Mayan Indian for "near the water."

Mindanao Mindanao is the largest southern island of the Philippine group. The spelling is the same in Spanish as in Malaysian, a contraction of *Magindanau*, a probable reference to a place on the shore of a lake, or to a principal lake. *Danau*, in the Malaysian language, means island.

Monrovia Liberia's capital takes its name from President James Monroe of the United States. A group of freed American slaves founded the city in 1822.

Morocco Geographically Morocco is the closest to Europe of any of the African nations. During the Persian Gulf War of 1991 the Moroccans sent a contingent to aid the United States and her allies to free Kurwait from the Iraqis. The name is a derivative of the Arabic *marukus*, originally a Berber word meaning fortified. (see Marrakech)

Mount Everest Everest is the highest peak in the Himalaya Mountains and, at 29, 028 feet, it is the highest spot on Earth. It was named in honor of Sir George Everest, Surveyor-General of India, maker of the first official survey of the region.

Mount Fuji Fuji is the highest peak in Japan, rising 12,389 feet above the countryside. In Japanese Fuji means "prosperous man," *fu* meaning prosperous and *ji*, man. *Fuji-Yama*, "Mountain of the Prosperous Man," is the full name. Another name in use is *Fujisan*, *san* also meaning mountain. *Fuji-Yama* is the name more popular among Europeans, while Fujisan is more readily used by the Japanese.

Mozambique The Arabs were familiar with this part of Africa at an early date and named it *Musa Malik*, King Moses. Portuguese sailors, who reached the area in the fifteenth century, recorded the name as *Mocambique* from which comes the alternative form, Mozambique.

Nagasaki On August 9, 1945 the second atomic bomb that was dropped on Japan hit the city of Nagasaki, on the west coast of the southern island. The name is a geographical description and it means long cape (*naga*, long and *saki*, cape).

Nairobi Nairobi is Kenya's capital and largest city founded in 1899. It is a large city with modern commercial and government buildings, and it hosts the headquarters of the United Nations Environmental Program. The name means swamp in the Swahili language.

Nepal Nepal is northeast of India, in the heart of the Himalayas. Mount Everest is within Nepal's borders. The name Nepal is both Hindi and Nepalese, a form of the Sanskrit *nepala*, from *nipat*, to fly down or to fly downhill. This probably refers to the mountain slopes that are so characteristic of this country.

New Brunswick This eastern Canadian region is known for its scenery, its cliffs along the coastline, and some of the highest tides on Earth, averaging over thirty feet. Originally a part of Nova Scotia, it became a separate province in 1794. It was named for King George III of England (1760-1820), a descendant of the House of Hanover or Brunswick, a part of Prussia.

New Caledonia This narrow island in the southwestern Pacific is a part of Melanesia. Captain Cook, the famous English explorer, discovered it in 1774 and named it after Caledonia, the Latin name for Scotland.

New Guinea New Guinea is an elongated island north of Australia and just south of the Equator. The people have retained a way of life that has not changed since the Stone Age as a result of their isolation. It is only recently that steel hoes and axes have replaced stone and wooden tools for agriculture. Most of New Guinea is covered with tropical forest. The Portuguese dis-covered it for Europeans in 1526, but it was I. Ortiz de Retes, a Spanish explorer, who named it twenty years later. He chose this name because some physical features of the natives reminded him of Africans. Guinea, a word used by the Portuguese and other Europeans for a part of the West African coast, comes from the Berber or Touareg *aginaw*, a reference to Blacks. *Giniya* is the Arabic form of *aginaw* and from this term comes the Europeanized Guinea.

New Zealand The two islands thàt comprise New Zealand, the north and south islands, are in the far southern Pacific, about four hundred miles southeast of Australia. Both islands are mountainous, scenic, and excellent for the grazing of sheep. During World War II New Zealand served as a military base against the Japanese. It was originally called *Staten Landt* by the Dutch sailor, Abel Tasman. Later on the name was changed to *Nieuw Zeeland* (Dutch) or New Zealand (English) after the Dutch city of Zeeland.

Nicaragua Nicaragua was caught up in civil strife during the 1980's. Gil Gonzalez, a Spanish explorer, reached Nicaragua in 1522. The Spaniards named the region for *Nicarao*, a chief of the main local Native American tribe.

Nile The Nile is the world's longest river at a length of 4,145 miles. As in ancient times, most Egyptians still live in the Nile Valley where they use the water for agriculture, industry, and in their homes. Nile is a Greek name, first appearing in a work of Hesiod called *Theogeny*, written around 750 B.C. Greeks, along with Phoenicians, were already trading in Egypt at this date. The Phoenician language was very much like Hebrew, and in Hebrew the word for a stream is *nachal*. Some linguists believe that that Phenician word was also *nachal*, and that the Greeks adopted it according to their own pronunciation. Greek had no equivalent of the *ch* sound, requiring the addition of a vowel to make pronunciation possible. It, therefore, became *Neil* with *os*, the Greek masculine ending, hence *Neilos*. The Greek *Neilos* became the Latin *Nilus*, and from this came the English name Nile.

Okinawa Taken from Japan during World War II, it was used as a base for long-range bomber raids during the Vietnamese War. The name of this Japanese island comes from *oki*, open sea and *nawa*, string or rope. According to some scholars, this may be a reference to an island that serves as a barrier against the ocean.

Omsk This city of western Siberia, founded in 1716, takes its name from the River Om, a word meaning calm in the Tatar language.

Ontario One of Canada's eastern provinces, its southern section has large population centers such as Toronto, Hamilton, Windsor, and Ottawa. Niagara Falls, Canada just across the bridge from Niagara Falls, New York, is also in this province. The Iroquois *oniatario*, from which the name stems, means sparkling or beautiful water.

Ottawa Ottawa, the Canadian capital, is in southeastern Ontario Province. According to Carl Waldman, an expert on Native Americans, the name probably has its origin in the Algonquian *adawe*, meaning to trade.

Pacific Ocean The Pacific covers about one third of the Earth's surface, and it makes up forty- six percent of the Earth's ocean surface. Its deepest spot is 36,198 feet, in the Mariana Trench. The sailor and explorer, Ferdinand Magellan, named it *Mar Pacifico* when he crossed it in 1520-21. He called it Pacific (peaceful) because he did not encounter any storms.

Pakistan Pakistan was created as a state in 1947 from the parts of India that had a Muslim majority. There are 83,000,000 people in Pakistan speaking seven languages and practicing four religions in addition to Islam. *Pak* is an acronym (P.A.K.) standing for the names of the country's three ethnic groups: Punjabis, Afghans, and the people of Kashmir.. The second part of the name comes from *ostan*, Iranian for land. There is a play on words, however, for *pak* is also an Iranian or Afghan word meaning pure, hence "land of the pure." Chandari Rahmat Ali created the name in the 1930's and it came into official use in 1947.

Palestine This name is a derivative of Philistine, a people mentioned in the Bible who dwelt in the southwestern part of Canaan, near the Mediterranean. Eventually the name was applied to the entire land of Canaan.

Pamir Mountains The Pamirs are shared by northeastern Afghanistan and southern Uzbekistan. The name may be a form of the Sanskrit *upa-Merou*, meaning "near to Mount Merou." Alternatively it may be an Iranian name in which case it could be *paye-mihr* ("foot of the sun"), *paye morg* ("foot of a bird"), or *paye marg* ("foot of death").

Panama Panama has the lowest population of all of the Latin American nations. The Panama Canal, opened in August of 1914, divides the country at the center. Panama is a name derived from the language of the Cuna Indians, the largest local ethnic group in pre-Spanish times. The name may be a reference to the country's abundance of fish, or it may simply be the Cuna Indian *panna mai*, meaning far away. If the second theory is correct, it was perhaps the answer that the Cuna gave to the Spaniards when they came in search of gold, telling them that it is far away, in order to get rid of them.

Papua This is the Indoneisan name for New Guinea, a form of the Malaysian *pua-pua*, curly- haired a probable reference to the hair texture of the people. (see New Guinea)

Paraguay Paraguay is a land-locked country with around three million people, many of them Guarini Indians. In the Guarani language *para* means water or river and *guay*, born, hence "born of a river."

Patagonia Patagonia is the name of the southern end of the South American continent. Most of it is Argentine, but the western part of it is Chilean. The climate is dry and the land is good for grazing sheep and growing wheat. During the Falkland War of 1982 the Argentines conducted military operations from bases in Patagonia. *Patagon* in Spanish refers to the Native Americans living on the Atlantic coast of Argentina. *Pata*, a word for an animal's foot or paw, is probably a description of the footwear made from the skins of llamas that these people had worn.

Peking *Pekin*, *Peiking*, and *Beijing* are the alternative renderings. The capital of mainland China, it means "capital of the North," and has been in use as a name since the fifteenth century. Before this time it was called *Khanbalik* "City of the Khan," the Mongol ruler of China.

Pernambuco The name of this eastern Brazilian city comes from the Guarani Indian *parana* (great river) and possibly *puku* (large). The second half of the name, however, may be another Guarani word *mbuku* (arms), "hence great river arms" or "arms of the great river." This is a fitting description, since the city is built on the delta of two rivers. Pernambuco is also known as Recife. (see Recife)

Philippie Islands These islands are the peaks of underwater mountains, composed of molten material from the interior of the Earth. It is a center of volcanic activity and one of the most unstable regions of the Earth's crust. In Tagalog, the official language of the country, the name is *Pilipina*. The Spanish is *Filipinas*, from *Felipe* or Philip II, king of Spain. Spanish sailors reached these islands in 1521, but the name was not given until 154

Phnom Penh Cambodia's capital, the city has an old section around the royal palace. There is a pagoda in this part of the city with a floor made of silver tiles. *Phnom* is a mountain or hill and *penh* means full or complete, hence "mountain of abundance" or "fullness."

Pitcairn Island Philip Carteret, an English naval officer, discovered this island in the south- central Pacific in 1767. The mutineers from the famous ship, *Bounty*, settled the island. It was named for Robert Pitcairn, an officer on Carteret's ship. It was Pitcairn who first viewed the island from the ship's deck.

Polynesia Polynesia is a triangular configuration of island groups and lone islands in the central and southern Pacific. Captain James Cook and Captain William Bligh of the ship, *Bounty*, visited some of these islands. The French coined the name Polynesia when they were exploring the region during the eighteenth and early nineteenth centuries. Polynesia simply means many islands.

Port Moresby The capital of New Guinea, it was named for the English explorer, John Moresby (1830-1922).

Pretoria This city serves as the administrative capital of the Republic of South Africa as well as the capital of Transvaal Province. The settlement started as Pretoria Philadelphia, and was named in honor of President A.W.J. Pretorious (1798-1855), the founder of Transvaal Province.

Punjab The Indus Valley Civilization flourished in this part of India over four thousand years ago, India's earliest civilization. There are over one hundred cities and villages, and the people used irrigation in the planting of their crops. Punjab is an administrative division of India, and is located in the far northwest. The name is Hindi and it means five rivers.

Quebec Canada's French-speaking province, Quebec was first settled in 1608. Quebec City is the provincial capital and Montreal, the largest city. The name is Algonquian and denotes the narrowing of a river, in this case the St. Lawrence. There is a legend, however, according to which Champlain, upon reaching the river bank across from present-day Quebec City, encountered a group of Native Americans who were shouting to him the word, "kabec," meaning debark.

Quito The Ecuadorian capital is built inside of a cup-shaped formation in the Andes. Quito was the name of the entire country until 1830, when it had gained its independence from Spain. Quito is a variation of *Quitu*, the name of the local ethnic group.

Rabat At one time the home of the Moroccan sultans, when the French made Morocco a protectorate in 1912 they built a new city there at the colonial capital. Rabat is a form of *ar-ribat*, Arabic for a "fortified building that guards a frontier."

Rangoon The Burmese capital has many Buddhist monasteries, and one of them is thought to be over two thousand years old. Buddhists believe that it is the only monument containing the relics of Gautama Buddha. Rangoon is an English form of *Rangun*, from *yangon*, a Burmese word for quiet or peaceful. The present name has been in use since the eighteenth century. Originally it was *Dagon*, from the Burmese *takun* (trunk of a tree).

Recife The Portuguese named this Brazilian city *Cidade de Recife* (City of Recife). It is a reference to a reef (*recife*) made of rocks. The Portuguese adopted their word from the Arabic *rasif*. (see Pernambuco)

Rhodesia Two African states have come out of the former Rhodesia. Northern Rhodesia became Zambia in 1964 see Zambia), and Southern Rhodesia became Zimbabwe in 1980. (see Zimbabwe) Rhodesia was named for Cecil Rhodes (1853-1902), a British colonial administrator and businessman.

Rio de Janeiro "River of January" in Portuguese, the sailors who first reached the bay on which the city would later be built made their landing on January 1, 1502. They believed that the bay was an estuary of a large river.

Sahara Desert The largest desert on Earth, it is a source of oil, iron, and natural gas. *Sahra* is the Arabic word for desert.

Saigon In 1954, when Vietnam split into North and South, Saigon became the capital of the South. On April 20, 1975 North Vientamese troops captured it, and it is now called Ho Chi Minh City. The city of Saigon took its name from the Sai-gon River, a Vientamese name that may refer either to a forest or to a sandy bank.

Sakhalin Island Sakhalin is an elongated island near the Siberian coast, in the Pacific Ocean. The name is of Manchu origin and it means black.

Samoa Islands Western Samoa is made up of two islands and American Samoa is one island to the east. Some scholars believe that the name comes from that of a chief, while others argue that it means "place of the moa," a large extinct bird that may have been a tribal totem.

Sargasso Sea This portion of the Atlantic Ocean lies between the West Indies and the Azores Islands. According to legend, ships got lost in the Sargasso due to the thick seaweed that would immobilize them. The seaweed is known as sargassum, hence Sargasso.

Saskatchewan A Canadian province since 1905, it produces livestock, wheat, petroleum, natural gas, and potash. Saskatchewan was originally the name of a river and it means rapid current in the Cree language (*kishika*, rapid and *djiwan*, current).

Senegal Senegal, on the coast of West Africa, is a country of over five million people who collectively speak six local languages. There are three possible explanations for the name: (1) it may have been named after the ancient city of Sanghana; (2) it could be a form of Zenaga, a tribal name; (3) it is possible that it comes from *Sanhaya*, a word denoting navigable.

Seoul This is simply the Korean word for capital. Seoul is the capital city of South Korea.

Seychelles Islands This island group is in the Indian Ocean, just over one thousand miles east of Africa and 350 miles south of the Equator. The Seychelles are a former British crown colony, independent since 1976. One of the local products is something known as patchouli, an oil used in the manufacture of soap and perfume. The Portuguese named these islands The Seven Sisters, but in 1742 the French seaman, Lazara Picault, renamed them Bourdonnais, for Bertrand Francois Mahe, Count of Bourdonnais (1699-1753), a naval officer. In 1756 the islands fell under the jurisdiction of the Company of the Indies, and were renamed once again. They took the name of the company's manager, Jean Moreau de Sechelles.

Shanghai Shanghai is the largest Chinese city, and it has served as a commercial center since the eleventh century. In 1921 the Chinese Communist Party had its start here. *Shang* is a Chinese preposition meaning on or above and *hai* means sea, hence "on" or "above the sea."

Siam Siam is the only nation in Asia never to have been colonized by Europeans. Siam is the traditional name, in use until 1939, when Thailand was adopted. *Sayam* is of Sanskrit origin, from *syama*, a word for black or brown, a reference to the color of the people. In this case brown, not black, would be more applicable.

Siberia Siberia includes the territory between the Ural Mountains and the Pacific Ocean. The terrain has a variety of features that make Siberia a land of abundant natural resources. Mountains, forests, tundra, and many great rivers yield minerals, timber, furs, and fish. *Sibir* is the name in the Russian and Mongol languages. It is possible that the name comes from that of a local tribe, but it may be a derivative of *sievier*, Russian for north.

Sinai The Sinai Peninsula is actually a bridge connecting Africa to Asia. The southern part of Sinai is a peninsula extending into the Red Sea. One of its features is the *Djebel Musa* ("Mountain of Moses") which is believed by some to be the Mountain Sinai of the *Bible*. Most likely the origin of the name, Sinai is *Sin*, a lunar deity of the ancient Sumerians, Akkadians, and Arabs.

Singapore A former British colony, Singapore is an island, or more accurately an island city. It is located near the southern tip of the Malay Peninsula. Its area is 226 square miles and its population is nearly 2,500,000. The five languages spoken in Singapore are Chinese, Malay, English, Hindi, and Tamil, a language of southern India. The name comes from the two Sanskrit words *simha* (lion) and *pur* (house or village), hence "village" or "house of lions." It is not known why the name came into use, since lions are not native to the island, but it is possible that *simha* (lion) was a name applied to a related animal that had lived there in early times. Singapore is the English form of the name, while *Singapura* is the Malaysian.

Sinkiang This large western Chinese province is a land of contrasts, with mountains over twenty thousand feet high and the lowest point in China at over five hundred feet below sea level. The name means new territory.

Somalia This nation of eastern Africa, on the Indian Ocean, has suffered because of rival war- lords who, intercepting humanitarian relief efforts, had exacerbated the problem of famine among the already starving inhabitants. Somalia comes from *as-sumal* or *as-sumaliyya*, the Arabic name for the people. It may be an Arabic form of the native word meaning dark, a reference to the local people. If it is a derivative of the African *soo mal*, meaning to milk, it would then refer to the native custom of bringing milk to guests. Another possibility is an origin in the Arabic *zamla*, meaning cattle, herd, or flock, which are abundant in this pastoral country. There is also the theory that the name may have been that of an important tribal chief.

Sri Lanka Formerly called Ceylon, this pear-shaped island lies off the coast of the Indian subcontinent. Sri Lanka is a Hindi name derived from the Sanskrit *sri* (good fortune, wealth, glory) and *lanka* (island). The name change took place in 1972. (see Ceylon)

St. Helena Island St Helena is in the South Atlantic, not far from the African coast. After having been defeated in Europe, Napoleon spent the rest of his life there in exile. The Portuguese sailor, John da Nova, discovered the island in 1502. He landed there on May 22, the feast day of St. Helena.

Sudan In early times this part of eastern Africa was called both Kush and Nubia, and during the Middle Ages, Dongola. It was the Egyptian Sudan in the nineteenth century and the Anglo- Egyptian Sudan from 1899 to 1952. Since 1952 this nation has had three different names: (1) Sudan (1952-56), (2) Sudan Democratic Republic (1956-85), and (3) Sudan Republic (since 1985). Sudan is an Arabic name and it refers to Blacks.

Sumatra This large, elongated island is a part of Indonesia. Its tropical forests produce rubber, spices, and coconuts. In Malay it is spelled *Sumatera* and may be a form of *Samudrad vipa*, Saskrit for "Isle of the Ocean."

Suriname The former Dutch Guyana, Suriname is on South America's northeastern coast. Most of the country's interior is tropical forest. It takes its name from the main river that runs through it, but the meaning of the name is unknown.

Sydney Australia's largest city, Sydney is the largest wool outlet in the world.. It was the first European settlement in Australia, founded as a penal colony in 1799. The city was named in memory of Thomas Townsend, first Viscount Sydney, who devised a plan for a convict settlement at Botany Bay. Arthur Phillip moved the penal colony to Port Jackson, at a place that he named Sydney Cove for Viscount Sydney. Sydney Cove was eventually shortened to Sydney.

Syria The earliest mention of this name is in reference to a place in Asia Minor called *Suri*, from a babylonian text dating back to 2000 B.C. *Assam*, an Arabic name for Syria, comes from *simaliyy* a word for left or north. The Hebrew word is *semol*. Syria lies north of both Arabia and Israel, and when one faces east, north is to the left.

Tabriz This city is located in the mountains of northern Iran. The name may be a form of the Greek Taurus, or possibly the Hebrew *tsur* (rock, stone, or mountain chain). A third possibility would be a derivation from *Tarwakisa*, a name mentioned in an Assyrian text.

Taiwan The island of Taiwan is ninety miles from the Chinese mainland, and in 1949 the government of the Chinese Republic relocated there. Taiwan has one of the highest standards of living in Asia. *Tai* is a Chinese word that suggests a high bank or a terrace and *wan* is a bay, hence "bay of the terrace." The name describes the terrain with its plateau, and its hills that descend onto terraces. (see Formosa)

Tangier Formerly in Spanish Morocco, Tangier is now in Morocco, on the Strait of Gibraltar. Tangier may come from Tingis, daughter of the mythical Atlas, or it may be a combination of the Berber *adji* (river) and the Semitic *tigris* (port).

Tanzania Tanzania is a former British colony where English is spoken along with the African languages. The name is formed by combining Tanganyika and Zanzibar, the two nations having been united in 1964. Tanganyika is the Swahili name for the lake that the country was named after. According to Sir Richard Francis Burton, the English explorer who reached the lake in 1858, the name comes from the Swahili *kou tanganyika*, to join or to meet, a place at which the waters come together. The British journalist, H.M. Stanley had a different opinion, however, claiming that the origin of the name is in *tonga* (island) and *hika* (smooth or flat). (see Zanzibar)

Tarim Basin This is the basin of the Tarim River in Sinkiang Province, China. From east to west it is nine hundred miles and from north to south, three hundred. It is surrounded by mountains, and it contains the Takla Makan Desert, one of the world's driest regions. Tarim is a name of either Mongol or Uigur origin and it means "river running in the sand." Uigur is an Altaic (Turkic) language spoken in Central Asia.

Tashkent Tashkent is the capital and largest city of Uzbekistan, in the former Soviet Union. It means stone village, from the Turkic *tash* (stone) and the Persian *kend* or *kand* (village).

Tasmania This island is separated from the Australian mainland by the Bass Strait, a channel of water approximately 150 miles wide. Tasmania, because of its geographic isolation, has some unusual fauna such as the Tasmanian Devil, a carnivorous marsupial that reaches three feet in length and weighs up to twenty-six pounds. There is also the so-called Tasmanian Tiger or Tasmanian Wolf, another carnivorous marsupial. This one has a dog-like appearance, grows up to five feet in length, and is now near extinction. Tasmania was named for Abel Janszoon Tasman, the Dutch sailor who sighted the island in 1642. He did not realize that it was an island, and it was years before geographers were sure. Tasman named it Anthoony van Diemenslandt in honor of the Dutch Governor General who backed the Tasman expedition. Until 1855 all official documents had Van Diemen's Land (in English) with references to the island. Nevertheless, as early as the 1820's Tasmania was gaining popularity as the island's name.

Tegucigalpa The capital of Honduras, it meant "mountain of silver" in the local Mayan or Lenca Indian language. When the Spaniards first arrived they mined silver and gold at the spot where the city would later stand.

Tehran Aga Muhammed Khan moved the capital from Shiraz to Tehran. Following World War II, when Iran was growing in wealth from its oil, the capital was becoming larger and more modern. The name may denote flat, level,

or uniform terrain, or it may come from a word meaning
pure or beautiful.

Tel Aviv Tel Aviv is a modern Israeli city founded in 1909, but
named after an ancient Babylonian city that had a Jewish colony.
The name is Hebrew for "hill of springtime" (*tel*, hill and *aviv*,
springtime).

Tibet This mountainous land became a part of China in 1951.
The Tibetans called their country *Bodyul* (yul meaning country), a
name related to the Sanskrit *bhota* (see Bhutan). Centuries ago
the Chinese called Tibet *Thupho*, but today they call it *Xizang*,
"the treasure of the West." The Arabs were familiar with this part
of Asia and they called it *At-Tubbat*, the direct origin
of the modern name.

Tigris The Tigris flows alongside the Euphrates, forming the
Fertile Crescent of ancient Mesopotamia. Baghdad, the modern
Iraqi capital, is on this river. The old Sumerian name was
Tigrusu meaning "river running with a conquering lance" (*tig*,
lance, and *ru*, to conquer).

Timor Occupied by the Japanese during World War II, in 1975 a
conflict arose between the leftist Revolutionary Front which wanted
an independent East Timor, and rival pro-Indonesian factions. They
declared independence from Portugal on November 28, 1975, but
Indonesian troops occupied East Timor and made it a province of
Indonesia in July, 1976. Timor is a form of *timur*, the Malaysian
word for east.

Tobago Columbus gave this island its name, a form of the Native
American *tambaku* (pipe), a device used to inhale the smoke from
burning tobacco leaves.

Tokyo One of the world's largest cities, it has served as a model for Japanese modernization. Today it is an international city with a service and computer-based economy. In Japanese *to* means east and *kyo*, capital, hence "east capital."

Toronto The first Canadian subway system was opened here in 1954. The name may be of Huron origin and it may refer to a meeting place. According to Carl Waldman, however, an authority on Native Americans, the name is Iroquois and may have one of the following origins: (1) *thoron-to-hen* ("fallen trees in the water"), (2) *de-on-do* ("the log floating on the water"), or (3) *onto* (to open, a reference to the entrance of Lake Ontario).

Tunisia This North African country is the site of the ancient city of Carthage, founded in 800 B.C. The country takes its name from Tunis, the capital city. Tunis is a Berber word that means to spend the night, a possible reference to Phoenician ships which used to rest there at the end of the day. There is also the possibility, however, that Tunis is a form of *Tanit*, the name of a Carthaginian female deity.

Upper Volta Known also as Burkina Faso, this country of close to seven million was once a part of French West Africa. Before the colonial era it was made up of small states and tribal lands. It took from 1894 to 1916 for the French to get firm control over the area. Upper Volta became an independent republic on August 5, 1960. The Portuguese called the local river the Rio de Volta, "river of return" or "curved river." The name Volta first appears on the map in 1741.

Uruguay This small South American country has more than three times as many cattle as people. The country was named for a river. The name is Native American and is probably a reference to a local long-tailed bird (*uru*, bird and *guay*, tail). Some linguists, however, say that it comes from a Guarani Indian word meaning "river of snails."

Vancouver The name applies to a city on the southwestern coast of British Columbia and to an elongated island separated from the shore by a narrow channel of water. Vancouver, the city is considered to be one of the most beautiful on the North American continent. The island of Vancouver is mountainous and heavily forested. Both the city and the island were named in honor of Captain George Vancouver, who reached the island in 1792. Vancouver became a British colony in 1859 and a part of British Columbia in 1866.

Venezuela Venezuela is one of the world's major producers of petroleum and it is the most wealthy of the Latin American nations. .The name is Spanish for "little Venice." Spanish explorers came upon a Native American village built on piles, reminding them of the Italian city. They called the village Venezuela ("little Venice") and over time the name was applied to the whole country.

Vietnam *Viet* is the name of an ancient state in southern China. In 208 B.C. the Chinese conquered a kingdom in northern Vietnam known as Hong-Bang. *Nam* is a word for south and is related to the Korean *nam* and to Chinese *nan*, also meaning south.

Vladivostok This Russian port on the Pacific, established in 1860, is noted for ship-building, canning, fishing, and whaling. The name means "rule of the east" (*vladi*, to rule and *vostok*, east).

Walvis Bay Walvis Bay is a port on the southwest African coast. In the Afrikaans (Dutch) language it is *Walvisbaai*, Walvis meaning whale, a place at which whales are hunted. The English form is Walfish Bay.

Wellington The capital of New Zealand was first settled in 1840 by British immigrants. It is a center of manufacturing, banking, and government. The city was named for the Duke of Wellington.

Winnipeg Winnipeg is the capital of Manitoba, and it is very close to the geographical center of Canada. At first there was a general store, the core of the original settlement, but by 1874, when it was still a small group of buildings, it was incorporated as a city. When the Canadian Pacific Railway arrived the community began to grow. The city takes its name from the lake. Winnipeg is a Cree Indian name meaning dirty water (*win*, dirty and *nip*i, water). Originally called Fort Garry, it became Winnipeg in 1876.

Yakustk This city goes back to 1632, and it is now the capital of the Siberian Yakut Republic. The regional economy is based upon fur, ivory, and leather. It is named for the Yakuts, a local people who refer to themselves as *Sakha*, speak a Turkic language, and breed livestock. These people reached their present home from farther south in the fourteenth century and became a part of the Russian Empire in the seventeen.

Yellow Sea This body of water lies between China and North Korea. The Chinese call it *Huanghai* (*huang*, yellow and *hai*, sea). It was so named because of the solid yellow particles or suspensions drifting in from the Yellow River.
Yemen Yemen differs from the other parts of the Arabian Peninsula in that the people have always lived a settled life and very few of them have been nomadic. *Al-yaman* is the Arabic name, with *yamin* meaning right side. In ancient times the right was symbolic of strength.

Yucatan Most of the people in this part of Mexico are of Mayan descent, and from 300 to 800 A.D. Yucatan was the site of the Mayan Civilization. One possible explanation for the name is the

Mayan *yuka* (to kill), a reference to the extermination of many Mayan Indians in the vicinity. There is also the story of the Spanish conquerors asking the local people the name of their country. Their answer was *yucatan*, meaning "I do not understand."

Zaire Formerly the Belgian Congo, Zaire became independent in June, 1960. There are around ten thousand species of flowering plants in this country. Zaire comes from *nzadi*, an African word for river. (see Zambia)

Zambia The former Northern Rhodesia, it takes its new name from the Zambezi River. The root *za* in Zambezi denotes a river. (see Rhodesia and Zaire)

Zanzibar Zanzibar is composed of two islands, Zanzibar Island and Pemba Island. During the nineteenth century it was a major commercial and political center of East Africa. In 1832, when the Arab ruler of Oman set up his capital there, it became a hub of the slave trade. Zanzibar has also been the world's greatest exporter of cloves. It is an Arabic name and it means "land of the blacks." Arabs have explored and traded in East Africa for centuries and have left many geographical names.

Zimbabwe At one time Southern Rhodesia, Zimbabwe became an independent nation on April 18, 1980. Victoria Falls, a tourist attraction, is on the Zambezi River, at the Zimbabwe-Zambia border. The falls drop abruptly over a 355-foot chasm and are 5,700 feet in width. *Zimba we bahwe* is Bantu for "house of stones," a name chosen because of an archeological excavation in the area.

Bibliography

Allen, Oliver E. *New York New York.*
New York, N.Y.: Atheneum, Macmillan Pub. Co., 1990.

American Scenic and Historic Preservation Society. *Annual Report.*

Armbruster, Eugene L. *Brooklyn's Eastern District.*
Brooklyn, N.Y.: Eugene Armbruster, 1942.

Armstrong, G.H. *The Origin and Meaning of Place Names in Canada.* Toronto: Macmillan Co. of Canada, Ltd., 1930

Avery, Catherine B., ed. *The New Century Classical Handbook.*
New York, N.Y.: Appleton- Century Crofts, 1962.

Bayles, Richard H., ed. *History of Richmond County (Staten Island), New York, From its Discovery to the Present Time.* New York, N.Y.: L.E. Preston Co, 1887.

Benzaia, Diana Fenichel. *Place Names in Selected Areas of Brooklyn. The Heart of New Utrecht.*
Brooklyn, N.Y.: A thesis presented to the Faculty of the Department of English, Brooklyn College. In Partial Fulfillment of the Requirements for the Degree Master of Arts, December, 1970.

Bergen, Teunis G. *Early Settlers of Kings County, L.I., N.Y.*
Greenport, La.: Polyanthos, 1973.

Blackie, C., and Blackie, J.S. *A Dictionary of Place Names.*
London: John Murray, 1887. 2nd ed.
Detroit: Gale Research Center, 1968.

237

Blumengarten, Jeannette G. *Flatbush Place Names.*
Brooklyn, N.Y. Unpublished Thesis, Brooklyn
College, 1960.

The Board of Aldermen of New York City. *Proceedings of the
Board of Aldermen of New York City.* New York, N.Y.:
The Board of Aldermen of New York City.

Cameron, Kenneth. *English Place Names.*
London: B.T. Batsford, Ltd., 1961.

Cannon, John, ed. *The Blackwell Dictionary of Historians.*
Oxford Basil Blackwell, Ltd., 1988.

Carpenter, Allan, and Lyon, Randy. *The Encyclopedia of the
Central West.* New York, N.Y. : Facts on File, 1990.

Cherpillod, André. *Dictionnaire Etymologique Des Noms
Géographiques.*
Paris: Masson, 1986.

City Council of New York. *City Council Proceedings*, Jan. – June,
1942.

Collier's Encylopedia.
New York: P.F. Collier, Inc., 1989.

Couling, Samuel. *The Encyclopedia Sinica.*
Hong Kong: Oxford University Press, 1983.

Craig, Robert. D., and King, Frank P., ed. *Histroical Dictionary
of Oceania.* Westport, Conn.: Greenwood Press, 1981.

238

Curtin Publishers. *Curtin's Directory of Long Island.*
New York, N.Y., 1865-66.

Custer, E.A. *Synoptical history of the towns of Kings County from 1525 to modern times.*
Brooklyn, N.Y.: E.A. Custer, 1886.

Deschampes, Pierre. *Dictionnaire De Geographie Ancienne Et Moderne A L'Usage Du Librairie Et De L'Amateur De Livres.* Paris: Librarie Firmin Didot Frères, Fils Et e, 1870.

Douzat, A., and Rostaing, Ch. *Dictionnaire étymologique des noms de lieux en France.* Paris: Librairie Larousse, 1963.

Ekwall, Eilbert. *The Concise Oxford Dictionary of English Place Names.* 4th ed. Oxford: Clarendon Press, 1960.

The Encyclopedia Americana. Danbury, Conn., Grolier, Inc., 1995.

Flint, Martha Bokée. *Long Island Before the Revolution.* 2nd ed. Port Washington, N.Y.: Ira J. Friedman, 1967

Freudenheim, Ellen and Wiener, Daniel P. *Brooklyn: Where to Go, What to Do, How to Get There.* New York, N.Y.: St. Martin's Press, 1991.

Fund for the Borough of Brooklyn. *The Brooklyn Neighborhood Book: Crown Heights.*
Brooklyn, N.Y. 1989.

Glare, P.G.W., ed. *Oxford Latin Dictionary.*
Oxford: Clarendon press, 1982.

Goldstone, Harmon H., and Dalrymple, Martha. *History Preserved. A Guide to New York City Landmarks and Historic Districts*. New York, N.Y: Simon and Schuster, 1974.

Grant, Bruce. *American Indians, Yesterday and Today*. Illustrated by Lorence F. Bjorkland. New York, N.Y.: E. P. Dutton and Co., Inc., 1960.

Gritman, Charles T. *Historical Miscellany*. New York, N.Y.: Unpublished Manuscript, 1910.

Grumet, Rovert Steven. *Native American Place Names in New York City*. New York, N.Y.: Museuem fo the City of New York, 1981.

Gudde, Erwin G. *California Place Names*. Berkely: University of California Press, 1974.

Hammond, N.G.L., and Scullard, H.H. ed. *The Oxford Classical Dictionary*. Oxford: Clarendon Press, 1970.

Harder, Kelsie B., ed. *Illustrated Dictionary of Place Names, United States And Canada*. New York, N.Y.: Van Nostrand Reinhold Co., 1976.

Hazan Ferrand. *A Dictionary of Ancient Greek Civilization*. London: Methuen and Co., Ltd., 1970.

Hazelton, Henry Isham. *The Boroughs of Brooklyn and Queens, Counties of Nassau and Suffolk, Long Island, New York 1609-1924*. New York, N.Y. Lewis Historical Publishing Co., Inc., 1925.

Heurgon, Jacques. *The Rise of Rome to 264 B.C.* Translated by James Willis. Berkeley: University of California Press, 1973.

Holt, Alfred H. *American Place Names.*
New York, N.Y.: Thomas Y. Crowell, Co., 1938.

Hopkins, Joseph E.G., ed. *Concise Dictionary of American Biography.* 2nd edition.
New York, N.Y.: Charles Scribner's Sons, 1977.

Ierardi, Eric. *Gravesend: The Home of Coney Island.*
New York, N.Y.: Vantage Press, 1975.

Johnston, James B. *The Place Names of England and Wal*
London: John Murray, 1915

Johnston, James B. *Place Names of Scotland.*
London: John Murray, 1934.

Kane, Joseph Nathan. *The American Counties.* 4th ed.
Metuchen, N.J.: The Scarecrow Press, 1983.

Kajubi, Senteza W., Lewis, L.J., and Taiwo, C.O., ed. *African Encyclopedia.* Oxford: Oxford University Press, 1974.

Knox, Alexander. *Glossary of Geographical and Topographical Terms.* 2nd ed. Detroit: Gale Research Co., 1969.

Lancaster, Clay. *New York's First Suburb: Old Brooklyn Heights Including Detailed Analysis Of 619 Century-Old Houses.*
Rutland, Vermont: Charles E. Tuttle Co., 1961.

Landesman, Alter F. *A History of New Lots, Brooklyn to 1887.* Port Washington, N.Y.: Kennikat Press, 1977.

Langstaff, Meredith B. *Brooklyn Heights Yesterday-Today-Tomorrow.* Brooklyn, N.Y.: Brooklyn Heights Association, 1937.

Leitch, Barbara A. *A Concise Dictionary Of Indian Tribes Of North America.* Algonas, Michigan: Reference Publications

Marlow, Nicholas J. *Bedford-Stuyvesant Place Names: A Thesis Presented to the Faculty of the Department of English, Brooklyn College.* Brooklyn, N.Y.: Brooklyn College, 1963.

Matthews C.M. *Place Names of the English-Speaking World.* London Weidenfeld and Nicolson, 1972.

McNamara, John. *History in Asphalt: The Origin of Bronx Street Names Place Names, Borough of the Bronx, New York City.* Harrison, N.Y.: Harbor Hill Books, 1978.

Miller, Rita Seiden, ed. *Brooklyn U.S.A. The Fourth Largest City In America.* New York, N.Y.: Brooklyn College Press, 1979.

Montanelli, Indro. *Rome: The First Thousand Years.* Translated by Arthur Oliver. London: Collins, 1962.

Moscow, Henry. *The Street Book: An Encyclopedia of Manhattan's Street Names And Their Origins.* New York, N.Y.: Hagstrom Company, Inc., 1978.

Moss, Joyce, and Wilson, George. *Peoples of the World: Latin Americans.* Detroit: Gale Research, Inc., 1989.

Mourre, Michele. *Dictionnaire D'Histoire Universelle.* Paris: Editions Universitaires, 19

Oliver, Roland, and Crowder, Michael, ed. *The Cambridge Encyclopedia of Africa.* Cambridge: Cambridge University Press, 1981.

Onderdonk, Henry, Jr. *Documents And Letters Intended To Illustrate The Revolutionary Incidents Of Queens County.* 2nd ed. Port Washington, N.Y.: Kennikat Press, 1970.

Paxton, John. *Companion To Russian History.* New York, N.Y.: Facts On File Publications, 1983.

Phillips, James W. *Alaska-Yukon Place Names.* Seattle: Unviveristy of Washington Press, 1973.

Queens Borough Historian. A/R, 1944.

Quimby, Myron J. *Scratch Ankle, U.SA. American Place Names And Their Derivation.* New York, N.Y.: A.S. Barns and Co., 1969.

Rashkin, Henry. *Bay Ridge Place Names.* Brooklyn, N.Y.: Brookyn College, 1960.

Reed, A.W. *Place Names Of Australia.* Wellington, New Zealand: A.H. and A.W. Reed, Ltd., 1973.

Reed, A.W. *Place Names Of New Zealand.* Wellington, New Zealand: A.H. and A.W. Reed, Ltd
Roberts, Robert B. *Encyclopedia of Historic Forts.* New York, N.Y.: Macmillan Publishing Co.., 1988.

Roller, David C. And Twyman, Robert W. *The Encyclopedia Of Southern History.* Baton Rouge: Louisiana State Unviersity Press, 1979.

Rosenthal, Eric. *Encyclopedia of Southern Africa.* Capetown, South Africa: Juta and Company, Ltd., 1978.

Smith, Rev. E.B. *Governor's Island: its military history uder three flags, 1637-1913.* New York, N.Y.: Pub. Rev. E.B. Smith, 1913.

Steinmeyer, Henry George. *Staten Island: 1524-1898.*
Staten Island, N.Y.: Statent Island Historical
Society, 1950.

Stewart, George R. *American Place-Names.*
New York, N.Y.: Oxford University Press, 1970.

Stewart, George R. *Names on the Globe.*
New York, N.Y.: Oxford University Press, 1975.

Stiles, Henry Reed. *History of the Country of Kings and the City
of Brooklyn, N.Y. from 1693 to 1884.*
New York, N.Y.: W.W.Munsell and Co, 1884. V

Streetname File Draw. Brooklyn, N.Y.: Brookllyn Public
Library, Main Branch, History Division, Brooklyn
Collection.

Strong, Thomas. *The history of the town of Flatbush, in Kings
County, Long Island.* New York, N.Y.: T.R. Mercein, Jr.,
Pub., 1842.

Thompson, Carol L.; Anderberg, Mary M.; and Antell, Jean B.,
ed. *The Current History Encyclopedia of Developing
Nations.* New York, N.Y.: McGraw-Hill Book Co.,
1982.

Utechin, S. V. *Everyman's Concise Encyclopedia of Russia.*
London: J.M. Dent and Sons, Ltd., 1961.

Véliz, Claudio, ed. *Latin America And The Caribbean: A
Handbook.* London: Anthony Blond, Ltd., 1968.

Waldman, Carl, and Braun, Molly. *Atlas Of The North American
Indian.* New York, N.Y.: Facts on File Publications,
1988.

Waldman, Carl, and Braun, Molly. *Encyclopedia of Native American Tribes.*
New York, N.Y.: Facts on File Publications, 1988.

Weed, Parsons, and Company. *Document Relating To The Colonial History Of The State Of New York.* New York, N.Y.: AMS Press, Inc., 1883. Vol. XIV.

Weld, Ralph Foster. *Brooklyn Village: 1816-1834.* New York, N.Y.: Columbia University Press, 1928

Wells James L. Haffen, Lewis F. Briggs, Josiah A.; and Fitzpatrick, Benedict, ed. *The Bronx And Its People: A History 1609-1927.*
New York, N.Y. The Lewis Historical Publishing Co., Inc., 1927.

Whibley, Leonard. *A Companion To Greek Studies.*
New York, N.Y.: Hafner Publishing Co., 1968.

Wilson, Rufus Rockwell. *Historic Long Island.* 2nd ed. Long island, N.Y.: Ira J. Friedman, Pub., 1969.

Wolk, Allan. *The Naming of America.*
New York, N.Y.: Thomas Nelson, Inc., 1977.

Works Progress Administration. *The WPA Guide To New York City.* New York, N.Y.: Random House, Inc., 1982. New Introduction by William H. White.

World Telegram

Travel Guide
Bibliography

Associated Students Of The Univesity of California. Europe
    On The Loose. New York, N.Y.: Fodor Travel
    Publications, Inc., 1994 and 1995.

Birnbaum, Alexander. *Birnbaum's 94 Great Britain.*
    New York, N.Y.: Harper Colins Pub., 1993.

Birnbaum, Alexander, ed. *Birnbaum's United States.* New
    York, N.Y.: Harper-Collins Pub., 1995.

Butler, Brian. *Europe For Free.* 3rd ed. Memphis: Mustang Pub.,
    1994.

Cabasin, Linda, ed. *Fodor's 96 Europe.*
    New York, N.Y.: Fodor Travel Publicaitons, Inc. 1995.

Crowther, Geoff, et. al. *Africia on a Shoestring.* Victoria,
    Australia: Lonely Planet Publications, 1992.

De Blaye, Eouard. *Frommer's Comprehensive Travel Guide
    U.S.A.* 4th ed. New York, N.Y.: Macmillan Travel,
    1988. English Translation, Simon and Schuster, Inc.,
    1995.

De Land, Antoinette, Dulles, Wink; and Pelton, Robert
    Young. *Far East 1944/5.*
    Redondo Beach, Ca.: Fielding Worldwide, Inc.,
    1994.

Feinsot, Louis, ed. *Walking Tours Of America.*
    New York, N.Y.: Collier Books, 1979.

Fodor's Travel Publications. *Fodor's 95 Europe*. New York, N.Y.: Fodor's Travel Publications, Inc., 1994.

Haberfeld, Caroline, ed. *Fodor's 95 U.S.A.* New York, N.Y.: Fodor Travel Publications, Inc., 1994.

Hughes, Holly, ed. *Fodor's Touring U.S.A.: Eastern Edition.* Fodor's Travel Publications, Inc., 1992.

Hundley, Adam R. ed. *Let's Go: The Budget Guide to Europe 1996*. New York, N.Y.: St. Martin's Press, 1996.

Kaplan, Frederic M., Sobin, Julian M., and de Keijzer, Arne J. *The China Guidebook.*

New York, N.Y.: Harper and Row Publishers Inc. 11th ed. Teaneck, N.J.: Eurasia Press, 1990.

Kurian, George Thomas. *World Data: The World Almanec Gazetteer.* New York, N.Y.: World Almanac Publications, 1983.

Moody, Mark D., ed. *Let's Go: The Budget Guide to the U.S.A. and Canada.*
New York, N.Y.: St. Martin's Press, 1994.

Munro, David, ed. *Chambers World Gazetteer.* 5th ed. Cambridge, England: Wand R. Chambers Ltd. and Cambridge University Press, 1988.

Patton, Marion, and Sherwin, Mary, ed. *Know Your America*. Vol. 1. Garden City, N.Y.: Doubleday and Co., Inc., 1978.

Paxton, John. *The Statesman's Year-Book: World Gazetteer*. 3rd ed. New York, N.Y.: St. Martin's Press, 1986.

Porter, Darwin, and Prince, *Danforth, Frommer's Comprehensive Travel Guide: Caribbean '95*. New York, N.Y.: Prentice Hall Macmillion Co., 1994.

Raff, Joseph and Judith. *Europa 94*. Redondo Beach, Ca.: Fielding Worldwide, Inc, 1991.

Ramey, Caitlin, ed. *Central America On The Loose*. 1st ed. New York: N.Y.: Random House, Inc. 1993.

The Reader's Digest Association, Inc. *Reader's Digest Off The Beaten Path*. Pleaseantville, N.Y.: The Reader's Digest Association, Inc., 1987.

Schmittroth, Linda. *Cities Of The United States*. 2nd ed. Detroit: Gale Research, Inc., 1994.

Seidenberg, Robert, ed. *Insight Guides: Crossing America*. Boston: Houghton Miffflin Co., Directed by Hans Hofer, 3rd ed. Hong Kong: APA Publications, Ltd., 1994.

Seligman, Craig, Paulus, Conrad Little, and Roth, Melanie. *Fodor's Southeast Asia*. New York, N.Y.: Fodor's Travel Publications, Inc. Random House, Inc., 1995.

van Hallie, Nancy, ed. *Fodor's Europe 1995*. New York, N.Y. Fodor's Travel Publications, Inc. Random House, Inc., 1995.

Wheeler, Tony, and Wheeler, Maureen, ed. *West Asia on a Shoestring*. Berkley, Ca: Lonely Planet Publications, 1990.

Williams, Roger, and Bell, Brian, ed. *Insight Guides: Continental Europe*. New York, N.Y.: Houghton Mifflin Co., 1994.

Wurman, Richard Saul. *Richard Saul Wurman's New Road Atlas: U.S. Atlas*. New York, N.Y.: Access Press, 1991.

Young, Margaret Walsh, and Stetler, Susan L., ed. *Cities Of The World*. 3rd ed. Detroit: Gale Research Co., 1987.

Printed in Great Britain
by Amazon